Changing consumer behaviour

Robert East
School of Marketing, Kingston Business
School, Kingston University

CASSELL

Cassell Educational Limited
Villiers House
41–47 Strand
London WC2N 5JE

First published in hardback 1990
First published in paperback 1991
Reprinted with corrections 1992
Repirnted 1993

British Library Cataloguing in Publication Data
East, Robert
  Changing consumer behaviour.
  1. Consumer behaviour
  I. Title
  658.8'342

  ISBN 0–304–32533–3

Phototypeset by Intype, London
Printed and bound in Great Britain by
Biddles Ltd, Guildford and King's Lynn

Changing
consumer behaviour

Contents

Figures

Tables

Exercises

Preface

This book is intended for students specializing in consumer behaviour, for colleagues in marketing, economics and psychology, and for practitioners in marketing, market research and advertising. The work examines the processes that underlie individual and aggregate aspects of consumer behaviour. It emphasizes the *dynamics* of consumption, the theories, methods and interventions that help us to predict, understand and bring about changes in consumer behaviour.

Textbooks in consumer behaviour are comprehensive, well illustrated and definitive but they often present the subject in a factual, cut-and-dried, rather uncritical manner. In practice there are competing explanations and methods and the existing textbooks fail to do justice to the changing nature of the subject. With this in mind I have tried to treat issues in some depth and to show where theories and evidence are in question. This approach narrows the coverage and means that some topics such as segmentation, personality, culture, family dynamics and the diffusion of innovation are omitted. For this reason this book is not a replacement for existing texts on consumer behaviour. I use it as the text for part of a course on consumer behaviour and use other books to complete the coverage.

The better-known textbooks in consumer behaviour are North American. As such they refer to *American* cases, market statistics, products, advertising, shops, governmental regulations, population changes and social institutions. British students using American texts are disadvantaged; they miss the findings of British and European research, the relevance and familiarity of our brands and shops, the cases based on our excellent advertising, and references to the organizations that operate in the British economy. This can only detract from the value and interest that our students assign to consumer behaviour and I have tried therefore to give emphasis to relevant British material.

The title of this work also supports a second meaning, to change some of the content in the subject of consumer behaviour itself. One new emphasis is on involuntary consumption. Many of the services used by people are provided by monopolies or near monopolies where the consumer has little choice or control over what is offered: energy supplies, telephones and medical provision are examples. Such services should take account of the consumers' needs and preferences and consumer research is a means of establishing these requirements.

Another expansion of the field of consumer behaviour occurs when we pay more than lip-service to research *on behalf of* the consumer. The main issues addressed in texts on consumer behaviour affect the interests of the promoter and supplier of goods rather than the consumer. Most texts do give a place to consumerism and to issues of consumer redress but the consumers' perspective is not the one that gets the funds. Consumers do not normally pay for research services nor do they employ the graduates of marketing courses. 'He (or she) who pays the piper calls the tune.' Fortunately there are several potential payers of the piper and this leads to some variety in the music. But even when non-profit agencies and government are using consumer research they often act as suppliers. Against this the consumer is quite well served by the product research of the Consumers' Association and from press and TV comment on goods and services. The government funded National Consumer Council and a variety of regulatory bodies also support the consumer interest but the great weight of consumer research remains in the service of those who want to supply the consumer and this affects the character of academic work.

Another extension of the subject involves a blurring of the boundary between consumer behaviour and other forms of behaviour. Marketing researchers have recognized that the techniques that are appropriate in commercial contexts can often be used in social and political fields (Kotler and Levy, 1969; Kotler, 1972). A similar argument applies to consumer behaviour: the prediction, explanation and change of social behaviour has much in common with prediction, explanation and change in consumption. Sometimes studies belong in both of these fields; for example when the object of research is alcohol consumption or the use of the oral contraceptive pill. Reflecting this, I have drawn examples from the social field, particularly the area of community health and I hope that the book will be of use to those in the field of health promotion.

Good education gives students a confidence about using and criticizing ideas. Wherever possible I have tried to enlarge this confidence by the use of appropriate exercises that help students to approach consumer behaviour from a practical standpoint. The exercises include self-appraisal, calculations, observations, measuring attitudes, analysis, finding applications and using computer programs. These exercises are placed where they are most appropriate to amplify the text. In many cases they are quickly done and the reader will benefit by doing them as they occur.

The computer programs are carried on one floppy disk, available free from the publisher.

Plan of the book

Chapter 1 introduces the reader to a description of different forms of consumption based on frequency, importance and freedom of action. Basic learning principles are sketched out and ideas behind high involvement purchase are explained. The belief that the consumer calls the tune in the exchange with the supplier is examined and it is argued that this over-simplifies the situation: consumer autonomy often involves an empty choice between equivalent brands and at other times there is little choice about the nature of the service provided. The effectiveness of competition at serving consumer interests is discussed and the function of brands is described.

Chapter 2 is concerned with the patterns that are found in repetitive purchase: it emphasizes British research in this field and shows how consumer research applies to a number of important marketing assumptions. Chapter 3 shifts interest to more important choices and to the scope for predicting these choices by measuring consumer preference. This approach is extended in Chapter 4 and the most widely accepted theory of behaviour prediction and explanation is described and applied; this is called the *theory of reasoned action*. Extensions of this work are covered in

Chapter 5.

Chapter 6 is a critical examination of attitude measurement practices in marketing research. Chapter 7 is concerned with a variety of theories from cognitive and social psychology that help us to understand how changes in thought, feeling and action come about and which must underlie, therefore, any changes induced by advertising. Chapter 8 turns to advertising and sales promotion. The chapter describes the measurable effects of these interventions, the attempts to explain advertising effects and the scope for testing advertising copy at an early stage in its development.

Acknowledgements

The groundwork for this book was laid at the Centre for Marketing and Communication at the London Business School during the 1986/87 academic year. I am particularly indebted to Andrew Ehrenberg for his careful reading of my drafts and for his advice and encouragement. I am also much indebted to Neil Barnard, Mark Uncles, Patrick Barwise, Jules Goddard and John Bateson who were very helpful and generous with their time.

I am grateful to researchers whose work I have used but particularly to Icek Ajzen for explaining his ideas in detail when I visited Amherst in 1985, and to Simon Broadbent and Gian Fulgoni who responded so supportively when I wrote to them seeking clarification of their work.

Finally I appreciate very much the comments of my undergraduate and postgraduate students at Kingston Polytechnic. With them in mind I have tried to be relevant and clear but any failure is entirely mine.

[1]
Concepts in consumer research

Forms of consumption

Which of the following are consumer behaviours?

- Buying a Bounty Bar
- Buying St Michael socks
- Buying a Bosch washing machine
- Buying a 500 megawatt generator set
- Going swimming in the local pool
- Opening an account with the Midland Bank
- Watching this week's *Dallas*
- Complaining about your car service
- Shopping at Tesco
- Going to the doctor
- Having the dustbins emptied
- Walking in Hyde Park
- Fare dodging
- Having children
- Voting in a General Election

Consumer behaviour covers the acquisition and use of goods and services by individuals or households. As such it is usually distinguished from industrial purchasing where organizations make the acquisition. Organizations buy 500 megawatt generator sets and sometimes they open bank accounts and buy confectionery. Many aspects of industrial buying parallel consumer purchase but the role of organizations is not explored in this text.

The focus here is on individual action; we want to explain how and why people do things. Some of the things people do, such as

1

shopping at Tesco, are consumer behaviour without question. Other activities such as fare dodging and walking in Hyde Park are less clearly so. From a commercial standpoint it may be necessary to distinguish consumer action from other activities but the explanation of behaviour jumps such boundaries.

In marketing much attention is devoted to the object of action, to the good or service. This must be so because profits are made when consumers buy one brand rather than another. But in consumer behaviour the focus is as much upon the action as the object. We note the distinctions between goods and services, brands and product types, but we are just as interested in the way people act towards these objects. This is reflected in the way we classify behaviours. There are three important ways of distinguishing actions:

1 Some actions are recurrent; others are done once or not at all.
2 Some actions are seen to have important and usually irreversible consequences while the outcomes of other actions are of little concern.
3 Some actions are freely chosen while others are involuntary.

Each of these distinctions is logically independent of the other two and this allows us to use the three descriptions frequent–infrequent, trivial–important, and constrained–free to local actions in a three dimensional psychological space. This is illustrated in Figure 1.1. Any action can be placed within these three dimensions: consulting the doctor, buying hairgrips, choosing a holiday, taking the bus to work. The points on the scales may vary from person to person, over time, and with the detailed nature of the action but these dimensions provide a first stage in the classification of consumption.

This approach to consumer behaviour gives attention to the more visible aspects of consumer decision making and avoids too much speculation about what goes on in the mind of the consumer. Like any classification it has its limitations. It is no more than a way of organizing the subject. It is certainly not an explanation of how people consume, though it leads on to different explanations of consumer action.

Using Figure 1.1 you can place actions in any one of eight different sectors but there is little interest in some of these, e.g. actions that are trivial and infrequent, whether these are free or

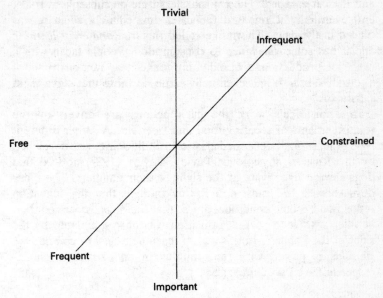

Figure 1.1 Dimensions of consumer action

not. For this reason the analysis to follow is focused on the three dimensions of frequency, importance and freedom of consumption, and not on the sectors. Each dimension is examined below in greater detail and the related theories of behaviour are explained.

Frequency

We learn from consumption experience. When the consumption is repetitive the learning can be used to modify our later behaviour. If the product or brand is unsatisfactory it can be avoided in the future. Conversely, satisfaction with the product increases the likelihood that it will be selected next time. Learning theory is a systematic description of the relationship between experience and subsequent behaviour.

Principles of learning

Early research on learning was done by Thorndike (1911) who confined a hungry cat to a cage and placed food outside. The erratic movements of the cat eventually released the simple catch and the cat escaped. The cat took less time on subsequent trials, and eventually it released the catch immediately when it was placed in the cage. Thorndike called this *trial and error learning* and it has some relevance to consumption. People faced with a range of products and brands may make near random trials of alternative brands and eventually settle on those that serve them satisfactorily.

In Thorndike's work the cat's actions are driven by the reinforcements of securing food and freedom. A rather different type of learning, later called classical conditioning, was developed by the Russian physiologist Pavlov. Pavlov (1927) noticed that dogs started to salivate at the sight of their handlers. The older dogs showed this most and Pavlov thought that the salivation reflex had become conditioned, i.e. that the dogs associated their handler with food so that salivation was now stimulated by the sight of the handler. In this sort of learning a new or *conditioned stimulus* is paired with the stimulus in an existing stimulus–response (S–R) sequence, i.e.

Food (unconditioned stimulus)   →   salivation

Food + handler   →   salivation

Handler (conditioned stimulus)   →   salivation

Pavlov set up a series of experiments to demonstrate this process of classical conditioning using a buzzer as the conditioned stimulus instead of the handler.

Pavlov's work was taken up enthusiastically by Watson, a psychologist at Johns Hopkins University who later became a vice-president of J. Walter Thompson. Watson and his colleague Rayner experimented on a child known as Little Albert. Watson and Rayner (1920) used the distress on hearing unexpected loud noises, a reflex possessed in some degree by all humans, as the initial S–R pattern. A white rat was the conditioned stimulus. Whenever the white rat became visible to the boy Watson created a loud noise by striking an iron bar behind him. Initially the white rat evoked no fear but after a number of trials the appearance of the rat caused Little Albert to react with the distress previously associated with the loud noise. Watson also noted that fear was shown when other white furry objects were shown to the boy showing that the learning had generalized.

These days Watson's treatment of Little Albert would not pass the Ethics Committee. Little Albert's mother certainly took a dim view of her child's treatment and removed him from Watson's care when she found out what was going on. Watson had intended to try to reverse the conditioning.

Classical conditioning has a place in consumer behaviour. Packaging, brand names, colours, music and contexts may become associated with the purchase of particular products. Some advertising is clearly intended to forge associations between brands and stimulus features, e.g. Benson and Hedges cigarettes and the colour gold, Esso petrol and tigers. The idea here is that the conditioned stimulus, the pack colour or tiger, may add to any purchasing tendency. Such learning may be generalized by family branding where a name like St Michael extends the positive associations of Marks and Spencer's products to a new line. Similarly new brand names may be chosen to capitalize on old associations.

Thorndike's work was developed further by B. F. Skinner (1938, 1953). Skinner's model of *operant conditioning* placed emphasis on the reinforcement associated with a response (or operant). Reinforcement is a pleasant or unpleasant experience and has most effect when it occurs at the same time or just after the response. Reinforcement changes the frequency of the response so that Skinner saw learning as a feedback system over time. In the model:

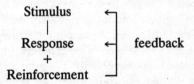

the arrows show how the likelihood of a response in later trials is affected by reinforcement in earlier trials. Skinner introduced the idea of *shaping*, the process whereby behaviour is moved from one form to another by successive reinforcement of small changes in the desired direction. Some shaping may be involved when people move up a product range.

Skinner also noted that reinforcers could lose their power to affect behaviour if they were heavily used. This satiation effect is one possible explanation for the loss of effectiveness of advertisements (called *wearout*). The power of a reinforcer returns when it is not used for a while and advertisers use this effect by resting advertisements and then bringing them back.

A satiation effect also occurs with stimuli so that they lose their power to elicit responses. Satiation with stimuli, called desensitization, helps people to put up with recurring unpleasant experiences. It is because the stimulus loses its power to evoke a response that surgeons suffer no qualms as they make an incision for the hundredth time. An important effect of desensitization in consumer behaviour is the way in which people get used to conditions that are inadequate or unpleasant and, as a result, rarely complain or demand compensation. Examples of this are the way people tolerate queues in banks, litter in streets and overcrowding on metropolitan transport.

Learning leads to habits. Something often done, such as going to work or buying detergent, requires little thought once the various alternatives have been tried. As a result people soon routinize their behaviour and follow an established pattern, no longer thinking out each step. Such habits economize on effort and leave attention free for novel aspects of the environment. This benefit of habit is balanced by a disadvantage: habit may stop people from taking advantage of improvements in service and technology that become available.

Learning can be reinforced each time a response is produced, i.e. continuously, or the reinforcement may occur intermittently. Learning is fastest if the reinforcement schedule is continuous but the final effect of a given amount of reinforcement is greater when it is used intermittently. Reinforcement schedules explain why people are prepared to lose money by gambling on fruit machines. A one-armed bandit is responsible for a regular negative reinforcement each time a coin is inserted and an intermittent positive reinforcement when the machine pays out. Although, over time, the payout is less than the amount paid in, the effect on behaviour of the irregular reward is greater than the effect of the regular payment.

When reinforcement stops there is a gradual extinction of the response but this extinction period is extended if the learning was made under an intermittent rather than a continuous schedule of reinforcement. Advertising is frequently put out as a burst followed by occasional exposures (called a drip). The burst is more like continuous reinforcement and produces fast learning which is then maintained by the intermittent drip.

Skinner noted that reinforcement could be used so that responses only occurred when very specific stimuli were presented. Such stimulus discrimination is a purpose of branding, the idea of which is that consumers associate benefits with a particular brand rather than the product type. This is emphasized by positioning which is the design and presentation of brands so that people think that they have particular benefits in comparison with other brands in the field. An example of positioning was the introduction of shampoo in three different forms for dry, normal and greasy hair. These subdivisions are now commonplace but when they were less common they were used by Elida Gibbs and helped All Clear shampoo to take a significant share of the market (see Broadbent, 1981).

Negative reinforcement or punishment discourages action and drives people away from the context in which it occurs. This is relevant to consumption. Unpleasant experience of products, e.g. a 'chemical' smell on a soap, or skin rash following use of a detergent brand, reduces the likelihood of further purchase of the brand. Such aversive learning can mean that a product is avoided and any improved formulation or other redeeming features may then remain undiscovered. This avoidance learning can be very costly to a supplier. Just one incident in which a product offends, e.g. when a restaurant makes its customers ill or a store gives bad after-sales service, can put people off for a long time. Promotion may get people to try again but it is better to maintain the quality of the product.

This very brief review of the concepts in learning theory has omitted the more controversial issues. In particular the whole-hearted behaviourism of Watson and Skinner has been much criticized for ignoring the capacities of insight and inference that people possess. Skinner did much of his work on pigeons and it is not surprising that he had no place for thinking and feeling as causes of human behaviour. This position is generally rejected today and later chapters examine the role of thought and feeling in the prediction and control of human behaviour.

Exercise 1.1. Habits

It is hard to detect habits that work against your own interests but consider two areas:

1 What do you write with? Most people use cheap throw-away ballpoint pens but are they worth using? More expensive pens with refills allow you to choose the size of point and often to write more smoothly. People who write a lot are almost certainly better off with such a pen; the extra cost is small in relation to time spent writing. Is this true for you?

2 Sugar in tea and coffee is a habit which adds to body weight and contributes to tooth decay. When people give up sugar they fairly soon get used to it and may prefer unsweetened tea or coffee after a few weeks. Is this not a habit worth changing?

Questions
What products or services do you use habitually?
What changes could you make in your habitual consumption?
What investigation of consumer practices is needed in a settled market?

Importance

Actions are trivial when a mistake is easily remedied or ignored. For example, with low cost products there is little risk because the wrong good can be discarded and a replacement bought. Even when a purchase is important the choice may be trivial. This occurs when there is little difference between two alternatives so that one will serve as well as the other. For example, it is important to get petrol when the tank is low but which four star brand is of no consequence to most people. Generally product purchase is more important than the brand choice but the distinction between the two is essential for any clear exposition of consumer behaviour.

Involvement
High involvement purchase has several features. The action is infrequent and not routinized. Once made the decision is not easily reversed, and the consequences of the choice are thought to be important. Krugman (1965) used 'high' and 'low' involvement to differentiate the types of cognitive activity that were elicited by purchasing and Engel, Blackwell and Miniard (1986)

use it as a pivotal concept in their treatment of consumer decisions.

There are some purchases that have more personal relevance than others. This partly reflects their cost but it also bears on the way in which some products enhance the consumer's self regard. Often a purchase decision reflects on the wider judgement of the purchaser. This is because possessions provide one clue to the way a person lives, thinks and feels. Possessions have symbolic value as first noted by Veblen (1899, 1949) who introduced the idea of conspicuous consumption to describe purchasing that showed to others what sort of person the purchaser was. This thinking separates the person from the role that he or she acts out in dealings with others. There is a real person and also a role person presented to the outside world through the symbolism of possessions. G. H. Mead (1934) used the role concept in his explanation of the social and individual nature of persons. Goffman (1959) extended this mode of analysis and introduced the concept of a 'managed situation', the idea that people manage the impression that others have of them by the way they present themselves. Forms of ownership are one aspect of self-presentation.

Products can be used by people in conspicuous consumption either because of their cost or because they are associated with particular ways of living and therefore describe the owner as a particular sort of person. The type of car, hand luggage and logos on clothes can all signify social memberships. Part of the skill of marketing is to give brands added value by associating them with attractive lifestyles. Even foods tell us something about the purchaser; who has not stood patiently in the checkout queue reflecting on the lifestyle of the person in front as it is indicated by the purchases in their trolley?

Engel, Blackwell and Miniard (1986) suggest that a high involvement decision is an elaborate procedure. They describe a process of extended problem solving with problem recognition, search for different alternatives and for information about each one, evaluation of alternatives, purchase, and post-purchase activities. The process is presented diagrammatically with arrows showing the flow of activity in Figure 1.2. This extended problem solving is contrasted with limited problem solving under low involvement where little thought is given to the choice, and problem recognition and search are minimal. If high involvement

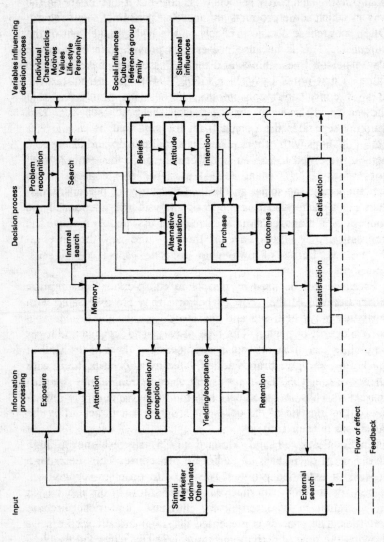

Figure 1.2 The complete decision process model (from Engel, Blackwell and Miniard, 1986, p. 35)

choices are repeated they settle down, according to Engel, Black-well and Miniard, into a routine problem solving pattern.

It is not hard to find fault with the extended problem solving model. An earlier form appeared in Engel, Kollat and Blackwell (1968) and it has much in common with the Howard and Sheth (1969) model which was criticized by Ehrenberg (1988). Such models cannot be precisely tested because the relationships between concepts are poorly specified and they lack agreed methods for measuring the concepts. At best they are indicative of the sort of activity that takes place in consumer decision making but even at this level they are inadequate. For example, it might be thought that industrial decision making would have much in common with extended problem solving, yet Simon (1957) has noted that much decision making at work is based on limited information search. Executives take an option if it is 'good enough' to abate a problem. He called this *satisficing* behaviour. The satisficing model may represent high involvement consumer choice too. Expensive choices are often made on the recommen-dation of sales staff and without recourse to *Which?*

There are also doubts about the sequence of decision making. It seems logical that one first gathers information, then evaluates it, and then finally moves to a decision. When Bales and Strodt-beck (1951) studied this process in group decision making they found some support for this order of activity. Specifically the most information gathering occurred in the first phase, the most evaluation in the middle phase and the most decision making in the last phase of the decision period. But they also noted that these different functions occurred in all phases of the decision process so that even near the point of decision the participants were still gathering and evaluating information. Such evidence is consistent with the idea that the processes involved in a decision do not follow a strict logical sequence. Problem solving is probably better explained as a series of associations of thought and feeling rather than as a logical inference.

Does the high/low involvement distinction help the analysis of purchasing? Certainly there are different sorts of purchase decisions. Some choices involve little thought while others bring about lengthy investigation and even distress. The response to advertising may also vary from inattention through to extended reflection, depending on the subject. Progress is being made in describing the processes of thought elicited by advertising and

decision making but this has been achieved by using simpler theories with well established methods for measuring the concepts.
Elaborate models such as Engel, Blackwell and Miniard's (Figure
1.2) reflect a normative approach, i.e. one that prescribes what
ought to happen. Consumer behaviour is concerned with what
does happen. This is a descriptive approach based on scientific
investigation.

Dissonance
Dissonance theory was introduced by Festinger in 1957 and is
concerned with situations in which people commit themselves to
an action that is important to them and which they find difficult
to justify; for example when people yield to pressure to do something they are reluctant to do, or when they make a difficult
choice. Such circumstances disturb people and lead them to
change their thought, feeling or actions in such a way that will
justify their behaviour and reduce their dissonance. For example
a person buying a car that turns out to give poor mileage may
justify the purchase by emphasizing the comfort.

   This theory is important in consumer behaviour because high
involvement decisions are likely to create dissonance and lead to
a search for relevant information. The theory implies that people
are often most receptive to information about a product after
purchase. This raises the importance of after sales service and
suggests that advertising may inform people most after they have
purchased the brand. Satisfied customers, who acquire more
understanding of the product that they have bought, may be
instrumental in getting other people to buy the product. Dissonance research is examined in greater depth in Chapter 7.

Involvement and consumer efficiency
There has been a tendency to regard low involvement purchases
as less soundly based than high involvement purchase. In fact the
reverse may be the truth. Infrequent purchase gives little scope
for trial and error so that people cannot learn from their mistakes.
Some mistakes can be avoided in high involvement choice by
reading reports, consulting other users and reflecting on needs,
but these activities may not give the understanding that is obtained
through direct experience of the product and there is evidence
that they are little used. Beales *et al.* (1981) noted three studies

indicating little overt search for information on expensive products such as major appliances and furniture.

Exercise 1.2. Involvement

Identify a purchase that you or others have made which is highly involving. What makes it so? Was your choice well made: How much investigation did you do before purchase and how much afterwards?

Identify a low involvement purchase that you have made. How much consideration did you give to the different brands?

Freedom of action

To be free, people need to have alternatives, to know what these options are, and not to be under pressure either to take any particular option or to have to choose when all alternatives are unattractive. Action taken without all these conditions applying is action under constraint. A purpose of this book is to extend the study of consumer behaviour to the study of consumption without choice because this is a large part of consumer experience and it often receives perfunctory attention in consumer behaviour texts. Here we are concerned with consumptions such as:

- commuting to work
- having a telephone
- using council services for rubbish collection
- using state educational services
- using state medical provision
- taking electricity and gas supplies
- keeping a bank account
- using the Post Office
- contributing to a pension
- getting a passport

Some of these actions may allow a degree of choice. Some people can afford private education and medical treatment and some people may do without a bank account or telephone but this causes problems in many occupations. There is a degree of choice at the brand level between Post Offices, banks, doctors, and modes of transport to work but when all options are unattractive the constraint still applies. There are also constraints on brand switching. Changing bank accounts or family doctors is complicated; alternative transport to work may be too slow.

Consumer researchers have tended to exaggerate the amount of choice that people have. For example Engel, Blackwell and Miniard (1986, p. 4) describe the consumer as one who can be informed, influenced, but in no way compelled in matters of consumption; they call this *consumer sovereignty*. Consumers are sovereign when they are knowledgeable and unconstrained and suppliers have to serve their interests or lose custom. If simple brand decisions about frequently purchased goods are taken as the exemplar of consumer choice then one may accept that consumers are sovereign in many fields. Buyers do have a large measure of autonomy over such decisions between brands and manufacturers of such goods have limited power to influence their choice.

But buyer autonomy is more restricted in other fields. Even with repetitively purchased goods there may be little freedom at the product level. People must put petrol in the car and detergent in the washing machine and the fact that they have a choice between near identical brands is usually a matter of indifference. Freedom of action is also limited by lack of knowledge, lack of money, and physiological dependence on products like cigarettes. People have limited time and access to alternatives. The claim that the consumer is sovereign must be set against the evidence that people do a great number of things that they would prefer to avoid, e.g. going to work, using congested facilities and queueing in banks and supermarkets. In many areas such as education, medicine and communications the opportunity to influence the service by withdrawing custom or complaining is limited. There are other areas where a lack of resources prevents people from doing the things they might wish to do. Large houses and luxurious cars are possible for only a few. There are some differences of opportunity between Britain and the USA but Engel, Blackwell and Miniard can only sustain their view of consumer sovereignty because they focus on the areas where suppliers must compete for the consumers' custom. Important though this is, it is only part of the picture.

Exercise 1.3. Constrained actions

List goods and services that you would like to avoid but which are forced upon you by other needs. Also list fields where the supply is monopolistic. How could you influence the suppliers of these goods and services?

Frustration

A number of psychological theories relate to restrictions on choice. The condition of blocked motivation called frustration examines the extreme situation where no options are available. A classic study by Barker, Dembo and Lewin (1941) explored the effects of frustration in children who were shown attractive toys but who were prevented from playing with them. Eventually the children were allowed to play with the toys and their behaviour was compared with a control group that had not been frustrated by first being prevented from playing with the toys. The experimental group behaved much more aggressively. A rather similar condition to frustration is *alienation*. Here people are compelled to do things that they do not want to do rather than prevented from doing what they do want to do.

Aggressive responses by consumers are most apparent when a service breaks down unexpectedly, e.g. when the telephone does not work or the traffic stops at times when it usually flows easily. Frustration and anger may also be present when consumers complain about goods and services.

The early work on frustration and aggression suggested a one-to-one relationship so that frustration always led to aggression and aggression was always the product of frustation (Dollard *et al*. 1939) but this is not so. The conditions of frustration and alienation need not result in aggression. Many problems are minor frustrations and these often elicit an effective problem solving approach. Some modes of consumption are rational responses to frustrations, e.g. replacing the unreliable computer or driving to work to avoid erratic public services. This suggests that one strategy in new product development is to look for recurrent frustrations, e.g. the way a stapler jams on the last staple, and to engineer a solution (perhaps a stop on the staple feed that prevents the last staple being used).

Attribution

When an action is freely taken it cannot easily be disowned. When the action is compelled by force of circumstances it is easy to say that 'I had to do it, I had no choice'. People take account of the conditions that affect freedom when they make these attributions of responsibility to themselves or to their environment. Suppose that you find yourself in a long queue at the supermarket on Friday evening. Who is to blame? You can attribute blame internally to yourself for going at a peak time, or externally to other shoppers, the supermarket staff for being slow or the supermarket management because some of the checkouts are unstaffed. How you see the situation affects your subsequent behaviour.

The internal or external attribution of responsibility does not just apply to yourself. The same processes affect the way that you regard the actions of other people. You may see them as personally responsible or you may see their action as the result of forces outside their control. One important finding is that people generally over-estimate the extent to which behaviour is controlled by personal disposition. Jones (1979) called this the *attributional error*. An effect of attributional error is that people will give insufficient attention to changing environmental constraints because they place too much responsibility for happenings on themselves and others.

Attribution theory was based on Heider's ideas (1958) and initially developed by Jones and Davis (1965) and by Kelley (1967).

Attitude and action

The relationship between attitude and action has been extensively researched and is examined at length in Chapter 3 and later chapters. When people act freely we expect their preferences and actions to correspond but when consumption occurs without choice there is no necessary relationship between what is liked and what is done. We might like to have an alternative supplier of gas to British Gas but we do not have that option. We would prefer to avoid queues but often we cannot. This means that consumers of British Gas and shoppers who wait at checkouts cannot be presumed to have positive views about either British Gas or queueing.

Widening the role of consumer research

In a free market, competition is a spur to manufacturers to conduct research and ensure that their brands are what people want. When consumption is constrained, as in public services, there is more need for such research because there is no competition and thus less pressure to remedy deficiencies. Can consumer research improve the public services we get? Probably, but inadequacies in a service can have a number of origins. Sometimes public agencies may be starved of resources, management may be poor, or industrial relations may be chronically bad. But the shortcomings of public services are so obvious that it must be doubted whether enough consumer research is being done. Would queues in Post Offices be eased if people were encouraged to buy stamps in greater quantity? Might public swimming pools be better used if information was published more widely on the times when they were least used? These are possibilities but research is needed to support such conjectures.

Control of public services

Competition

When public services are unsatisfactory the problem of effective control can be approached in two ways. The first approach is to free the market, to stop monopolies and to facilitate switching between suppliers. The problem here is that it is precisely in areas where competition does not work easily that we have the greatest problems of control. An example of this is bus deregulation. This is claimed as a success by Government but a survey by the Metropolitan Authorities showed that the policy was associated with substantial increases in fares and a 12.5 per cent reduction in patronage (*The Independent*, 2 Sept 1988). Transport systems can work better when parts of the system are subsidized by other parts. Deregulation can produce piecemeal competition that destroys cross-subsidy.

Thus the benefits of raising competition vary from application to application and may have costs that make this approach ineffective. The fierce competition that occurs between supermarkets or consumer electronics stores may be unobtainable in other areas.

For example, in 1988 with falling sales, British unit trusts raised their management charges. Even when competition is effective there is a cost. Badly managed resources that lose the battle for custom are wasting assets that provide little benefit to society. But sometimes competition is an excellent solution. In the USA gas can be bought from any supplier who is required to meter into the distribution system the amount of gas that has been sold. This creates real competition quite simply and the only monopoly is the supply system. In principle the same method could be used for electricity.

Management and regulation

The second remedy for many of the unsatisfactory services is managerial. Services that are ill-designed and poorly resourced can be improved by better management that consults its users and ensures that they have effective means of influencing decision makers. This approach uses professionalism, external regulation, and publicity to ensure that standards are high. Like competition, however, managerial remedies may fail. For instance, professionalism will not guarantee same day service in the Passport Office. Good management, however, has many aspects and more relationship between pay and performance in the public sector might help. When public offices such as the Post Office are adequately capitalized it is reasonable that employee pay should reflect the amount of business transacted.

More regulation

Governments and their agencies frame the rules within which public activity takes place and this has an effect on the consumer. Government policies often affect consumer opportunities: freer trade, rules on monopolies and restrictive agreements, intervention on interest and exchange rates, the resourcing of the public sector, and privatization of public assets, laws on labelling and shop hours; all of these impact upon the choices available to the citizen.

Despite the fact that rules are often seen to inhibit competition there is an important role for Government regulations that will

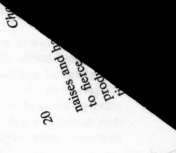

raise competition. Rules against ca
example of this, and other example
prices (as in a French bar), stating th
on the reverse of receipt notes, requirin
of bank accounts easy, making the chai
such as unit trusts more related to their
formance, and restricting the level of ci
choice is limited.

Brands and product type

ref

[The distinction between brand and product type is well understood
but it has implications which should be considered. Kotler (1986,
p. 302)] defines a brand as:

> a name, term, sign, symbol, or combination of them intended
> to identify the goods or services of one seller or group of
> sellers and to differentiate them from those of competitors.

Thus branding serves to differentiate products from other similar
products so that they can be marketed separately. This was of
course the original use of branding with cattle. Brands may differ
in their properties, sometimes very little as with petrol or detergent and sometimes substantially in the case or confectionery or
biscuits. Advertising may add value to brands by associating them
with important social groups, with style and excitement. Many
brands are sub-divided into *varieties*. For example I can buy Crest
toothpaste in two different flavours, as a gel or paste and in
standard and tartar control formulations. The class that a brand
belongs to, e.g. toothpaste, is called the *product type* or (in the
USA) *category* and all the brands of that type are called the
product field.

Branding can be looked at from the position of the producer
or the consumer. From the standpoint of the producer, branding is
a necessary prerequisite for effective marketing. Unless consumers
have in mind the particular branded version of a product and
distinguish it from other versions the supplier is easy prey to
competitors and to price bargaining from retailers. [Thus an
important function of advertising is to establish brand identity.] Cole
The case of Hellmann's mayonnaise (Channon, 1985) illustrates
this point. This brand was priced well above competitive mayon-

...d such a large share of the market that it was open ...competition from other brands, particularly own label ...ucts in the supermarkets. This meant that strong brand iden-...ty was essential to reduce the extent of substitution and the advertising used the term 'Hellmann's' rather than 'mayonnaise' to differentiate it from other commercial mayonnaises. The campaign was successful in stemming the loss to own brands but it is likely that the quality of the product helped here. Hellmann's uses lemon juice in the formulation whereas the competitors often use spirit vinegar and the difference in taste is distinct.

It is not always possible to establish a strong brand identity. Some products like vegetables are difficult to brand because of the variability in supply. Others are so invariant that they are treated as commodities. Sugar and salt, for example, are available as branded goods but it makes little sense to advertise them by brand name. Some goods are not easily recognized as different brands. Beds, for example, have brand names such as Myers or Slumberland but members of the public would not normally know the difference between them. Sometimes this problem is overcome by design features that differentiate a brand from other brands in the field. Perrier water chose a distinctive bottle and the Swiss firm, Zehnder, did this with central heating radiators using bright stove enamelling and distinctive shapes.

Consumers have other criteria than brand when they differentiate products, e.g. price, size, freshness, origin, or colour. When consumers ignore brand differentiation the promotion of one brand has the effect of promoting all brands, i.e. the product type. Under these circumstances producers must decide whether to devote advertising resources to trying to establish brand identity or whether to use price, product design, sales promotions or distribution to secure the market. When distribution is assured, promotion can often be limited and therefore branding is less important. This underlies the growth of retailer brands that has taken place in recent years.

In some areas a sale may rest heavily on intermediaries. Industrial goods and insurance are examples for which the manufacturer's name is more important than specific brands. This is also true of famous retailers like Harrods. Thus, depending on the product, distribution and supplier, and the way consumers respond to the product field, a decision must be made on brand emphasis. When specific branding is not a commercial strategy an

alternative may lie in the promo
(e.g. St Michael), the supplier's n
advertising), or, using a consort
Board, the generic product. The la
the absence of a trade body capabl
suppliers.

Branding has some value to con
one variation of the product type. W
the branding helps consumers to ob
may not be present in other brands.
well. Stilton or Brie vary quite widely
what you are buying is achieved by opting for a brand name such
as St Ivel or Cambozola.

In many frequently purchased goods markets the differences
between brands are small both objectively and in consumers' perceptions. The interest of the manufacturers is in their brand share
but their influence on the consumer is weak. The buyer wants
detergent, sugar, cooking oil, etc. first and often does not care
whether the brand is Persil or Surf, Tate and Lyle or Silver Spoon,
Mazola or an own brand. In some cases the brand may be so
unimportant that it is ignored. For example you are more likely
to know the country of origin of olive oil than its manufacturer.

Other brand choices have more substance: Mars Bars versus
Bounty Bars, Bath Olivers versus Jacob's Cream Crackers,
Mother's Pride versus Hovis, Roger et Gallet soap versus Pears'.
There are more brand differences in the consumer durable market
where particular household appliances or cars have features of
performance, reliability, and after-sales service which may be of
central importance in the consumer's choice. A number of studies
have shown differences in consumers' perceptions of brands. Cowling (1973), Ryan and Etzel (1976) on toothpaste, and a pro-
prietary investigation by Tuck on detergent referred to by Ajzen
and Fishbein (1980) have measured differences between the
beliefs associated with different brands. Consumers' ideas about
brands may also differ from their ideas about the product type.
Mazis, Ahtola and Klippel (1975) found that the beliefs about
cars in general omitted many beliefs that were confined to brands,
e.g. their status symbolism and country of manufacture.

Human processes

...ssion on branding underscores an important point. We ...cerned with human choice which depends upon perceptions ...ut alternatives. Judgements are related to these perceptions and not directly to the objective features of alternatives. Objective features are important because they affect perceptions but there is no simple one-to-one relationship between the physical features of a brand and the way it is perceived. A study by Schlegel, Crawford and Sanborn (1977) reflects on this. They found that the attitude to drinking different alcoholic beverages depended upon the social contexts in which the drinking was to take place whether at home with parents, at a party with friends, or at a pub.

Many brand features may not be known and some beliefs about alternatives may not fit the facts. A study by Wheatley, Yalch and Chiu (1980) illustrates this latter point. Subjects were informed that two alternative new brands of cola contained an identical product. Brand A and Brand B were presented in the same way except that Brand A had a 10 cent coin taped to each can. The subjects were given money to buy six cans. Even though the subjects had tasted the colas they still lost money by selecting, on average, more than two cans of Brand B out of every six chosen. Clearly the ideas that subjects had about the colas went beyond the objective facts.

Such evidence shows that assumptions about human choice can easily be mistaken. If we measure beliefs and preferences rather than making assumptions about these variables we shall have a better basis for the design and promotion of products and services.

Summary

Actions can be described according to their frequency, importance and freedom. Three types of action are particularly relevant to the analysis of consumption. The first is repetitive, free and relatively unimportant and includes brand purchase in the fast moving goods sector. The repetitive nature of this choice makes learning principles relevant. The second type of consumption is important, relatively free and infrequent and covers durable purchases and major personal decisions. High involvement consumption belongs to this type. Theories about the way consumption affects the purchaser's image are relevant. Also difficult choices raise psychological stress and dissonance theory may explain some post-purchase behaviour.

The third type of consumption is constrained and covers the actions forced upon us in monopolistic markets and as a consequence of earlier decisions. This is called consumption without choice. Lack of choice may be frustrating; people may act aggressively or make efforts to overcome the constraints. Another response to unpleasant modes of consumption which are recurrent is for people to become desensitized and not to be affected by what they have to do. This has the unfortunate consequence that they do not complain. When people feel they have no control they attribute responsibility to their environment and their preferences lack correspondence with their actions. The effective control of monopolistic services has a political aspect.

When consumer choice is limited, research on consumer preferences is needed since there is no market competition to operate in the consumer interest. Consumer behaviour is a descriptive subject concerned with what *is*; in this respect it differs from the normative approach of marketing where the focus is upon what *ought to be*.

Further reading

Engel, J. F., Blackwell, R. D. and Miniard, P. W. (1986) *Consumer Behavior*, 5th ed. New York, The Dryden Press, ch. 1.

[2]
Regularities in buying behaviour

Overview

This chapter is a review of British research on repetitively purchased goods. This work has direct relevance to strategic decisions in marketing but it has not been given the prominence it deserves in textbooks on consumer behaviour. Part of the reason for this absence from student texts is the demanding nature of the material. To simplify the presentation I have adopted a question and answer format and have kept back some of the issues raised by this research until the last section.

Learning theory, outlined in Chapter 1, applies to frequent purchase because previous consumption experience can reinforce later purchase. In fact learning theory suggests two different models. The first is one of constant updating in which all previous purchases and brand experience bear on current purchase propensity. This implies a *fluctuating propensity* to buy. The fluctuation arises from any variation in experience and from satiation and extinction effects. The second model from learning theory is based on the way in which habit takes over in human behaviour. People form *stable propensities* to act in particular ways which are unaffected by minor variations in the reinforcement experience.

A third model for explaining patterns in frequent purchase comes from popular assumptions about buying and fits the idea that we have attitudes for and against different brands. In this approach people keep allegiance to particular brands until they switch and then they give the same allegiance to a new brand. This is the *switching* model. This model gives promotion the role of engineering the switch and is a working assumption for many people engaged in marketing.

Of the three models the one which applies best to frequent purchase is the second. The basic pattern in frequent purchase markets is a *stable propensity to purchase*. Of course purchase dispositions do sometimes change and people do stop using some brands and start using others but this activity is comparatively rare. Because marketing practitioners tend to work on a switching model they are liable to make errors in marketing strategy.

Stable propensities help to make purchase behaviour predictable so that, for example, repeat purchase, the distribution of heavy and light buyers, and the pattern of purchase within a brand field are derivable from other measures. Many articles have been published on these subjects, e.g. Ehrenberg (1959, 1969) and Collins (1971). This work was brought together by Ehrenberg (1988) and less formally by Ehrenberg and Goodhardt (1979). These authors attacked many of the conventional wisdoms of marketing, and have forced a reappraisal of traditional ideas about brand loyalty, brand image, brand segmentation, the effects of advertising, and the way in which sales grow.

The methods of analysis used by these authors are mathematical and can be applied to other forms of repetitive behaviour. Goodhardt, Ehrenberg and Collins (1975, 1987) have applied these methods to the study of television audiences. Barwise (1986) and Ehrenberg and Goodhardt (1986) have made other contributions to the study of television audiences. Another application has been to store choice, treating stores like Sainsbury as a brand, e.g. Kau and Ehrenberg (1984).

Ehrenberg and his co-workers look at the buying that takes place over a defined period of time. Data on such purchases are gathered for households in panel studies such as those run by Audits of Great Britain Ltd (AGB) and the Market Research Corporation of America (MRCA). With a panel the same people are surveyed at intervals and their purchases can therefore be related to their own previous and subsequent consumption. Many of the markets studied in this way are found to be approximately stationary, i.e. there is no overall trend for brands, and total purchases in two equal time periods are therefore the same. Of course a market is never exactly stationary; there is often some seasonality or a slight trend and there may be substantial short-term fluctuation as a result of promotions.

Stationarity in the market occurs either because the same people buy the same amount or because the increase in the tendency to buy among some people is matched by a decrease among others. Particularly over shorter periods there is some variation in what individuals buy, but this is due to chance fluctuations rather than changes in the underlying propensity to purchase. Over long periods panel data show little change in what individuals buy. Also it is found that purchase levels return to near normal after price promotions and temporary stockouts. This again suggests an underlying propensity to purchase which is relatively unchanged by disturbances in the market. Evidence supporting this has been gathered in marketing experiments (England and Ehrenberg, 1986, 1988).

Because individually and collectively the purchases of a brand in two equal time periods tend toward the same amount a probabilistic model of purchase can be constructed which describes purchase behaviour. This gives an explanation of how people act rather than why. Ehrenberg does not suggest that individuals lack specific wants and purposes but says that such motivations produce aggregate effects that can be measured and calculated without knowledge of the precise nature of the motivation.

Some of Ehrenberg's critics argue that the lack of attention to motivational issues limits the application of his work and that this is particularly so when people change. What do you put in advertisements if people's motivations are unknown? Why do some people respond more to price cuts than others? Do those who buy more have different reasons from those who buy less? Some markets do expand and contract over time and such changes may sometimes reflect changes in motivations. Ehrenberg and Goodhardt do not claim to cover all the problems that arise in marketing, and specifically exclude the qualitative aspects of motivation. However recent work at the London Business School has shifted to the dynamics of consumption (for example, how people change their buying in response to price changes) and this may raise more detailed questions about motivation.

The following sections of this chapter examine the panel evidence on the nature of single brand purchase, the mathematical theory which can be used to predict this purchase, and purchase effects across brands in the same product field; later sections show how this work relates to advertising and examine more critically some of the issues raised.

The purchase of a brand

Definitions

The reader should be clear about three definitions and their relationship.

1 The *penetration*, b, which is the proportion of all potential buyers in a population who buy a brand at least once in a period.
2 The *purchase frequency*, w, which is the average number of purchase occasions for those who purchase at least once in a period.
3 *Sales*, m, which is the average number of purchase occasions in the period made by an individual potential buyer. When b is expressed as a percentage m will be the sales per hundred buyers.

These variables are linked by the sales equation:

$$m = bw$$

When average sales by weight, value or number of units purchased are required the equation must include a factor which converts a purchase occasion into the appropriate variable, e.g.:

$$m_v = bwv$$

where m_v is the sales value and v is the average value of a purchase. In most fields people buy one unit at a time and we do not distinguish between purchase occasions and the number of units bought.

Exercise 2.1. Applying the sales equation

1 Suppose that in a stationary market the penetration of Bic biros is 0.07 over 24 weeks. Given that 21 units are sold per hundred potential buyers, what is the purchase frequency?

2 How many units will be sold per 100 potential buyers in 48 weeks?

3 If the purchase frequency for the 48 week period is 4.6, what will be the mean sales and penetration?

4 In 24 weeks 105 biros of all types are sold per hundred buyers. What is Bic's market share?

Questions about consumer purchase

In the rest of this section the following questions are answered:

- Do people buy habitually?
- How does the nature of a product affect sales?
- What fraction of buyers in one period will buy again in another?
- How many people buy once, twice, etc. in a period?
- What fraction of sales come from heavy buyers?

Buying habits

Do we buy at regular intervals? Habitual purchase would show up in panel data as an individual tendency to buy a brand every week or month. Habits of this sort would mean that a purchaser's probability of buying rises sharply at intervals. This model may fit some frequent purchases such as newspapers or cigarettes but in general the evidence approximates to the simpler stable propensity model of purchase. Purchase is like the fall of raindrops: we cannot predict when the next raindrop will strike from when the last one fell and we cannot predict when the next purchase will be made from when the last one was made. The incidence of purchase is quasi-random. This sort of incidence is described mathematically as having a Poisson distribution.

However, people rarely buy a brand again immediately after purchasing it and people buy little at night. Habits do have some effect and the Poisson distribution does not fit purchase over periods that are much shorter than the average inter-purchase interval. Over the longer periods covered in panel research the fit of the Poisson assumption is close and provides a basis for the mathematical model described in the next section.

Do some people regularly buy more than others? Yes, they do;

the people who are heavy consumers in one period tend to be heavy consumers in another period though the actual sales show a stochastic variability. So there is habit in the *level* of consumption.

How does the type of product affect purchase? Obviously some products have higher penetrations and purchase frequencies than others; such differences are not at issue. But, for example, is sole brand loyalty or repeat purchase affected by the type of product or the brand? Many manufacturers think so and may be proud of the loyalty that customers show in buying their brand. However panel research shows that sole brand loyalty and repeat purchase depend mainly on purchase frequency and slightly on penetration so that a knowledge of these variables is sufficient to predict repeat purchase for any brand. A few products do show higher levels of repeat purchase than would be expected from their purchase frequency, cigarettes for example, but generally the type of product or brand need not be known for the prediction of a number of important measures like repeat purchase. This means that a mathematical theory applying to most frequently purchased goods is possible and this theory (Negative Binomial Distribution Theory) is explained on pp. 32–4.

Repeat purchase

Stationarity in the market means that the same total amount is bought in any two periods but this does not mean that the same people buy in each period. Some of those who buy in one reference period will not buy in another and 'new' buyers will enter the market to make up for these 'lapsed' buyers. The quotation marks for 'new' and 'lapsed' are a reminder that they may not be new or lapsed when other periods are considered. New buyers may have bought in other periods than the reference period and lapsed buyers may return in later periods.

Panel studies reveal the proportion of repeat buyers, i.e. those buyers in one period who also bought in a previous reference period. Earlier it was noted that repeat purchase proportions depend mainly on the purchase frequency. Reflection suggests that this should be so since purchase frequency is some sort of index of the disposition to buy and more strongly disposed buyers are more likely to buy in the next round. Repeat purchasers buy at a somewhat higher rate than they did in the reference period while new buyers purchase at a low and fairly constant rate of about 1.5 purchases in any period.

Table 2.1 *Repeat purchase for given purchase frequencies and penetrations*

Penetration (%)	2	2	20	20
Purchase frequency	2	20	2	20
Repeat purchase (%)	57	85	60	86

Penetration does have a small effect on repeat purchase rates which is illustrated in Table 2.1. Table 2.1 shows that when penetration is constant a tenfold difference in purchase frequency has much more effect on repeat purchase rate than a tenfold difference in penetration when purchase frequency is constant. Note that it is the repeat purchase *rate* that is only slightly affected by penetration. The *number* of repeat purchasers is directly affected by penetration.

The weak relationship between penetration and repeat purchase rate may be used to estimate the effective number of purchasers available to a market. For example the number of purchases of Whiskas by non-owners of cats is very low and the base on which penetration should be calculated is more realistically the number of households owning a cat, not the total number of households. Apparent distortions in repeat purchase may be due to unrealistic base assumptions.

To illustrate the Whiskas example suppose that 20 per cent of the population buys Whiskas with a purchase frequency of 5 times a month. The repeat purchase expected is 77 per cent for this penetration and this purchase frequency. But if only one household in three has a cat and the penetration of Whiskas is 60 per cent of this group, the repeat purchase expected is 83 per cent. Thus evidence of high repeat purchases may indicate that the potential purchasing group is smaller than that which has been assumed.

If the purchase frequency for Quarter 1 indicates a repeat purchase rate of 50 per cent, then approximately this figure will be found in Quarters 2, 3 and 4 under stationary conditions with no seasonality. A repeat purchase that is much different from 50 per cent, or one that shows a trend, indicates that the market lacks the normal stability. Repeat purchase is therefore an important diagnostic measure. For example it helps to find out what to do about a heavily advertised new brand that has stationary sales. Is the advertising ineffective? Or is the brand failing to create repeat purchasers so that sales are made up by a disproportionate number of trialists who are encouraged by the advertising? Evidence that repeat purchase is normal favours the first explanation and means that the advertising should be changed. Evidence that the repeat purchase is below the normal level supports the second explanation and indicates that the brand is a loser.

Heavy buyers
For quite long periods most people might never buy a brand at all. Of those that buy, most do so infrequently and relatively few buy heavily. Table 2.2 shows that over a 13 week period 93 per cent of a sample of households did not buy Shredded Wheat at all, 4 per cent bought once, 1 per cent bought twice and less than 2 per cent bought three or more times. Although few people buy frequently these people are responsible for a lot of the sales. Table 2.2 shows that for every 59 purchases of Shredded Wheat by those buying once there are 30 by those buying twice (i.e. 15 × 2), 39 by those buying three times, 12 by those buying four times, 30 by those buying five times and at least 24 from those buying six or more times. In general a substantial proportion of purchases are made by very few heavy buyers; one rule of thumb is that the lighter buying 50 per cent are responsible for about 20 per cent of all purchases while the heavy buying 50 per cent are responsible for about 80 per cent of all purchases.

Table 2.2 *Sales of Corn Flakes and Shredded Wheat by a sample of 1420 US households (from Ehrenberg and Goodhardt, 1979)*

	Penetration %	Purchases in 13 weeks (% of those purchasing)						Purchase frequency
		1	2	3	4	5	6+	
Corn Flakes	20	55	22	8	5	5	5	2.1
Shredded Wheat	7	59	15	13	3	6	4	2.0

This breakdown of purchase shows that heavy buyers are an attractive segment in many markets and marketers may therefore try to focus their efforts on the heavy buyer. However it is doubtful whether such efforts can be more than marginally successful. Success would mean that the usual distribution of purchases between heavy and light buyers would no longer be found. Sometimes it is possible to target the heavy buyers by adapting the distribution system. For example the 'wine warehouse' selling by the case may secure a larger proportion of heavy buyers.

Negative Binomial Distribution (NBD) theory

In the previous section it was explained that two quite different brands in any product field will have approximately the same repeat purchase rate if they have the same purchase frequency and penetration. NBD theory is a mathematical model which permits the prediction of repeat purchase and other measures from data on the penetration, purchase frequency and period. The theory is based on the assumptions that total purchases of a brand are stationary, that individual purchases follow a Poisson distribution, and that the long run average purchase rates of individuals follow a Gamma distribution. These assumptions are set out by Ehrenberg (1988, ch. 4). Within these assumptions it is possible to derive an expression for the probability of making r purchases in a period, p_r.

$$p_r = (1 - m/(m+k))^{-k}$$

where m is the sales and k is a factor that is estimated from the purchase frequency and penetration. Expressions of the form $(1+x)^n$ are called binomial. The equation for p_r is a negative binomial because the exponent is negative.

The calculation of the NBD requires the solution of the equation

$$1 - b = (1 + m/k)^{-k}$$

(where b is the penetration) to obtain the factor k. This can be done using tables or with a computer program called 'NBD'.

Program NBD

Using data on the penetration, purchase frequency and period, this program solves the equation to obtain k and computes repeat purchase and new purchase rates for different periods. The distribution of people buying once, twice, etc. is worked out for each period and the proportion of sales attributable to different rates of purchase is also calculated. These figures are displayed on the screen and the user has options to change the rounding, and to express figures as proportions, percentages or actual numbers. The tabulated figures can then be printed.

The program is easy to use but has one technical limitation: when the penetration is high and the purchase frequency is low the mathematical procedure for estimating k breaks down and the user must then extrapolate from results obtained with lower penetration figures. The program is needed to answer questions in Exercises 2.2 to 2.5.

Exercise 2.2. Using Program NBD: How the period affects the data

It is assumed that the reader is familiar with personal computers. After the machine is booted the program is loaded by typing NBD<return>.

1 Assume that 5 per cent (0.05 as a proportion) of the population buys an average of 1.5 KitKats in each 4 week period. Enter the penetration, b, and the purchase frequency, w, for the given period and fill in the table below:

Weeks:	1	4	12	24	48
b:					
w:					

How do these variables change over time?

2 The maximum penetration is 1, but because many people buy very rarely, b is usually much less than 1, even for long periods. Can you compute the proportion of the population who buy *no* KitKats in four years? (Hint: If you enter the 4 week data as 1 week data all results will be for four times the tabulated period.)

3 Notice that the purchase rate for new buyers is relatively constant for different periods. See whether it remains so for different b and w input data.

Real data and theoretical prediction

Estimates using the negative binomial theory are very close to the figures obtained from panel data. NBD theory is therefore very useful for calculating benchmark data for stationary conditions. Changes produced by promotions can then be evaluated by comparing real data with these benchmarks.

It is important to see that the calculations correspond with real findings under stationary conditions. You can generate theoretical data to compare with the real data in Table 2.2 for example. Use Program NBD and enter the penetration, purchase frequency and period for each brand. The theoretical distributions obtained are very close to the empirical figures.

Exercise 2.3. Collecting panel data for comparison with NBD predictions

NBD predictions can be tested in class. You and others must keep a diary and record, for instance, how many times you phone your friends or drink lager each day. The data should be accumulated for a period greater than the average inter-purchase interval because the theory may fail when the duration is shorter than this. In this respect telephoning works well. Table 2.3 is derived from such data obtained from 224 students for one day.

Table 2.3 *Number of students making one or more telephone calls in a day*

No. calling:	1	2	3	4	5	6+ times
Predicted:	75	28	8	2	0	0
Found:	75	30	8	0	0	1

Derived from the findings in this table $b = 0.509$ and $w = 1.456$.

Exercise 2.4. Exploring the relationships

1 Use the KitKat data from Exercise 2.2 to work out w_R/w which is the ratio of the purchase frequency of repeat buyers to the general purchase frequency (both given by Program NBD). Note that NBD theory makes this approximately constant at about 1.2. Try this for other data inputs.

2 What proportion of all KitKat purchases are made by people buying more than once a month? How might you promote the product to such people?

3 Suppose that the theory indicated that 60 per cent of those purchasing a brand should buy again in the following period but the evidence showed that 80 per cent did. There is no evidence that the market is disturbed; in fact 80 per cent is regularly found for this brand. What would this departure from NBD prediction suggest?

Exercise 2.5. Marketing analyses

1 Brand R was launched 18 months ago. With continuing advertising support it has maintained a stable penetration of 4 per cent and a purchase frequency of 1.4 per quarter. Panel research shows a repeat purchase rate of 21 per cent. Should you stop the advertising? Withdraw the brand? Maintain both? (To answer this you need to work out whether the stationary sales show the theoretical repeat purchase for a stationary brand (see Ehrenberg 1988, p. 97–8).)

2 The consumption of soup rises in the winter and falls in the summer. Find out whether all those who buy soup reduce consumption in the summer or whether there are two groups: those who buy it all the year with much the same frequency, and those who buy it only in the winter. Panel data show that those who buy soup in the summer show a penetration of 32 per cent and a purchase frequency of 5 over 12 weeks. When these people are followed into the higher consumption winter period, panel data show that their quarterly repeat purchase is 79 per cent. What do you conclude? (You need to work out whether this repeat purchase is the norm for a stationary market. If it is then you have two separate groups: the year round stationary buyers and seasonal buyers who only enter the market in the winter. For more information see Goodhardt and Ehrenberg, 1979, Section 2.8.)

3 In January 5 per cent of the population bought brand C on 4.4 occasions. In February when C was promoted 8 per cent of the population bought C. Panel data show that 79 per cent of January buyers bought again in February. How did the promotion affect repeat purchase and new purchase respectively? Fill in the table showing the figures that would be expected under stationary conditions and those that were obtained with the promotion. Start with the totals.

	For every 100 buyers in January the buyers in February will be:	
	Expected (stationary)	Obtained (promotion)
Repeat purchasers:		
New purchasers:		
Totals:		

Product field effects

The focus now shifts from the brand to the product field and we address the following questions:

- How do purchase frequencies vary in a product field?
- What are the characteristics of more popular brands?
- Which changes more when market share changes: penetration or purchase frequency?
- Can we predict the purchase frequency and penetration of a new entrant to a market for a given market share?
- Are people mostly loyal to one brand or do they spread their purchases across several brands in the product field?
- Who buys more: single brand buyers or multi-brand buyers?
- When people buy more than one brand do they buy particular alternatives so that a pattern of brand substitutions emerges?
- Does the evidence favour a 'niche' or a 'me too' strategy in new product introduction?
- Is television watching like brand purchasing?
- Can we analyse markets on other bases than brand?
- How can multi-brand purchase patterns be modelled mathematically?

Purchase frequencies and penetrations

Purchase frequency variation and popular brand characteristics

From Table 2.2 it can be seen that one cereal has three times the market share of the other. This difference appears mainly through penetration; the purchase frequencies are very similar. This indicates an empirical regularity that is generally found: that different brands in the same product field have similar purchase frequencies. Differences of brand share are marked mainly by difference in penetration. Thus big brands have large market share mainly because they have higher penetrations than others in the same product field.

To explore this further consider the data on US coffee consumption in Table 2.4. These data show some tendency for purchase frequency to increase as penetration increases but penetration is much more variable than purchase frequency in the range illustrated. The relationship between purchase frequency and penetration fits approximately the equation:

$$w_X(1-b_X) = w_Y(1-b_Y)$$

where X and Y are brands in the same product field. In many product fields the brand penetrations are quite low so that $(1-b)$ is close to unity for all brands. This explains why the purchase frequencies show little difference in Tables 2.2 and 2.4. The relationship between penetration and purchase frequency in a product field is also described by the law of *double jeopardy*: that less popular brands are bought by fewer people and those that do buy these brands buy them less often. The principle of double jeopardy was described by McPhee (1963, pp. 133–40) who credits the original idea to the broadcaster Jack Landis. McPhee was concerned to explain popularity and in particular how the liking for broadcasters (among those who had heard of them) fell with the proportion of the population who had heard of them. McPhee explained double jeopardy thus:

> On top of the initial disadvantage that such an unpublicized alternative is unknown to many people, who therefore *cannot* choose it, there is a second disadvantage that the few people who do know the lesser alternative apparently *do not* choose it, not proportionately as well as they do others.

Table 2.4   *Brand penetration and purchase frequency for instant coffee sales over 48 weeks in the USA (MRCA Panel Data, 1981)*

Brand	Purchases per 100 households	Penetration	Purchase frequency
Maxwell House	86	24	3.6
Sanka	69	21	3.2
Taster's Choice	62	22	2.8
High Point	57	22	2.6
Folgers	49	18	2.7
Nescafe	38	13	2.9
Brim	18	9	2.0
Maxim	16	6	2.6

Double jeopardy may occur in part because of the effects of repeated exposure. More popular brands tend to be more widely exposed so that more people are aware of them. Those who do see the brands do so more often and there is evidence (Zajonc, 1968) that stimuli are liked more if they are seen more. If people choose what they like the effect of double jeopardy is supported. Brand double jeopardy is discussed by Ehrenberg, Goodhardt and Barwise (1988).

The nature of brand popularity has been further explored by Goddard (1978). He accepts that brand size is related to penetration but he also found that the more popular brands were bought by people who bought the product class at a lower purchase frequency. Goddard found that the ratio:

$$w/w_p$$

is closely related to popularity. This is because w, the brand purchase frequency, is larger for purchasers of more popular brands because of double jeopardy while w_p, the product type purchase frequency, is smaller for purchasers of the more popular brands. Goddard's finding is restricted to one data set dealing with detergents but his evidence is consistent with a second McPhee principle called the law of natural monopoly: that more popular items are disproportionately favoured by those choosing few alternatives in a given period of time. For example the more popular the newspaper that people read the less likely they are to read other newspapers (McPhee, 1963, p. 126–33).

Market share changes

Table 2.4 also shows the way in which consumption data might be expected to change if market share alters. From the figures in Table 2.4 it is unlikely that Brim could equal Folgers by getting all existing buyers to use nearly three times as much. The relative constancy of brand purchase frequencies means that sales have to grow mainly by increases in penetration. Sometimes a gain in frequency may be possible by persuading consumers to find new uses for a product, e.g. pouring bleach down drains to disinfect them, but this is a new use of the product type which is likely to raise all brand purchase frequencies so that they remain in step.

The relative constancy of purchase frequency within a product class is an empirical finding. People could buy more of a brand, even without altering their total purchases in a product field. For example, in the US instant coffee market people buy twice as much of other brands than they do of their preferred brand so that a brand that secured 100 per cent loyalty could raise its purchase frequency by three times but such effects are not found. It is not suggested that purchase frequencies remain relatively constant throughout the turbulence of a promotion. It is argued that once sales have stabilized after a market intervention any change in market share will show up mainly as a change in the penetration variable.

Motes and Woodside (1984) found gains in both penetration and purchase frequency during the period of a package advertisement campaign. In this case there was no long-term gain in market share and these gains disappeared when the campaign stopped. Another study (Channon, 1985, p. 168) examined the growth in popularity of Curly Wurly, a price competitive toffee strip liked by children. In 1982 advertising substantially raised purchase which stabilized after 4 months and remained constant for the rest of the year. From the published data it appears that the increase in sales was 70 per cent among 7–11 year old children and in this group the two-monthly penetration shifted by an average of 60 per cent which implies a marginal increase in purchase frequency in line with the double jeopardy effect. Among adults the sales gain was 150 per cent, penetration doubled and purchase frequency rose by about a quarter. Thus this extreme test indicated, as predicted, that penetration carried most of the increase.

Treasure (1975) has pointed out that the fact that brands differ mainly by penetration is a consequence of the fact that most penetrations are low. The picture changes if longer periods are considered. Obviously the longer the period, the larger will be the proportion of the people who try the product at least once so that penetrations rise with the length of the period considered. As the penetration approaches its maximum so increases in sales must come more from increases in purchase frequency. Thus the way that sales growth appears depends upon the penetration level. When penetrations are fairly low, say less than 20 per cent, a sales change appears predominantly as a penetration change. This evidence has bearing on marketing strategy. It is unrealistic for marketers to expect to see large increases in purchase frequency as a result of their intervention. However, this does not mean that a 'use more' strategy is necessary unwise.

Prediction of purchase frequency and penetration
Table 2.4 indicates the pattern of consumption that can be expected from a new entrant to the market which reaches a given market share. For example a new instant coffee with a market share like that of Brim is going to have a purchase frequency of the order of 2.5 for the period if it is bought through the same distribution systems as other instant coffees. Any other marketing assumptions are simply unrealistic.

Exercise 2.6. Inferences about purchase frequency

Suppose that after a determined advertising campaign the penetration over 12 weeks of Kleenex Velvet toilet paper rises from 20 per cent and stabilizes at 25 per cent. Initially the purchase frequency was 5 for this period. What purchase frequency would you expect now? Use the equation:

$$w_X(1-b_X) = w_Y(1-b_Y)$$

where the X and Y indicate values for Kleenex Velvet toilet paper before and after the campaign.

The brand portfolio

Table 2.5 presents data reported by Ehrenberg and Goodhardt (1979) on the extent of 'other brand buying'. Most buyers of a given brand also buy other brands on a regular basis and their selection is called the *brand portfolio* or *brand repertoire*. Most people are not sole brand loyal therefore but the evidence supports a looser meaning of brand loyalty: i.e. continuing to buy the same portfolio of brands in much the same proportions over long periods of time.

Some people are loyal to only one brand but this depends partly on the duration of the period being considered. In a short period most buyers are loyal to one brand because they have no time to buy anything else. The evidence of multiple brand buying shows that a person can have several propensities to buy in a product field. An important consequence of this idea is that people do not 'switch' when they buy a brand which is different from their last purchase. Switching implies a change of sole brand loyalty. If people have several brand propensities in a product field they can buy different brands with no change in these propensities.

Table 2.5 *Average frequencies of purchase of cereals in a year (from Ehrenberg and Goodhardt, 1979)*

Brand	Average purchases by buyers of stated brand	
	Stated brand	Other brands
Nabisco Shredded Wheat (USA)	4	37
Nabisco Shredded Wheat (UK)	7	33
Kelloggs Corn Flakes (USA)	5	29
Kelloggs Corn Flakes (UK)	10	23

When both single brand buyers and multi-brand buyers purchase a brand the single brand buyer buys a little more of the brand than the multi-brand buyer. But the total purchases of the product type made by a multi-brand buyer are larger than those of a single brand buyer. As such the fully loyal purchaser is of less value to the professional marketer; the person who buys more presents more opportunity of extra sales. Despite this fact manufacturers continue to attach great importance to the level of sole brand loyalty that their brand commands.

Brand segmentation

One explanation for multi-brand buying is that people see certain brands as substitutable for each other and therefore they buy them interchangeably. If brands X and Y were substitutable in this way we would find that the buyers of brand X were more likely to buy brand Y than would be predicted on the basis of the brand Y market share (and vice versa). Such an effect is called *brand segmentation*. Ehrenberg and Goodhardt (1979) demonstrate that this effect can occur, for example, in pre-sweetened cereals where those who buy one sweetened cereal are more likely to buy another of that type than an unsweetened brand.

However for most of the product fields studied there is little brand segmentation. When segmentation does occur it can usually be connected with distinct product features like price and sugar content rather than to the less tangible features of the brand identified in advertising. Collins (1971) has reviewed this issue in a succinct paper.

How then do we describe how people distribute their second and third choices in a product field? The evidence shows that, in aggregate other purchases are proportional to the market share of other brands. This is a logical consequence of the fact that brand segmentation is low. If people do not cluster purchase on brand sub-groups then the aggregate effect of their secondary purchasing must reflect the way in which purchases are generally distributed, i.e. market share.

One consequence of this evidence is that new brands do not need to have some unique formulation to succeed. Product positioning may be over-valued and it may be unnecessary to search for some combination of product attributes that has not been offered in the existing product range and then to base a new product on this unique sub-set of attributes. Since consumers appear not to make subtle distinctions between brands the 'niche' strategy may be ill-founded. When this strategy does succeed it may be because the product is generally perceived to be equivalent to other brands rather than different from them. Thus Ehrenberg recommends that manufacturers do not rule out the strategy which is often called 'me-too', i.e. copying existing successful brands. This is a strategy much used by retailers with their own brands.

Despite this analysis the niche approach is well established in marketing and the evidence that there is little brand segmentation surprises brand managers and those responsible for new product development who give careful attention to the positioning of their brands. They are clearly right to do so when the brand features can shift the product from one category to another. For example, ice cream brands can range from confectionery-like products to thirst-quenching frozen fruit juice and thus they compete with both chocolate and squash. What is more at issue, however, is whether the minor differences between brands have much effect on sales. This matter arises again in the discussion later in this chapter about the way in which individual preferences may be obscured in aggregated data.

The close association between secondary purchase rates and market share is probably mediated by brand distribution. If you cannot obtain one brand the availability of other brands is likely to affect your choice of alternatives. If this is so, one would expect local variation in distribution to produce local variation in other brand purchases. Those who prefer John Smith's beer in Yorkshire may sometimes find themselves drinking Tetley because this brand is abundant there; in Surrey the second choice might be Courage. Uncles and Ehrenberg (1987) have shown this effect with stores: in the USA the duplication of purchase between Safeway and Lucky is higher than the prediction from theory because these chains tend to have stores in the same areas.

Watching television

The watching of television has similarities to purchase and it has been studied by Goodhardt, Ehrenberg and Collins (1987). When the programmes are serials, repeat viewing is similar to repeat purchase of a single brand and we can ask how much programme loyalty exists. If there was no loyalty we would expect last week's viewers to watch at a level predicted from market share (i.e. the TV rating). The evidence shows that there is loyalty, particularly for the serial with a very high rating. This loyalty may be rather lower than most people would expect. In Britain an average of about 55 per cent of an audience will repeat view in the following week but not much less than this would be watching the same channel at the same time the following week *even when the programming had changed*. This effect occurs partly because some people watch more television than others and watching in the

previous week is an indicator of heavier viewing, partly because
people have tendencies to watch at the same times during the
week, and partly because there is a degree of channel loyalty
irrespective of the programme. The authors also found that people
watch a range of programmes and that specialist programmes are
watched by a large number of non-specialists which augurs badly
for 'dedicated' cable or satellite channels. This confirmation that
television is a broadcast and not a 'narrowcast' medium is surprising to many programme planners who think that they are
addressing a particular discriminating audience with some of their
specialist work. They have 'programme positioning' assumptions
similar to the brand positioning assumptions of marketers.

The opportunity to watch (or record) a serial is restricted to
the time when it is transmitted and this makes television viewing
different from purchase which is less time constrained. This difference is allowed for in the mathematical theory used to predict
viewing rates which is the *betabinomial* model.

Dividing product fields

The product field is divided into brands but it may also be divided
by pack sizes, price ranges or some other criterion and purchases
of these divisions of the product field will fit the predictions of
NBD theory. Thus, for example, purchases in a product field may
be analysed:

- by pack size, either of the same brand or of different brands;
- by groups containing some or all brands;
- by place of purchase, treating purchases made from a particular store like a brand.

This flexibility in the way in which repetitive behaviour is analysed can be illustrated with the use of cash dispensers. People
may withdraw £5, £10–£20, or more than £20 and there is no
reason why these different sums should not be regarded like pack
sizes. People may use the dispenser nearest home, the one most
convenient at work, or some other dispenser and these classes
could be treated like brands. It is also possible to treat 'with-
drawals of £5 from the dispenser nearest home' as an activity that
can be analysed using NBD theory. Marketing problems may
justify such analyses. For example banks might be concerned

about the queueing that is produced by frequent small with-
drawals.

Store patronage

Uncles and Ehrenberg (1987) looked at instant coffee purchase
in US retail chains. They found that brand purchase by store
mirrored many of the effects found with brands. As penetration
increases with time for brands so does store patronage, the double
jeopardy effect occurs with people buying less per visit at the
stores that they patronize less often. Shoppers also have a 'store
portfolio' like a brand portfolio. In effect store chains can be
treated like brands and show the consumption patterns expected
from brand purchase models. This was also found by Wrigley and
Dunn (1984) who looked at store choice within a single city.

Very accurate evidence on the use of shops is now available
from scanner panels which are described in Chapter 8. These
panels record actual purchases of a household at all the stores in
a township. The brand portfolio effect is clearly shown. Over a
12 week period 8 per cent shop at one store only. If loyalty is
defined as 85 per cent or more of purchases then 36 per cent are
loyal to one store over 12 weeks (see Totten and Block, 1987).
In these studies 85 per cent loyal shoppers are important to the
store. Totten and Block found that for large stores 17 per cent of
shoppers were 85 per cent loyal and made 37 per cent of all the
purchases. In small stores 9 per cent of shoppers were 85+ per
cent loyal and made 28.5 per cent of all the purchases.

The Dirichlet model

The Dirichlet model (Goodhardt, Ehrenberg and Chatfield, 1984)
is a mathematical model that predicts the likelihood of purchase
for *all* the brands in a product field. The assumptions are similar
to those for the single brand NBD model but in addition it is
assumed that the market is unsegmented. The model does not
apply if there is appreciable evidence of brand clustering on any
other basis than market share. The model specifies how many
purchases of the product class a purchaser makes in a period and
with what probability a consumer chooses a brand from those

available. Research is proceeding on the accuracy of Dirichlet predictions.

A computer program for Dirichlet predictions, called BUYER, is now available (Uncles, 1988). This program requires the following inputs:

1   the penetration for the product type, B, i.e. the proportion of households that buy the product at all in a given period.
2   The purchase frequency for the product type, W, i.e. the average number of purchases made by households that buy the product at all in a given period.
3   The average number of brands bought and the market shares of individual brands (or individual b and w values for each brand).

Alternatively the program will accept raw data and will use this to derive the measures above. The output of the program can give predictions of b, w, sole buyers, sole buyer purchase frequency, proportions of buyers at different frequencies and sales distributions for single brands or the whole field. This output therefore illustrates the theoretical market position of a brand in relation to other brands and is useful for evaluating actual brand performance.

Inducing change in the market

This section describes how Ehrenberg and his co-workers have answered questions about market intervention. A fuller examination of promotional effects appears in Chapter 8. The questions are:

● What effect do price changes have?
● Does advertising convert people from one brand to another?
● Does advertising make people aware of brands or get them to try them?
● Does advertising support existing purchase?

Price changes

Recent work at the London Business School (England and Ehrenberg, 1986, 1988) has examined the effect of price changes and stock-outs using two field experiments. In the first study, teas, cereals and biscuits were offered for purchase via house visits to 240 housewives at fortnightly intervals. No changes were made to the brands on display for the first few visits and repeat purchase showed the usual stationary market pattern. When the price of a brand was reduced there was an abrupt increase in purchasing which reversed just as abruptly when the price was restored to the previous level. A reverse pattern occurred for a price rise followed by a fall. When a brand was withdrawn for a period and then restored the sales re-established at about their former level indicating that the disposition to purchase a brand endures over long periods. It was also found that a price change for one brand had only limited effect on the sales of other brands and had limited effect upon later price changes for the same brand. This supports, in a dynamic context, the Poisson assumption that one sale does not have much effect on the probability of others.

The second study by England and Ehrenberg (1988) extended the range of brands studied. All brands had a similar price elasticity coefficient of approximately -2.6, i.e. a 10 per cent cut in price induced approximately 26 per cent increase in sales. Other work by Castleberry and Ehrenberg (1986) has generalized results to other product fields.

A number of questions are raised by this sort of evidence. There is a practical problem of generalizing the findings to shop settings where the promotions may be less noticeable and may be presented rather differently. England and Ehrenberg tentatively suggest that 'the sales response to a price change may not depend on the product' because the elasticities they obtained were so similar, but evidence from other research opposes this view. For example Telser (1962) found a range of long run elasticities (-3.0 to -5.7) for four different products and the brands within the categories also showed a range of elasticities which contrasts with the near uniformity obtained by England and Ehrenberg. More recent studies have found price elasticities as low as -0.5 (Cadbury's Fudge, Channon, 1985). Finally scanner research in the USA shows wide variation in the response to price promotions between product categories; this is reviewed in Chapter 8. One explanation for this difference between experimental and field evidence is that experiments compare the responses of the same people to different products whereas the elasticities obtained from natural settings reflect the fact that different people buy different products, and brands like Cadbury's Fudge may attract price-insensitive people.

An explanation is required for the change in purchasing rates that occurs when prices are changed. England and Ehrenberg support the simplest account, that people make reference to the other prices displayed at the time of purchase. They argue that people do not refer to the previous price (on the last call) of the brand because the purchase rate is the same for a given price irrespective of how close the previous price was to the new one or whether it was higher or lower. But another hypothesis about price change response is that people set up a norm based on their long-term experience of the brand. It is also worth noting that a study in real shop settings by Doob *et al.* (1969) did show effects of previous price. Doob *et al.* found that there were more sales when prices started high and went low than when they started low and went high. This effect is explained if the initial price set some reference level for the worth of the good. This issue is not yet resolved but one useful step would be to ask panel members about their reasons for buying a brand; this may help to reveal what reference processes are at work.

Conversion and reinforcement

Even in marketing, many people still assume that consumers are sole brand loyal until they are converted and switch their loyalty to another brand; this is the leaky bucket theory of consumption which gives advertising the role of maintaining the level in the bucket by converting non-buyers and the buyers of other brands to the advertised brand. The evidence on multi-brand buying disposes of this idea for stationary markets. A consumer who buys a different brand from the last time may simply be expressing his or her stable propensities to buy several brands and therefore has not switched. Thus conversion does not explain the effect of advertising in frequent purchase markets.

So what does advertising do if it does not switch brand preference? Ehrenberg (1974) argues that for repetitively purchased brands most of the reasons for purchase are to be found in the qualities of the brand purchased and that this is particularly true when frequent purchase and trial of different brands makes purchasers well aware of the similarities and differences of available

brands. Under these circumstances advertiseme
to transform the perception of products. Instead the ad
adds a little to the natural reinforcement provided by t
sumption of the brand. This is the 'weak theory of advertisi
giving it a role in *reinforcing* existing purchase tendencies rather
than converting people. One consequence of this analysis is that
advertising acts *after* purchase to justify buying and to confirm
later repeat purchase, rather than *before* purchase to inform
buyers about where their needs might be satisfied. Ehrenberg
(1974) stresses that awareness and trial of products are necessary
before repeat purchase can become established but since most
purchase is repeat purchase by established buyers in stationary
markets he shifts the emphasis onto reinforcement in the
sequence:

Awareness → Trial → Reinforcement (ATR)

The advertising of new products and infrequently purchased
goods requires more emphasis on awareness and trial. But even
for infrequent purchases advertising may be more effective after
the purchase than before it; people often search for useful or
reassuring information after buying. But what effect can this have
on consumption? People do not go and buy a second washing
machine if they like the model they have just bought. In spite of
this there is substantial word-of-mouth influence in this sort of
market and advertising may increase the social influence exerted
by satisfied customers on other prospective buyers. This account
is plausible but it should be noted that the recipients of word-of-
mouth information must do something with it before it affects
their purchase. They may accept it, change it or reject it and may
or may not relate the information to their needs. This information
processing and attitude changing needs more examination if we
are to understand how advertisements produce their effect on
sales.

Brand image

Advertisers and their agencies use the concept of brand image, a
set of ideas about the brand which affect its value to the consumer.
Brand image is a rather loosely used term and three emphases
emerge:

...ciations of the brand: e.g.
...ic and sensible, Golf GTis are
...who eat Cadbury's Bourneville
...ned, only Grannies drink Horlicks
...ead the *Daily Telegraph*. This kind
...ussed in Chapter 1 and is relevant
...nts the values of the user.

...ives from advertising recall studies such
...lward Brown Market Research Ltd. Rice
...r children' and go 'snap, crackle, pop' when
...d. This approach to brand image picks up
quite ...advertising playback but it also covers more
general iss... such as 'value for money', 'healthy' and 'good
quality'.

3   The third, more scientific, concept of brand image, is less used
    commercially. This scores each brand on the advantages and
    disadvantages of purchase, using criteria that cover all brands
    in the product field. These criteria should be drawn from
    consumers of the product type. Criteria that are drawn from
    brand advertising or from an objective assessment of the
    brand's properties may make little sense to people who use
    the brand for other reasons. An extended discussion of this
    subject appears in Chapter 6.

Barwise and Ehrenberg (1985) base their research on the second
concept of brand image. They show that people do differentiate
between brands on certain descriptive criteria, e.g. the crispness
of Rice Krispies, but these descriptions have little bearing on
consumption. The evaluative judgements such as 'good value for
money' do relate to consumption and here they find that people's
evaluations tend to follow from their use. Barwise and Ehrenberg
find that people evaluate the brands that they use in very similar
ways. The brand leader gets a higher score mainly because there
are more people who use that brand but if only the users of a
brand are polled then it is found that more popular brands have
only slightly stronger brand images. This finding is similar to the
evidence that brands in the same product field have similar purchase frequencies and shows the same double jeopardy effect.

This evidence on brand image is a shock to advertising people
who see their work as 'adding value' to the individual evaluations
of a brand. Barwise and Ehrenberg (1985) indicate that much of

the added value comes about by adding to the number of people who assign a positive value to the brand and that these evaluations may follow rather than precede usage. However, this issue remains open. Other measures may give more support to the advertising agencies' assumptions about added value and, in any case, the different explanations may co-exist to some degree.

Critical review

The issues discussed in this section divide into two groups. The first deals with some technical problems discussed in relation to the following questions.

- Does the research have a wide enough range of application?
- Are the findings of panel research suspect?
- Could the NBD predictions be improved by a different mathematical model?

A second group of problems affects strategic decisions in marketing and relate to: advertising, brand loyalty, brand avoidance, 'buy more' strategies in promotion, and 'niche' strategies in product positioning. The questions are:

- Does the analysis of data in an aggregated form tell us enough about individual behaviour?
- What is the role of attitude in repetitive purchase?
- How can inferences about market change be drawn from a theory about stationary markets?

Research application range

A very wide range of applications has now been accumulated. NBD and double jeopardy predictions have been found to apply to a great variety of repetitively purchased goods, in different countries, in industrial markets, when the purchases were individually made and when they were made by households. There are, however, some exceptions: departures from NBD predictions occur as a result of regular shopping habits and sometimes there are bursts of enthusiasm for particular products. These are all noted by the authors but they can nonetheless point to 'significant sameness' in the patterns obtained from a wide range of applications.

The marketer wants to show that his or her brand is an exception, that it commands more brand loyalty than others, or that it is only substituted by certain other brands, or that a promotion designed to increase purchase frequency can work. In the main such aspirations tend to be confounded by the evidence but to take them seriously we must look for the exceptions.

One potential exception was the case of Hellmann's mayonnaise where the avowed purpose of the advertisers was to encourage new uses for the brand. The manufacturers found that the British used Hellmann's mayonnaise on salads, unlike the rest of the world which uses salad dressings. This British habit had been learned from earlier experience with salad cream, a concoction peculiar to the British market. The main concern in the advertising for Hellmann's was therefore to expand the number of uses of the product. The case report (Channon, 1985) shows that, following the advertising, 40 per cent of users were trying the product in new ways suggested in the campaign and were doing this more than buyers of competitive products. This suggests that there was some gain in purchase frequency relative to other brands but exact figures are not reported. However, there was also a substantial gain in penetration which accounted for much of the increase in sales. This case provides some evidence of brand specific gain in purchase frequency but it also underlines the importance of penetration in making sales gains.

Application to smoking cessation

When looking for wider applications of NBD theory it occurred to me that the recurrent attempts to stop smoking might show the negative binomial distribution. We know that most attempts to stop smoking are short lived so that few smokers leave the 'market'. Are brief episodes like this distributed like purchases? If so we can work out the proportions of people trying to stop in different periods given data for one period. We have little evidence on unaided attempts to stop but one study was made by Marsh and Matheson, 1983; Table 2.6 incorporates their findings. The data are quite close to NBD predictions and permit estimates of the proportions of the smoking population who attempt to stop over different periods. Using the NBD program we find that 8 per cent of smokers make at least one attempt to stop during one month and 52 per cent try to stop during the year, making on average just over two attempts each.

Table 2.6 *Number of smokers making 0, 1, 2, 3 and 4+ attempts to give up over a six month period and expected figures predicted from NBD theory*

Attempts to stop	Actual number of persons	Theoretical number of persons
0	818	818
1	304	290
2	88	103
3	29	37
4+	30*	21
Totals: all:	1269	1269
triers:	451	

Proportion making attempt (penetration) is 451/1269 = 0.355
Frequency of attempts among those trying is 702/451 = 1.557
* Assuming an average of 4.5 attempts in this group.

Panel research findings

One argument mounted against research based on panel data is that the purchase patterns obtained in this way will contain certain measurement biases. There may be selection effects that affect those willing to take part in panels and those who drop out and there may be systematic errors in the recording of purchase. Sudman and Ferber (1979) have reviewed many of these problems of diary panels. Fulgoni and Eskin (1981) have compared diary panels with the new, more accurate scanner panels in the USA. They found biases in reporting and changes in consumption produced by panel membership (detailed in Chapter 8). However, using the new scanner data, the predictions of NBD theory continue to be supported.

Some panel and survey data are now available covering short periods of sales from one store. This single source data has highlighted the high degree of variation in sales over short periods that may be produced by sales promotions. Marketers can point to this and ask how NBD theory with its assumptions of stationarity can be relevant to them. In response it can be said that most of these markets appear to be approximately stationary when fluctuations are evened out by taking a longer period and combined sources. The ball is in the marketer's court; he or she must show how the longer term market share can be shifted by using promotions. Available evidence shows a return to base levels when sales promotions stop.

NBD prediction improvement

One suggestion is that NBD theory might be modified to allow for the temporary loss of buying interest following a purchase. Such modifications might affect predictions but any gain would be marginal since the theory is already very close to panel evidence. Usually the random variation in the data is rather larger than any difference between the predictions of competing mathematical models. In a comparison of theories Schmittlein, Bemmaor and Morrison (1985) concluded that the NDB model was hard to beat.

Another suggestion is that purchase has the effect of modifying the purchase probabilities in the brand portfolio, i.e. a return to the fluctuating model of purchasing. This makes little sense for frequently purchased goods but it might affect the way we buy important purchases like cars; for example my previous purchase of a Citroën may raise the likelihood of buying a Citroën next time. When account is taken of the last purchase, the model is called *first order*. NBD theory is *zero order* because it assumes that previous purchase has no effect on purchase probabilities. The most popular first order approach is the Markov model. Ehrenberg and Goodhardt (1979, Essay 13) point out that the Markov model has not been supported by evidence and that the assumptions permit no change over time in purchase probabilities and allow for no distribution of consumer preference. The Markov model has mathematical appeal because the eventual market share can be calculated from given inputs but this remains a mathematical exercise and lacks empirical support. It seems unlikely that such support will be found if, as one suspects, the effect of brand experience is variable between products, consumers and over time. Bass *et al.* (1984) have researched the order of brand choice. They found that three quarters of consumers could be classified as zero order.

Individual and aggregate effects

A more complicated criticism concerns the inferences that are made from aggregate data about the behaviour of individuals. The evidence that there is little brand segmentation means that in aggregate secondary purchases are distributed by market share. This does not require that each individual distributes secondary purchases in this way. I might, for example, always buy Macleans toothpaste if I cannot get Crest. If everyone did this there would be evidence of Crest–Macleans segmentation at an aggregate level but this would not be seen if there is a range of secondary preferences to Crest. If the individual substitutions range over the market the aggregate effect will show no segmentation. This example shows that aggregate data do not reveal individual patterns and may not reveal some sub-groups with regular preference combinations. Such sub-groups could be the target of promotional campaigns. Another strategy might be to create such segmentation; for example a new brand might be deliberately associated with the brand leader. This argument indicates that brand positioning assumptions may have more importance than is indicated by aggregate patterns of secondary purchase.

2nd big one.

The role of attitude

Attitudes as causes

Barwise and Ehrenberg (1985) suggest that brand attitudes are probably best seen as an outcome of usage, i.e. the behaviour leads to the attitude. Their work raises doubts about the assumption that advertising changes attitude or some other mental condition which then changes usage. This behaviourist approach confines attitude or brand image to the sideline and suggests that point-of-sale promotions and better distribution may be more profitable emphases in marketing because these methods directly affect usage.

The causal priority of attitudes and actions is examined in detail in Chapter 3 but it should be noted here that the causal process may be two way. Even if the dominant effect is for usage to determine brand attitude there can still be some control of usage through the beliefs and feelings about a brand. The beliefs and feelings that are not formed through experience with the brand may be produced by communication via the mass media or through face-to-face contact. Advertising does have some effect on sales and must achieve this by changing some individual disposition. The point to note here is that advertising operates for the most part in a different time and context from purchase. This means that its effect must be carried forward through some change in the person experiencing the advertisement. Attitude is one candidate for carrying this effect of advertising.

Loyalty as an attitude

In many areas the lack of sole brand loyalty comes as no surprise. In some product fields people want variety; in others, products are bought on a commodity basis so that branding has no consumer relevance and different brands are bought without thought, e.g. sugar. But in many fields people have difficulty in accepting the evidence of multi-brand buying. For them brand loyalty is a matter of preference and they say that they themselves prefer one particular brand of toothpaste, tea, etc. How can this feeling be reconciled with evidence of brand portfolios? In this area it is necessary to distinguish brand loyalty as an attitude from brand loyalty as a behaviour; a loyal attitude to one brand may co-exist with multi-brand buying.

A first explanation for multiple brand purchase is that people change over time. I used to prefer razors with one blade; now I prefer the two bladed design; for a while I bought both. A second explanation is the mechanism of satiation which can operate to diminish preference temporarily. I may try a different coffee for this reason but later return to my normal choice. In other cases the attractions of experimenting may overcome customary preference, particularly when the trial brand is on offer. A further reason for multiple brand purchase is that different members of a household may have different preferences so that, for example, three different toothpastes may be used though each person in the household may be faithful to only one brand. Yet another reason is that people buy different brands for different contexts. Supermarket canned beers are often acceptable at home but would be rejected in a pub so here people may have two distinct attitudes that are lost in the aggregation of beer purchases. Perhaps the most important reason for multiple brand purchase, however, is the impact of distribution. Retailers know that the mere fact of stocking a brand will usually ensure that it is sold, often because it is available when a favourite brand is not. For example I prefer a Sainsbury brand of shampoo but will settle for equivalent brands when I am in another store.

This is an area where self-examination is possible. Look at your preferences for tea, toothpaste, bread, cereals, beer, etc. and ask how much your brand preferences are expressed in your household purchases. Often the number of product categories where we would claim to have single brand loyalty is small. We forget the fields like petrol where few people would claim loyalty to one brand.

This issue affects marketing strategy. If there is more stated support for sole brand loyalty than the purchasing statistics reveal we need to know how the discrepancy comes about with different products. Was the different purchase because of a change of preference, satiation, variety seeking, a different household member doing the purchasing, a different context of consumption or inability to find the preferred brand? Answers to these questions relate to distribution and promotion. Distribution may be especially important in fields where variety seeking is common and if consumption is related to different contexts it may make sense to show these in advertising.

Attitude may also affect non-buying. There may be brands in a product field which are automatically discounted by some potential shoppers, a non-purchase loyalty. Such attitudes need to be revealed if advertising copy is to raise the likelihood of trial.

These considerations suggest that brand loyal attitudes may be more sharply demarcated than brand loyal purchase. 'So what?' is the tough minded response, 'it is sales that make profits.' But advertising may affect sales by modifying attitudes and this makes attitude important.

Dynamic effects

How can research on stationary markets be useful to people in marketing who are trying to disrupt the stationary pattern? One answer to this question is that promotions can only be evaluated relatively to what would have happened without such intervention and that stationary market research can supply the necessary comparison. Another answer is that the theory specifies realistic marketing goals. For example the double jeopardy formula can be used to calculate the expected penetration and purchase frequency if sales increase by 100 per cent. These are valuable managerial applications but the comparison of two stationary conditions does not tell us exactly what process of change occurs. Do the new buyers enter across the range of purchase frequencies as a result of a promotion or do they enter at low purchase frequencies (as under stationary conditions) while the old buyers increase their purchase frequency to maintain the average? The answer to this question is crucial to the issue of whether it is worth trying to get existing users to buy more frequently.

To explain the point further I use a much simplified example. Suppose 10 people buy a brand and that they all buy with a purchase frequency of 2. After a promotion the position stabilizes with 20 people now buying the brand and the average purchase frequency is still 2. Consider two possibilities: either all the old buyers kept their purchase rates and the new buyers entered the market at the same rates, or the old buyers moved to a purchase frequency of 3 and the 10 new buyers entered with a purchase frequency of 1. In the first instance the old buyers do not alter their purchase frequency but in the second case both old and new buyers increase their purchase frequency from 2 to 3 and from 0 to 1 respectively. In both cases there is no change in overall purchase frequency.

How can individual purchase frequencies all rise without any change in the aggregate figure? This effect occurs because purchase frequencies are calculated on a changing base. An alternative way of looking at the market change is to keep the base constant and to consider anyone who buys in either of the two periods. In the simplified example this gives us twenty people whose mean purchase rises from 1 before the promotion to 2 in the second period. This explanation does not dispute the evidence on purchase frequency as it is conventionally presented. Purchase frequency is nearly constant at low penetrations, but marketing intervention can increase, or reduce, the purchase rates of a subset of a brand's buyers.

We do not have information on how old and new buyers move when consumption levels change. This is because large movements in sales which stabilize at new levels are rare. When they occur, e.g. the case of Curly Wurly (Channon, 1985), the purchase patterns of old and new buyers should be revealed by panel studies but I have been unable to find any study that examines individual purchase behaviour when consumption level shifts for an established brand. One study of a new launch showed that new buyers were entering the market like old buyers across the purchase frequency range (Wellan and Ehrenberg, 1988). We need more evidence about individual purchase when aggregate consumption changes; it would assist our understanding of what advertising does. If advertising has the effect of introducing new buyers at low purchase frequencies then this raises the importance of trial. Conversely, the reinforcement role of advertising is stressed if the new buyers enter the market with purchase rates that are similar to old buyers.

Summary

The tradition of consumer research led by Ehrenberg, Goodhardt and Collins focuses on observable effects in repetitive consumption. Many of these effects are predictable from two theories: the Negative Binomial Distribution and the Dirichlet. These theories are based on assumptions about constant individual propensities to buy and about the stationarity of the market. When changes do occur in the market (for example as a result of a promotion) the theories provide a comparison against which the changes can be assessed. However, the mechanisms of change are not yet well understood.

Panel research shows that consumers buy more than one brand and that their secondary purchases are distributed by market share and not clustered. In any product field the brand purchase frequencies are fairly constant, tending to increase slightly with penetration. Most sales come from repeat purchases and it is argued that a principal function of advertising is to maintain this repeat purchasing by reinforcing existing patterns of consumption.

This type of research emphasizes the numerical description of markets, not the explanation of individual consumer action. Recent work, in which brand price changes are experimentally studied, demands some explanation in cognitive terms of how consumers react to the price changes. Similarly advertisers need evidence on attitudes in order to decide on themes in campaigns. Attitude research that has been conducted by Ehrenberg and his co-workers has suggested that attitude is dependent on product experience but this evidence is limited. Subsequent chapters explore attitude theory and measurement. There seems to be no inherent discord between the numerical and attitudinal approaches to consumption.

Further reading

North American textbooks have largely ignored this work. It is instructive to look up topics like brand loyalty and brand switching to note the rather traditional assumptions.

Easiest to follow is:

Ehrenberg, A. S. C. and Goodhardt, G. J. (1979) *Essays on Understanding Buyer Behavior*. J. Walter Thompson Co. and Market Research Corporation of America

Some of Ehrenberg's ideas are explained in:

Foxall, G. (1983) *Consumer Choice*, London, Macmillan

The ATR model of advertising effect is explained in the following two papers:

Barwise, P. and Ehrenberg, A. S. C. (1987) Consumer beliefs and awareness. *Journal of the Market Research Society* **29**, 1, 88–94

Ehrenberg, A. S. C. (1974) Repetitive advertising and the Consumer. *Journal of Advertising Research* **14**, 25–34

[3]
Attitude and behaviour

This chapter is concerned with the definition and measurement of attitudes and their relationship to behaviour. This relationship has two aspects: the causal priority between attitude and action and the strength of any relationship between the two.

The attitude–behaviour relationship is relevant to the prediction of consumption. At the broadest level there is the use of measures of business sentiment to predict change in the economy. Somewhat narrower in focus is the cross-sectional prediction of consumption, e.g. whether demand is likely to concentrate on VCRs or washing machines, and how the prospective demand for a product type is spread across different demographic groups. A further concern is the demand for new products, like satellite television or mobile phones, before they are placed on the market. Can we use people's intentions to predict consumption? Yet another application is to compare the attitudes of users and non-users to see how they differ. If attitudes affect consumption this sort of analysis may help in the modification of product design and in the choice of promotional strategies. We may even be able to compare the attitudes of prospective users and non-users and thereby to anticipate shortcomings in a product. The specific form of these applications is the province of market research and this chapter is addressed to the fundamental issues involved in such applications.

Attitudes and concepts

Attitudes are what we feel; actions are what we do. Actions can be observed when they happen; attitudes are inferred from what people say or do. Attitudes are *about* some concept which may be a brand, a person, an ideology, a behaviour or any other entity which we can think of and to which we can attach feeling. In our thinking, concepts may be seen as a single entity or as a cluster of attributes and we can have an attitude to both. For example I may like apples but also I may like the taste, the convenience and the dietary value of apples. These ideas are expressed more formally later in this chapter.

Reasons for action

When alternatives are well differentiated and the choice is free we expect people to predict and to explain their preferences by referring to features of the alternatives that they like and dislike. This leads us to treat this sort of consumption as rational within the limits imposed by knowledge, habit, effort, etc. People can make an informed choice between brands which are valued and quite different (confectionery for example), they may decide carefully between holidays, and they may take some trouble when they decide between brands of dishwasher. They may also make more fundamental choices such as whether to cut out confectionery from their diet, whether to take a holiday at all and whether or not to have a dishwasher.

This rational treatment of consumption will fail when choice is constrained, when the outcomes of choice are so trivial that people do not bother to think about them (e.g. some brand choice), or when the choice is so new to people that they lack relevant knowledge. Rationality is favoured when the choice is repetitive because it can then evolve by a selection process; people do not continue with unsatisfactory products when they think that there are better alternatives available and eventually they come to have good reasons for the purchases that they continue to make. Conversely, choices that are unrehearsed may be poorly reasoned.

Behaviourism and cognitivism

The behaviourist rejects the idea that thought and fe
initiators of action and explains action only by refer
circumstances that applied to previous examples of   ...c
action. When earlier action has been rewarded the propensity to
repeat the action is strengthened. If past action has been negatively reinforced then the potential to repeat the action is diminished. This behaviourist approach was endorsed by Watson (1913)
and Skinner (1938) whose work was introduced in Chapter 1. To
a behaviourist thought and feeling are epi-phenomena, *caused but
not causing*; like ripples on the surface of a pond they indicate
the fish's movements but do not move the fish. If this account is
correct we can use attitude data only as an indicator of behaviour,
to *predict but not to explain*.

Such narrow behaviourism is usually rejected today. One reason
is that it takes no account of the different sorts of action which
have been discussed above and which may have rather different
causation. A second reason is that thought and feeling are needed
to define many of the most powerful reinforcers that operate upon
us; words become insults or praise only through understanding.
Similarly, movements become actions by virtue of the understand-
ings of the people who witness them. The widely accepted position
that opposes behaviourism is that thought and feeling can produce
change in action directly. This is *cognitivism*; in its strongest form
attitudes control behaviour, and reinforcement only acts by changing attitudes. Behaviour may also be affected when communication directly modifies attitudes. Without such a process it is
difficult to see how advertising can affect the more involved consumer choices. Advertising can affect the way consumers interpret
the benefits received from a product and it can inform people
about product advantages about which they were unaware. In
both cases it may operate through thought and feeling to produce
an impact on buying behaviour.

Examples

Some support for the cognitivist position can be found in the
impact of the news media. For example reductions in the consumption of tobacco followed the publication of the USA Sur-

geon-General's reports on the risks associated with smoking. Perhaps one of the most remarkable effects of information was in Japan in the early 1950s. In one year the birthrate fell from the usual 18 or 19 per thousand to 11 per thousand. This was caused by a widely believed legend that children born in this year would be ill fated.

There are also examples where behaviour precedes attitude. Clare and Kiser (1951) asked parents of completed families about the number and sex of the children that they would have if they could start again. There was a strong tendency to prefer both the size and the sexual composition of the family that they already had. At the time of the study there were no ways of controlling the sex of offspring so the preference for the same sexual composition can be explained only as a product of experience, as attitude following behaviour. In many other cases the priority between attitude and behaviour may be in doubt. The preferred number of children is a case in point. In the last example the parents might have had two children because they wanted two, or, having had two children, they might have come to prefer this number. Such alternative explanations affect many social and economic issues.

For example Marx argued that it was not man's ideology that determined his system of social relations but his social relations that determined his ideology. This is the sociological equivalent of the primacy of behaviour over attitude. It was the basis for Marx's claim that he had turned Hegel, who espoused the primacy of ideas, on his head. But in later work Marx placed less emphasis on such social determinism. It was difficult for Marx to invoke a revolutionary ideology in support of change when all ideologies, including Marxism, were the product of social forces.

Many economists avoid explanations where mass attitude change has causal primacy; most prefer to find a material basis for social changes, an approach that might be described as macro-behaviourist. Economists do use attitude measures to predict economic change. Leading indicators of industrial growth are based on what industrialists expect but these expectations may be based on economic factors and may not be causes of economic change. But some elements of consumer confidence may have a causal as well as predictive status in determining consumer trends (see for example the review by Pickering, Greatorex and Laycock, 1983). Curtin (1984) gave similar precedence to collective thinking when he argued that growth in the economy was stimulated by consumer willingness to incure debt. This suggests that the economy may be 'talked up' by nationally respected people who bring about growth by inspiring confidence that it will happen. No doubt this process is much helped by more objective indicators of likely growth which add credibility to any predictions.

Detailed evidence

A study by Bird and Ehrenberg (1966) indicated that with frequently purchased brands it was usage that preceded intention to buy. This study took evidence from the British Market Research Bureau's (BMRB) Advertising Planning Index (API). The study showed that a fading brand gets a higher intention rating than a static brand with the same usage and that a rising brand gets a correspondingly lower intention rating. This study employed the API's terms 'use', 'buy' and 'serve' to measure either current or recent usage in twenty different product fields.

Bird and Ehrenberg found that two thirds of those who have used the brand at some time express an intention to buy it. A fading brand has a long tail of past users who express an intention to buy whereas a new brand has few users, past or current. The much larger group of past users for a fading brand thus creates a 'tail effect' enlarging the number of stated intentions. The Bird and Ehrenberg analysis does suggest that there is a causal process from usage to stated intention and the authors found no evidence for the reverse process that intention leads to purchase in a subsidiary analysis in the study. Sandell (1981) examined the relationships between purchase and brand attitudes using panel data and found that attitudes were aligned with purchase immediately after buying but then, over time, reverted to the pre-purchase pattern. This also suggests that attitudes are changed by purchase and implies that in the fast-moving consumer goods (fmcg) field we should be wary of attitude data. Current consumption may be a more reliable predictor of future consumption.

However, finding no evidence is not the same as there being no evidence and the Bird and Ehrenberg research does not prove that there is *no* causal effect from attitude to action in the fmcg field. From the standpoint of advertising the issue is not whether purchase is led by previous purchase or by attitude. With frequently purchased goods most purchase is very likely to be strongly affected by previous purchase experience. What is at issue is whether a change in attitude which is brought about by communication will have any impact on behaviour. Any such effect can co-exist with a causal process in the reverse direction from behaviour to attitude.

Systematic research into the causal order between attitude and action has related measures of one with later measures of the other. This is called cross-lagged correlation. A panel is used so that changes in the attitudes and actions of the same people can be tracked. When changes in behaviour always follow changes in attitude it is unlikely that behaviour is causing the attitude change and likely (but not proven without experimental control) that attitude change is causing new behaviour.

Kahle and Berman (1979) used a panel to explore the causal order of attitude and behaviour on four issues. On two of the relationships (Table 3.1) 'voting for Carter' and 'voting for Ford' (as Presidential candidates) the attitude change preceded the behaviour; on the other two, drinking and religious observance, the results were ambiguous but still favoured the primacy of attitude.

Table 3.1 *Cross-lagged correlations relating changes in attitude (A) and behaviour (B) (from Kahle and Berman, 1979)*

Issue	A → B	B → A
Carter's candidacy	0.53	0.18
Ford's candidacy	0.57	0.13
Religion	0.57	0.49
Drinking	0.58	0.48

The above example suggests that precedence in the attitude–behaviour relationship varies with the subject matter. In stationary fmcg markets it is likely that attitudes to brands rest heavily on the experience of past purchase and use; Foxall (1984a, 1984b) certainly thinks so. But in other fields the cognitivist account is better supported by the evidence. When purchase is rare, past experience cannot explain attitude so easily. Pickering (1984) found that purchase expectations for consumer durables were correlated with later purchase. In this field it is harder to argue that experience forms attitude since the opportunity to try the durable is not available to all prospective purchasers.

ew more

A number of studies illustrate the attitude–behaviour relationship in different fields. Korgaonkar, Lund and Price (1985) found that attitude predicted store choice but that the reverse effect was insignificant. Newcomb (1984) found that attitude predicted sexual behaviour in women rather better than the reverse. Horst and Jarlais (1984) examined a range of attitudes and behaviours among students. Changes in this group took place slowly, many taking more than a month, and the authors argued that the attitude and behaviour changes overlapped and that this ruled out any simple 'A causes B' or 'B causes A' accounts. Marsh and Matheson (1983) looked at smoking attitudes and subsequent behaviour. Interestingly this study found support for both behaviour and attitude determinants of later smoking cessation. The number of previous attempts to quit (behaviour) was positively related to quitting later. Also those who saw large benefits for themselves if they stopped smoking (attitude) were more likely to stop. Other research has looked at the relationship between liking other people and associating with them. There is little doubt that we seek out those we like and avoid those we dislike but Homans (1961) also noted that those who are brought together by force of circumstances tend in most cases to come to like each other.

The competition between cognitive and behavioural explanations permeates the social sciences; each side can claim some support and it is realistic to assume that causal priority, when it can be detected, will depend upon the person, action and context. But this review also indicates that it may be mistaken to assume any simple causal primacy. Thought and feeling seem interwoven with behaviour so that any change in one component is likely to affect the other components of the system.

The relationship between attitude and behaviour is important because we want to know how to intervene to change action. If we narrow the issue to this problem the key question is:

Are there differences in the subsequent behaviour between those who have changed their ideas as a result of communication (including advertising) and those who have changed them as a result of experience?

A study by Smith and Swinyard (1983) found that attitudes were changed much more by trial than by advertising and that subsequent purchase was better predicted by attitudes derived from trial. However it is difficult to make a fair comparison between trial and advertising communication. In this case trial involved taste which cannot be conveyed adequately in an advertisement. Some advertisements are better than others which makes the generalized comparison of trial and advertisement impossible without many examples of each.

Fazio and Zanna (1981) found that evidence generally supports the view that direct experience of an object leads to more strongly learned associations between attitude and behaviour. Regan and Fazio (1977) and Fazio and Zanna (1978) provide supporting studies. Fazio (1985) explains relationships between attitude and behaviour as a result of selective perception driven by attitude; what people do is constrained by what can be called to mind. The link from attitude to behaviour is stronger when the attitude is activated more easily and Fazio argues that this is so when the attitude–behaviour association has been laid down by experience. This research is reviewed by Eiser (1986, pp. 72–7).

When experience has more effect this may be because (following Fazio) it induces responses that are stronger, or it may be because it introduces more information. A study by Clore and Jeffery (1972) found that role play induced about the same attitude change as passive observation of that role play; since both role players and observers obtained much the same information in this case, the findings are consistent with the idea that different methods of influence have more or less success in affecting behaviour because of the *amount* of information that is received. In many situations one might expect that trial would be a powerful agent of change because of the amount of relevant information that could be imparted through such experience. In other situations where the item is intangible, long term, or complex, e.g. an investment advice service, it may be difficult to engage in trial, and information through news, advice and advertising may have more impact.

Multi-attribute alternatives

A feature of many decisions is that the alternatives are *multi-attribute*. Do I go to Corfu or Wales? To choose between them I have to take account of weather, cost, travelling effort, food, opportunities for recreation and more. To maximize objective value in multi-attribute choices it is necessary to take the option with the highest likely return which is calculated by multiplying the probability and value of each attribute and summing these products, i.e.

$$p_1 v_1 + p_2 v_2 + p_3 v_3 \ldots + p_i v_i$$
or more briefly, $\Sigma_1^i p_i v_i$

In consumer choice people have only their subjective judgements of probability and value but they can still engage in processes that produce a subjective optimality by choosing the alternative with the highest subjective value. The subjective value of an attribute is given by the product of expectancy (denoted by b) and evaluation (e). The subjective value of the option is given by the sum of these products, i.e.

$$\Sigma_1^i b_i \, e_i$$

This approach accommodates the marketing idea that, in acquiring products, a person acquires a bundle of expected benefits and disbenefits. Edwards (1954) was one of the first to express these ideas, calling his theory the subjective expected utility (SEU) model of decision.

Expectancy-value theory of attitude

In this theory the attitude to a concept is the subjective value that a person associates with that concept and this in turn depends upon the subjective values that the person has for the several attributes of that concept. Rosenberg (1956) supported this account when he found that the evaluation of an object was closely related to the expectations that the object would help or hinder the attainment of valued goals. In a further test of this approach Fishbein (1963) used semantic differential scaling (see next section) to measure the evaluation (e) and the subjective probability (b) of factors that were associated with an ethnic group. Aggregate scores for each subject were calculated by multiplying the belief strength by the evaluation and summing the products, i.e.

$$\Sigma_1^i b_i \, e_i$$

Fishbein also measured the overall attitude to the ethnic group (the attitude to the object, A_O) using the semantic differential. In this way the attitude theory could be tested by correlating the aggregated score with the overall attitude measure. A high correlation was found ($r = 0.80$) which gave support to the idea that global attitudes are based on the sum of the expectancy-values of the attributes. The theory can be expressed by:

$$A_O \propto \Sigma_1^i b_i \, e_i$$

Fishbein's expectancy-value treatment of attitude has been supported in a large number of published studies and can usually be verified in students' practical work; e.g. the correlations between $\Sigma b_i \, e_i$ and A_B in Table 4.5.

The semantic differential

The semantic differential was developed by Osgood, Suci and Tannenbaum (1957) as a technique for measuring meanings. The technique uses seven-point scales with opposite terms flagging the ends of each scale, e.g.

bad $\underline{\quad -3 \mid -2 \mid -1 \mid 0 \mid 1 \mid 2 \mid 3 \quad}$ good

slow $\underline{\quad -3 \mid -2 \mid -1 \mid 0 \mid 1 \mid 2 \mid 3 \quad}$ fast

weak $\underline{\quad -3 \mid -2 \mid -2 \mid 0 \mid 2 \mid 2 \mid 3 \quad}$ strong

The scales may not show numbers and may have other verbal referents such as 'extremely', 'quite', 'slightly', to aid response.

Any two concepts measured in this way are deemed to have the same meaning if they score the same point on each scale. Thus difference of meaning between concepts is indicated by the discrepancy between measures. Osgood, Suci and Tannenbaum used about twenty scales and found that the responses obtained could be reduced to three basic dimensions: *evaluation, potency* and *activity*. Evaluation accounts for most variance in the definition of meaning and corresponds with its everyday meaning; it is measured by scales using referents such as good–bad, favour-able–unfavourable and pleasant–unpleasant.

It is inevitable that psychological measurement procedures do some violence to the nature of human response. There are problems about the exact concept being measured, what verbal descriptions to use on scales, what numerical subdivisions to use, whether scales are uni-polar (e.g. 1 to 7) or bi-polar (e.g. −3 to +3), and whether summations of products are appropriate.

Compensation

Fishbein's treatment of attitude assumes a process of compensation, i.e. that negatively valued attributes are compensated for by the positive values attaching to other attributes. (The unspoilt beaches of Wales can offset the bad weather there; the cheapness of Greece can be set against the extra time and cost of getting there.) At best this psychological accounting is likely to be approximate. Just taking account of the main outcome of an action requires some thought. When several alternatives are present the assessment is even more complicated. This sort of extended thought before choice is a rarity but we probably consider more attributes when important decisions are taken, particularly when circumstances extend the decision making period. In general compensation is likely to be limited and this view is supported by the finding by Wilkie and Pessemier (1973) that multi-attribute theories gave better predictions in market research when relatively few attributes were used.

Exercise 3.1. The expectancy-value matrix

Use the computer program ATALYS to exhibit the features of the expected value model for a multi-attribute action. This program shows how principal attitudes may be changed by altering their components. ATALYS records an expectancy value matrix from the data that you give which can be printed and used in class discussion. What are the limitations of this sort of rational analysis of decision making?

Modal salient beliefs

Fishbein's theory of attitude is about what *individuals* think and feel. People vary in their attitudes but it would be laborious to use a different questionnaire for the different thoughts and feelings of each person. Fortunately on many issues there is substantial agreement on the factors that are important even though the value which different individuals attach to these factors may differ. This degree of agreement between people justifies the use of the same questionnaire for all respondents. This procedure obviously introduces some error because people have to answer some questions about outcomes that are not salient for them.

To establish the commonly held beliefs about a concept it is necessary to perform an elicitation. This is a series of questions about the positive and negative associations of the concept which are put to members of the relevant sub-group of the population. The beliefs that come easily to mind are called *salient*. Fishbein and Ajzen (1975) (Ajzen is pronounced 'Eye-zen') argue that non-salient beliefs which have to be dredged up from the recesses of the mind are unlikely to have much effect on behaviour. The salient beliefs that are commonly found in a sub-group are called *modal salient beliefs*. After similar responses have been grouped together the list of modal salient beliefs is usually quite short. Complex issues, such as getting married or using oral contraceptives, may have a dozen or more items salient; others, such as subscribing for a new issue of shares, appear to have few salient items. The procedure for eliciting individual salient beliefs probably understates the number. Belson (1988) has noted that the percentage of people offering any particular idea is far smaller than the percentage that either believes the idea or regards it as important.

Exercise 3.2. Eliciting salient beliefs and salient referents

(Note: This procedure also covers the elicitation of salient referents, i.e. establishing the people and groups whose assumed views have an influence on behaviour. This is explained in Chapter 4; here there should be little difficulty in following the procedure.)

1 Define clearly the action that you are concerned with; e.g.

'buying Mars Bars', 'buying wine at Sainsbury's', 'giving blood when the blood transfusion service comes to the campus'.

2 Define clearly the sub-group that you are concerned with. For example you might be particularly interested in males under 25 buying Mars Bars, or women wine buyers.

3 *Elicit salient beliefs.* Ask each person (in a sample of people from the sub-group) questions about the advantages, disadvantages and other associations of the defined action. After each response prompt with: 'anything else?' but do not press hard for ideas. Record the responses for each person. A typical encounter might be:

Q: 'Can you tell me what you think are the advantages of buying wine at Sainsbury's?'
A: 'It's cheap'
Q: 'Anything else?'
A: 'There's a good choice'
Q: 'Anything else?'
A: 'Not really'
Q: 'Can you tell me what are the disadvantages of buying wine at Sainsbury's?'
A: 'It's difficult to buy cases'
Q: 'Anything else?'
A: 'No'
Q: 'Is there anything else that you think of about buying wine at Sainsbury's?'
A: 'No'

4 *The negative action.* Certain actions may have different salient beliefs associated with *not* doing the action. For example not having children and not taking drugs may be seen as actions with their own rationale, not just as opposites to having children and taking drugs. When this is likely it is wise to elicit salient beliefs to the negative action from another sub-group. This is because the propensity to act is usually measured on a scale that ranges from taking the action to not taking the action. Since both of these alternatives are investigated the salient beliefs about both should appear in the questionnaire.

5 *Salient referents.* Ask each respondent in the sample whether there are people or groups who think the respondent should do the defined action. Repeat with 'should not'. Ask if there are other people or organizations that come to mind when they think of the action. Use the prompt 'anyone else?' but do not press for responses.

6 Using other people as judges work through the responses and combine similar beliefs. Compile a list of modal salient beliefs using the ones most frequently mentioned. The decision to include a belief depends on the frequency with which it is mentioned and the time and money available to support the research. When the questionnaire is intended to be used both before and after exposure to advertising or experience of the product it is important to include beliefs that may become salient as a result of this exposure.

7 You can use the computer program PREACT to make up an Ajzen and Fishbein questionnaire. Ajzen and Fishbein's full theory is explained in Chapter 4.

When attitudes fail to predict action

In the earlier discussion about the direction of causation between attitude and action the possibility that there was no relationship between the two was ignored. However in 1969, when Wicker reviewed the matter, he concluded that:

> It is considerably more likely that attitudes will be unrelated or only slightly related to overt behaviors than that attitudes will be closely related to actions.

Wicker's conclusion was based on 47 studies and cast doubt on the competence of social psychologists to predict behaviour from measures of attitude. Following Allport (1935), attitude is usually seen as predisposing behaviour, indicating 'a preparation or readiness for response', and thus should be a predictor of action if there is little constraint on behaviour. The inability to show reliable relationships between attitude and action indicated a deficiency in either measurement or theory.

Often quoted in this context is the study by LaPiere (1934).

LaPiere accompanied a Chinese couple on a tour of America and observed that hotel proprietors nearly always provided a courteous service. Later, in response to a letter from LaPiere, many of these proprietors indicated that they would be reluctant to have Chinese guests. Another example was provided by Vroom (1964) who found little overall correlation between the evaluation of 'one's job' and measures of job performance (median of 15 studies $r = 0.14$). But among the studies reviewed by Wicker there were a few strong relationships, for example Newton and Newton (1950) found that the attitude to breast feeding did relate quite well to the amount of breast milk taken by the infant. In the face of this evidence researchers adopted different positions.

Abelson (1972) took the extreme position that attitudes could not be used to predict behaviour. Another group of researchers, e.g. Schuman and Johnson (1976), took the approach called 'other variables' by Ajzen and Fishbein (1980). This emphasizes the involuntary nature of much action and stresses the control on behaviour exerted by the environment. The other variables in a situation can pre-empt action and swamp the volition of individuals so that they cannot express their preferred mode of action. This might apply in organizational settings and could help to explain Vroom's findings. Another effect of the environment is to provide a choice: one may like an alternative but not choose it because another one is better. Other factors mentioned under the 'other variables' heading are personal abilities (or the lack of them) and uncertainties about the outcomes of action.

Discrepancies between attitude and behaviour may also arise when the measures are taken at different times. People may change their attitudes and intentions over time in response to new information so that a measure of attitude at one time may fail to predict action taken at a later time. For example, the intention to vote for a political party may be affected by political events and a measure of voting intention close to an election has more predictive value than one taken years before.

Correspondence

These explanations help to explain the low correlation between attitude and action measures but much of the failure in this area can be traced to poor *measurement* of attitude. This arose in part because attitude was badly conceptualized by the *multicomponent* concept of attitude (Rosenberg and Hovland, 1960) which is illustrated in Figure 3.1. In this approach attitude is seen as a disposition that is expressed by affective (evaluative), cognitive and behavioural responses. A positive attitude to cheese is shown by statements about liking cheese, statements about the valued properties of cheese and by actions such as purchasing and eating it.

With this definition the indicators of the attitude concept would be inconsistent if a person who did not like cheese proceeded to buy it. But should we expect a close correspondence between liking cheese and buying it? People buy cheese for a variety of reasons which go beyond personal preference. This sort of thinking was expressed by Campbell (1963) when he pointed out that the hoteliers who were moderately hostile to Chinese in LaPiere's study might say that they would not take a hotel booking by letter but would not demur when face-to-face with a Chinese couple because of the embarrassment that would be created by expressing prejudice under such conditions. What they said in response to LaPiere's letter was not inconsistent with their later behaviour taken under circumstances not implied in the letter. On the other hand it would have been inconsistent if they had stated that they would turn away a Chinese couple under particular conditions and not to have done so under those conditions.

Fishbein and Ajzen (1975, 1977) clarified this issue. Firstly their theory rejects the multicomponent model and treats attitude as an evaluative concept only, not as an aggregation of evaluations, cognitions and behavioural dispositions as in the multicomponent view of attitude. They then introduce the idea of *corresponding* measures of attitude and behaviour. They argue that the attitude to an object (A_O) is not necessarily related to the attitude to behaviour toward that object, A_B. People who dislike cheese may still buy it to serve at a dinner party or as an ingredient in cooking. People who like cheese may not buy it for other reasons, e.g. allergic reactions or the objections of other members of the family. Therefore we should not expect high correlations between attitudes to objects and action toward those objects. On the other hand an attitude to a *behaviour*, such as buying cheese, should be consistent with that behaviour. This is because the attitude to *buying* cheese is based on salient outcomes that include its use in

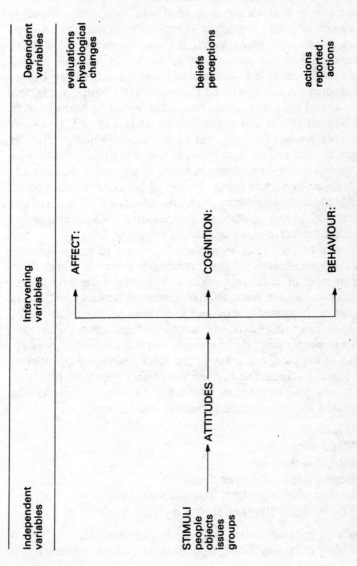

Figure 3.1 The multi-component model of attitude (from Rosenberg and Hovland, 1960)

Independent variables	Intervening variables	Dependent variables
	AFFECT:	evaluations physiological changes
STIMULI people objects issues groups → ATTITUDES	COGNITION:	beliefs perceptions
	BEHAVIOUR:	actions reported actions

dinner parties and the objections of others; these may not be salient beliefs for the attitude to the object.

This simple lesson about using corresponding measures based on the same concept has not been well learned. In consumer research it means that attitudes to the purchase, hiring, etc. of the product must be measured since it is these attitudes that relate to the actions that we are concerned with. When the product is developed it is also important to study the attitude to using it, eating it, etc. since repeat purchase rests heavily on a satisfactory experience with the product. Often there is substantial overlap between the attitude to the product and the attitude to buying the product but, as Ajzen and Fishbein show (1980, Ch. 13), this is not always so. Also relevant here is the finding by Mazis, Ahtola and Klippel (1975) that the beliefs about brands and the beliefs about the product type may not be the same. Similarly, attitudes to generalized actions like smoking may have little relevance to the specific action of a smoker in giving up cigarettes. The attitude to giving up cigarettes covers a range of personal concerns about tension, loss of concentration and the likelihood of relapse. For this reason plenty of smokers are negative about smoking but reluctantly positive about continuing to smoke.

From these examples we can see that some of the 'other variables' are measured when the corresponding attitude is measured. The notion of correspondence is a powerful methodological advance in attitude research. The history of attitude research in marketing, health education and social science, has tended to be a tale of measuring the *wrong* variable. All too often the attitude measure simply fails to correspond with the behaviour measure. This was the case with many of the studies reviewed by Wicker. The more closely the attitude and behaviour measures correspond, the higher their correlation. The rules of correspondence can be illustrated with an example. Consider your attitude to:

- Wine
- White wine
- Buying white wine
- Buying white wine from Tesco
- Buying white wine from Tesco this weekend
- You buying white wine from Tesco this weekend

Which of these attitudes is going to correlate best with your likelihood of buying white wine from Tesco this weekend? It is not hard to recognize that the last attitude is most likely to capture the factors behind this action. Ajzen and Fishbein (1977) summarize the aspects of correspondence under five headings: Target, Action, situation or Context, Time (remember: TACT) and the personal nature of some action. Applying these headings to the example above:

- The *target* is the focus or object of the action, i.e. the white wine;
- The *action* is buying;
- The *context* is Tesco;
- The *time* is the weekend;
- The *personal aspect* is ensured by using terms like 'For me' and 'I' in measures.

Ajzen and Fishbein (1977) used these five criteria to check on the correspondence of attitude and action measures for 142 attitude–behaviour relations reported in 109 investigations. They sorted the data into three groups: those with low correspondence between the measures; those with partial correspondence and those with high correspondence. The last group was subdivided because some measures were not clearly specified. Table 3.2 shows their findings.

Table 3.2 *Effect of correspondence on the attitude–behaviour (A–B) relation (from Ajzen and Fishbein, 1977)*

	Number of A–B relations		
Correspondence	Not significant	Low[a] or insignificant	High[b]
Low	26	1	0
Partial	20	47	4
High:			
Questionable measures	0	9	9
Appropriate measures	0	0	26

[a] $r < 0.40$
[b] $r \geqslant 0.40$

Exercise 3.3. Correspondence test

Circle the numbers that are closest to your feelings:

Swimming is:

bad | -3 | -2 | -1 | 0 | 1 | 2 | 3 | good
extremely   quite   slightly   neither   slightly   quite   extremely

For me, going swimming in my local swimming bath is:

bad | -3 | -2 | -1 | 0 | 1 | 2 | 3 | good
extremely   quite   slightly   neither   slightly   quite   extremely

I will go swimming in my local swimming bath:

unlikely | -3 | -2 | -1 | 0 | 1 | 2 | 3 | likely
extremely   quite   slightly   neither   slightly   quite   extremely

Sports cars are:

bad | -3 | -2 | -1 | 0 | 1 | 2 | 3 | good
extremely   quite   slightly   neither   slightly   quite   extremely

For me, buying a sports car in the next three years is:

bad | -3 | -2 | -1 | 0 | 1 | 2 | 3 | good
extremely   quite   slightly   neither   slightly   quite   extremely

I intend to buy a sports car in the next three years

unlikely | -3 | -2 | -1 | 0 | 1 | 2 | 3 | likely
extremely   quite   slightly   neither   slightly   quite   extremely

Tesco supermarkets are:

bad | -3 | -2 | -1 | 0 | 1 | 2 | 3 | good
extremely   quite   slightly   neither   slightly   quite   extremely

For me, going shopping at Tesco next week is:

bad | -3 | -2 | -1 | 0 | 1 | 2 | 3 | good
extremely   quite   slightly   neither   slightly   quite   extremely

I will go shopping at Tesco next week:

unlikely | -3 | -2 | -1 | 0 | 1 | 2 | 3 | likely
extremely   quite   slightly   neither   slightly   quite   extremely

Rail travel is:

bad | -3 | -2 | -1 | 0 | 1 | 2 | 3 | good
extremely   quite   slightly   neither   slightly   quite   extremely

For me, going home by rail is:

bad | -3 | -2 | -1 | 0 | 1 | 2 | 3 | good
extremely   quite   slightly   neither   slightly   quite   extremely

I will go home by rail:

unlikely | -3 | -2 | -1 | 0 | 1 | 2 | 3 | likely
extremely   quite   slightly   neither   slightly   quite   extremely

In an exercise like this we cannot measure behaviour so a measure
of intention is used as a guide. This is the third measure in each
of the four trios of measurement, the other two being A_O and A_B.
In general you will find that the intention measure is closer to the
second than to the first measure in each trio. This is because there
is more correspondence between these measures; they both refer
to the action, not the object, and are personal. In some cases time
or place is specified.

The rank order correlation between correspondence and the
magnitude of the attitude–behaviour relation in this table was
0.83. Retrospective analyses such as this may carry some benefit
from hindsight but Ajzen and Fishbein's evidence on correspondence has been supported in subsequent studies.

Purchase intentions

Closely related to the attitude to purchase is the intention to
purchase. The nature of the relationship is described in Chapter 4
but here we note the usefulness of intention measures in predicting
behaviour. There is now substantial evidence that an 'intention
to buy' measure shows the propensity to purchase. The literature
on purchase prediction goes back to research by Katona (1947)
and Ferber (1954). Juster (1966) showed that people could
respond to a range of likelihoods that they would purchase a
consumer durable so that a scale was more accurate than a 'yes/no'
response format. In new product development Infosino (1986)
found that purchase likelihood could forecast new product sales
though Tauber (1975) found that intention only predicted the first
purchase of new products; any repeat purchases were presumably
decided by reference to the initial purchase experience.

The intention measure has been well tested in the field of
consumer durable purchase. Pickering and Isherwood (1974)
found that only 5 per cent of respondents who expressed no
intention to purchase a durable in the next 12 months actually did
make a purchase. Among those expressing 100 per cent likelihood
of purchase the probability rose to 61 per cent. These findings
were close to those obtained by Gabor and Granger (1973) from
a Nottingham sample. This shows that intention to buy discrimi-

nates quite well between prospective buyers and non-buyers and indicates that worthwhile cross-sectional research can be done comparing prospective purchasers and non-purchasers in the same way that users and non-users are compared. This suggests that purchase can be anticipated and market research may discover why people *will* buy before they have actually done so.

Although intention discriminates between those likely and unlikely to purchase, it is not much value in forecasting total purchase potential (Pickering, 1984). With durables the great majority of people express no purchase intention so that even a small percentage of buyers in this group yields a large fraction of the total number of buyers. Pickering and Isherwood found that 55 per cent of all buyers came from the group expressing no intention to buy. This compares with findings in the USA by Theil and Kosobud (1968) that 70 per cent of purchasers were in this category and by Gabor and Granger (1973) that 65 per cent of purchases came from those stating a zero purchase probability.

This subject has been reviewed by McQuarrie (1988) who assembles data from 13 studies. He notes that those who did plan a purchase did so, on average, 42 per cent of the time whereas those planning not to make a purchase fulfilled this prediction 88 per cent of the time. This asymmetry is probably related to the much larger numbers who state that they are not going to do something (the double jeopardy principle leads us to expect the more popular choice will be made with more thoroughness). McQuarrie shows that predictions may be improved by including behavioural measures along with the intention measures but prediction of this sort is limited by unexpected events; Pickering (1975) found that failure to act according to stated intention could usually be traced to unanticipated conditions.

Summary

There is substantial evidence that attitudes lead to action when behaviour is unconstrained. The evidence on repetitive brand purchase suggests that in this case the action depends mainly on previous experience with the product. In general it is likely that there is mutual causation between attitude and action.

Developments in attitude measurement have supported the expectancy-value model. In this approach the concept is seen as a bundle of associated attributes and the attitude to the concept is derived from the sum of each attribute evaluation multiplied by the attribute likelihood. The attributes are found by an elicitation procedure.

Many of the early studies showed little relationship between measures of attitude and behaviour. Some of these discrepancies can be attributed to the influence of external factors which limit choice. Sometimes attitude changes during a time lapse between measures. Many of the claimed discrepancies arose because the attitude and action concepts were different. High correlations are obtained when *corresponding* measures are used.

Further reading

Ajzen, I. and Fishbein, M. (1980) *Understanding Attitudes and Predicting Social Behavior*: Englewood Cliffs, NJ, Prentice-Hall, chapters 1, 2, 4 and 12 and Appendix A

Eiser, J. R. (1986) *Social Psychology: Attitudes, Cognition and Social Behaviour*. Cambridge, Cambridge University Press, ch. 3

Pickering, J. F. (1984) Purchase expectations and the demand for consumer durables. *Journal of Economic Psychology* **5**, 4, 342–52

[4]
Predicting and explaining action: reasoned action theory

A major objective of marketing and applied social science is to influence behaviour. To do this economically researchers try to understand the bases of action from a theoretical standpoint and to develop appropriate measures for these bases. The evidence reported in Chapter 3 shows that there is often a close association between attitude and behaviour when these variables are appropriately measured. In this chapter beliefs, attitude, intention and behaviour are related in an extended *theory of reasoned action* (Ajzen and Fishbein, 1980). This theory and associated measurements are explained and illustrated with a number of studies and applications. In Chapter 5 the theory is examined more critically.

Assumptions

The theory of reasoned action fits the actions of a 'reconstructed economic man'. Traditional economic man was knowledgeable, selfish and optimizing. By comparison, 'reasoned action person' has limited knowledge of the outcomes of action and takes account of only some of these known outcomes (the ones that are salient, i.e. easily brought to mind). Secondly, actions are done partly in response to the normative influence of other people and groups; this element is similar to the idea of conscience. Thirdly, although people seek personal benefit they have limited power to realize their preferences. For this reason their *intentions* rather than their actions are predicted in the theory. Often action will follow intention but circumstances may intervene to change intention and action.

History

The theory of reasoned action was given this name by Ajzen and Fishbein in a 1980 statement of their work; the authors had presented much of the theory in earlier publications, e.g. Ajzen and Fishbein, 1969; Ajzen, 1971; Ajzen and Fishbein, 1972; and (the most complete account) Fishbein and Ajzen, 1975. Before 1980 the theory was known as the *Fishbein–Ajzen behavioural intentions model* or as the *extended model*, i.e. an extension of Fishbein's (1963) theory of attitude which remains part of reasoned action theory.

In the early 1970s Fishbein's work was in vogue among British consumer researchers such as Sampson, Tuck and Cowling and the 1971 ESOMAR Seminar in Madrid was devoted to the Fishbein model (Fishbein, 1972). The theory was not always well tested in early applications. Inappropriate measures for some of the components were used and there was some disappointment with the results. In commercial practice the theory gave way to other methods such as factor analysis and conjoint analysis which were aided by greater computing power. Meanwhile those with less numerical inclination made increasing use of qualitative research. The result of these new directions was research without theory and consumer understanding has probably been held back as a result.

In America the theory of reasoned action was used more in academic consumer research but there were disagreements between the authors and those seeking to apply it. See for example Bass and Talarzyk (1972); Cohen, Fishbein and Ahtola (1972); Sheth and Talarzyk (1972) and Sheth (1972); see also an exchange between Songer-Nocks (1976a, 1976b), Fishbein (1976) and Fishbein and Ajzen (1976a, 1976b). These disagreements show that the theory is quite complicated in application and this deters its use in commercial consumer research. A second factor making the theory less suitable for application arose in Chapter 1; this is the need to emphasize brand choice in much consumer research. The theory of reasoned action has relevance to choices where consumers can give reasons for their preferences. When there is little difference between brands (in the view of the consumer) the theory is of little value in explaining brand preference though it may serve to explain why the product type is bought. Reasoned action theory has been widely used in social research, particularly in health and voting applications. It is now a standard element in texts on consumer behaviour (e.g. Engel, Blackwell and Miniard, 1986, ch. 6).

Determinants of intention

The theory of reasoned action treats people as rational within limits. Their attitude to a voluntary action (A_B) is one determinant of whether they *intend* to perform that action (see Figure 4.1). In other words people seek to act in ways that will bring benefits and avoid costs.

However, this explanation does not cover altruistic behaviour or action done out of a sense of social obligation. Such action may bring external costs rather than benefits. For example blood donors sometimes feel weak for a while or are bruised where the needle is inserted but this does not usually stop them from giving blood. Counteracting these hazards are feelings of self-respect or pride from giving blood and possibly shame or self-reproach from not giving. These *internal* states are often produced when we do things that meet or fall short of what we think certain other persons or agencies think we should do. The agencies may be friends, parents, doctors, priests, political parties etc. Fishbein and Ajzen called this internally mediated pressure the *subjective norm*; subjective' because it is what we think, and 'norm' because it is what we think others think we should do. The subjective norm (usually abbreviated to SN) does not operate through external reinforcement, e.g. the overt congratulations or hostility of others. Such external factors may be responsible for implanting the subjective norm in the past but any present or anticipated external social consequences operate through the A_B, not the SN.

Just as attitudes can be decomposed into the perceived likelihoods (b) and evaluations (e) of a set of outcomes so also can subjective norms be unpacked into two components. One, called normative belief (NB), is the belief that another agent thinks that you should do the action; the second, called motivation to comply (MC), is the willingness to do what the other agent thinks you should do. The product of each pair of measures gives the effect of each referent; the aggregate of the products determines SN.

Some actions, such as giving to charity, may be strongly influenced by SN while other actions, such as buying a calculator, rest

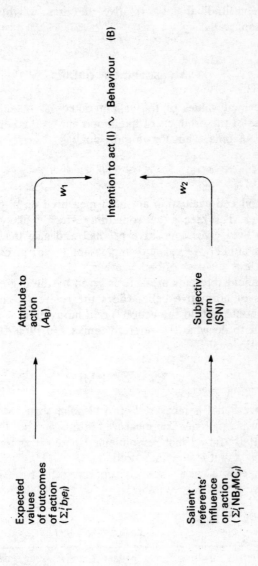

Figure 4.1 The theory of reasoned action

more heavily on the expected benefits and hence A_B. Some actions such as voting and fashion purchase may reflect both influences. Thus the theory must incorporate weights for the two paths of influence, attitudinal and normative, and these weights are established empirically.

Measurement details

The expected values of the salient outcomes of action are an aggregate of the products of likelihood and evaluation in respect of each outcome. Thus for an individual:

$$A_B = \Sigma_1^i b_i e_i$$

Likelihood and evaluation are both measured on bi-polar (–3 to +3) scales. This means that something which is likely (+ve) and valued (+ve) gives a positive product and also that something which is unlikely (–ve) and unpleasant (–ve) gives a positive product, e.g. low risk of bad weather.

The salient referents measure is given by the aggregate of the products of normative belief (does the referent think that you should/should not do the action?) and motivation to comply (do you want to do what the referent thinks you should do?). Thus for an individual:

$$SN = \Sigma_1^j NB_j MC_j$$

Normative belief is measured on a bi-polar scale. Motivation to comply was originally also measured in this way but Fishbein and Ajzen (1981) found that respondents treated it as uni-polar and this is the way it is now measured.

A_B is measured as a whole concept using the average of several evaluative scales. For example,

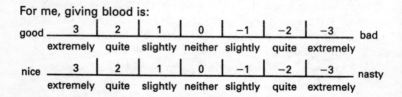

For me, giving blood is:

good	3	2	1	0	–1	–2	–3	bad
	extremely	quite	slightly	neither	slightly	quite	extremely	

nice	3	2	1	0	–1	–2	–3	nasty
	extremely	quite	slightly	neither	slightly	quite	extremely	

Other scale references that are frequently used are pleasant-unpleasant and attractive–unattractive.

SN is also measured as a whole concept. Usually one scale is used with the phraseology:

Most people who are important to me think that I should give blood:

likely	3	2	1	0	−1	−2	−3	unlikely
	extremely	quite	slightly	neither	slightly	quite	extremely	

The weights w_1 and w_2 may be determined by regression analysis. The relationships between elements of the theory may be expressed by correlations. More recent work has used the LISREL program by Joreskog and Sorbom, 1978, which takes the whole theory for testing, makes allowance for measurement error, reports the overall fit between data and model and gives path coefficients that indicate the strength of relationships in the model.

Intention is measured as a likelihood using the phraseology: 'I intend to give blood' or the self-prediction form 'I will give blood'. For example,

I will give blood:

likely	3	2	1	0	−1	−2	−3	unlikely
	extremely	quite	slightly	neither	slightly	quite	extremely	

The tilde sign (~) in Figure 4.1 indicates that the relationship between measured intention and behaviour is contingent upon external factors. As explained in Chapter 3 one effect of such factors may be to change beliefs and hence intention so that a different action is performed than the one predicted from earlier measures. The longer the gap between measures of intention and action the weaker will be the relationship. Another way in which intention and action may correlate poorly is when the environment presents little opportunity for action; in other words when the action is not fully voluntary. Fishbein (1966) illustrated this in a study of premarital sexual intercourse. The study showed that men were less successful than women in realizing their sexual ambitions. In the cultural climate prevailing at the time of the study a woman could more easily persuade a man to become her lover and she could refuse such offers from men; men found it harder to persuade women and therefore had less freedom of action.

Exercise 4.1. Analysing the bases of charity giving

The diskette carries a set of files which cover the different aspects of an investigation into giving money to charities like Oxfam.

CHAR.TXT is the questionnaire that was used; you can print it out and work out which items measure intention, A_B, SN, b_i and e_i.

CHAR.DAT is the data that was gathered from a small number of respondents. Look at this on the screen; each line is the data for one respondent. The first four digits are the number assigned to the respondent. The next two are reserved for the *condition* in case the study was used to compare two different groups, e.g. people who had seen tragic footage on famine in Africa and those who had not. The remaining numbers are the ones checked by the respondent in the order in which the items appear on the questionnaire.

CHAR.SPS is an SPSSX program for analysing the data on a mainframe computer. This may need some modification if you want to run the program on the PC version of SPSS. If you are unfamiliar with SPSS you should still be able to work out what each line is concerned with. For instance you will see that numbers 1 to 7 are recoded to -3 to $+3$ for the b, e and NB measures before products are computed.

CHAR.LST is the output from the SPSS analysis. Inspect this and work out (for discussion in seminar):
(a) Is charity giving most related to A_B or SN?
(b) Do A_B and SN correlate with their supposed determinants, i.e. $\Sigma_1^i B_i e_i$ and $\Sigma_1^j NB_j MC_j$?
(c) Which factors correlate most with the intention?
(d) Which factors might be used in advertising, if any?
(e) What are the shortcomings of this study and analysis?

Illustrating the theory

Using the pill

The use of oral contraceptives by women is an important aspect of family planning. The pill is also a product of major commercial importance to pharmaceutical manufacturers. From both standpoints there is a need to understand the reasons why some women use the pill and others do not. These reasons will vary between different population segments. Two American studies, by Jaccard and Davidson (1972) on unmarried college women and by Davidson and Jaccard (1975) on married women with children, explored this matter. These studies may have less relevance in Britain today but this work still illustrates the power of reasoned action theory as an explanation and as a source of ideas for changing behaviour.

Jaccard and Davidson found that measures of intention correlated strongly with reported pill usage a year later ($r = 0.85$) so that 93 per cent of the women acted according to their stated intention. Beliefs and salient referents were elicited and were measured in a combined questionnaire together with attitude, subjective norm and intention to use birth control pills.

A comparison between the two studies showed that those in the unmarried sample were concerned about side-effects, morality and effectiveness whereas in the married sample women were less concerned about morality and more concerned about family size and sexual pleasure. For both samples husbands/boyfriends and doctors were powerful referents while parents, friends and the 'religion in which I was raised' had little influence. This last finding may surprise some readers but it is consistent with other research showing the waning influence of religion (e.g. Westoff and Ryder, 1970) and confirms the value of the Ajzen and Fishbein method.

Levels of explanation
The correlations between components of the theory of reasoned action are shown for the college women in Figure 4.2. Three levels of explanation are possible from this kind of study. The first level is the extent to which intention falls under A_B or SN control, the second level looks at the expectancy-values, i.e. $b_i e_i$ products, most closely associated with the intention and the third level assesses whether it is the likelihood, b_i, or the value, e_i, that is most related to the intention.

At the first level of explanation Figure 4.2 shows that for unmarried college women A_B is more important than SN in determining the intention to use birth control pills. This probably reflects the importance of avoiding pregnancy for this group. Davidson and Jaccard (1975) found that, compared to the unmarried women, the married women with children placed somewhat more emphasis

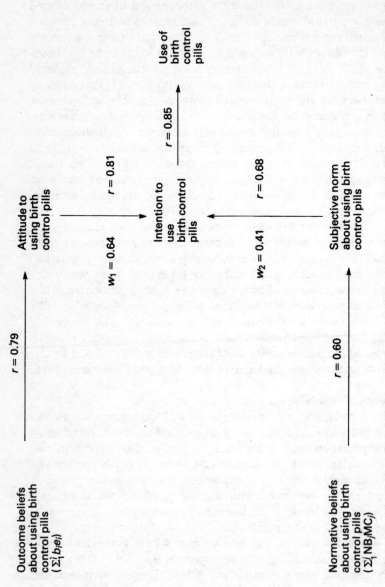

Figure 4.2 Birth control pill usage among college women: relationships between components of the theory of reasoned action (from Jaccard and Davidson, 1972)

on the normative component. The second and third levels of explanation for pill usage come from a comparison of users and non-users. Table 4.1 does not show the expectancy-value of the different outcomes, only the likelihood and evaluation measures separately. This restricts the explanation to the third level.

Table 4.1 *Mean beliefs and outcome evaluations for college women who intend and do not intend to use birth control pills (scales −3 to +3) (from Ajzen and Fishbein, 1980, p. 146)*

| | OUTCOME LIKELIHOOD | | EVALUATION | |
| | Intend: | | Intend: | |
Using birth control pills:	to use	not to use	to use	not to use
Leads to major side-effects	−0.4*	1.2	−2.5	−2.5
Leads to minor side-effects	1.4	1.3	−1.1	−1.8
Produces children who are born with something wrong with them	−2.4*	−0.4	−2.5	−2.5
Is using a method of birth control that is unreliable	−2.3*	−1.1	−2.5	−2.0
Is using the best method available	2.0*	0.9	2.7	2.1
Would remove the worry of becoming pregnant	2.4*	1.1	2.8	2.2
Would affect my sexual morals	−1.9*	−0.4	−1.4	−1.6
Is immoral	−2.7*	−0.7	−1.8	−1.8
Would give me guilt feelings	−2.3*	0.1	−2.4	−2.4
Is using a method of birth control that is expensive	−0.9	−0.8	−1.1	−1.6
Is using a method of birth control that is convenient	2.6	1.8	2.7 *	1.7
Would enable me to regulate the size of my family	2.7	2.2	2.7 *	1.8
Would enable me to regulate the time interval between pregnancies	2.7	2.2	2.7	1.9
Would regulate my menstrual cycle	2.4*	0.8	2.1	1.4
Would increase my sexual pleasure	0.5	−0.1	2.2 *	1.1

Data have been rounded to one decimal place
* Significant difference ($p < 0.05$) between intenders and non-intenders

We can see which likelihoods and which evaluations are most closely connected with the use of oral contraceptives. The connections may be because people who have these beliefs tend to become users, or because users learn to have these beliefs, or the relationship may arise through some common cause such as family sub-culture. Such data are far from conclusive about what makes people likely to use the pill. A stronger support for the theory would be given if it was found that non-users who tended to think like users were more likely to become users. In the absence of stronger evidence we have to use judgement in assessing data like those in Table 4.1.

Using the findings

The information in Table 4.1 can help in interventions designed to change behaviour. Though these data show no certain causal routes for influencing action they do provide some basis for deciding what to put in advertising. Ajzen and Fishbein point out that the list of salient beliefs in Table 4.1 lacks any reference to biological processes underlying reproduction or to population control. This suggests that these issues would not help in mass communications promoting oral contraceptives. Ajzen and Fishbein argue that many public education programmes get the emphasis wrong because they do not pay attention to the relevant motivation. The mistaken procedure is:

1 identify the problem;
2 identify the behaviour change that will lessen the problem;
3 promote the behaviour change as a solution to the problem.

For instance, excess fertility might be seen as a problem and the use of a more effective method of birth control the solution, but the evidence suggests that some other reason than excess fertility must be given if the education programme is to be effective.

This problem of choosing relevant reasons applies to the British anti-AIDS campaign promoting the use of condoms by heterosexuals. When the campaign ran in 1988 the risk to heterosexuals of getting AIDS was extremely low and was not a sound reason *at that time* for using condoms in irregular sexual intercourse. A credible campaign needed to give credible reasons for condom use. In this case a good reason was available. Condoms operate as a barrier to the spread of diseases like genital herpes and warts. Warts are thought to be related to cervical cancer which is responsible for the deaths of 2000 women every year in Britain and there has been an alarming rise in the incidence of this disease in younger women. This is a good reason for condom use and if this use reduces the prevalence of genital warts it may also help in a second way to reduce the spread of AIDS because it is likely that AIDS transmission is assisted by diseases like warts which can cause bleeding during intercourse.

Giving up cigarettes

In 1978 the Joint Committee on Research into Smoking, set up by the Social Science Research Council and the Medical Research Council, recommended that a new study should be undertaken on attitudes towards smoking and in particular of the relationship between smoking attitudes and smoking behaviour. Available at the time was a 1977 report on attitudes and smoking behaviour prepared by Fishbein for the US Federal Trades Commission. The DHSS commissioned the Social Survey Division of the Office of Population Censuses and Surveys to carry out the study. The field work was done in 1981 and the report, *Smoking Attitudes and Behaviour* by Marsh and Matheson, was published in 1983. Much of the research was based on the theory of reasoned action and it is therefore one of the most substantial tests ever given to a theory in social psychology.

The Marsh and Matheson Report is an impressive piece of research and this review touches on only a small part of the findings. The study used a sample drawn from the first three-quarters of the 1980 General Household Survey (GHS) supplemented by respondents from the Electoral Register. Six months after the main study was completed the 2667 smokers in the sample were recontacted by postal survey and were asked about their smoking status and any serious attempts to stop. A 70 per cent response rate was obtained which was raised to 74 per cent by follow-up of a quarter of the non-respondents. Finally a representative sample of 1355 returns were analysed.

A feature of the Marsh and Matheson research was the care that was taken to measure attitudes to the different options of stopping, cutting down, increasing consumption and continuing to smoke though in practice the analysis focused on stopping and continuing to smoke as the principal options. The researchers predicted behaviour on the basis of the difference between the expected values of these two options. It is this difference that shows the personal gain or loss of taking one option rather than the other. An example clarifies the point. Most smokers accepted that smoking causes lung cancer (73 per cent) and heart disease (59 per cent) but the study showed that most of these people believed either that they did not smoke enough to do any damage or that any damage was already done and was irreversible; for such people cessation held no promise of reduced risk. For heart attacks only 14 per cent, and for lung cancer only 11 per cent, of smokers believed both that they had an enhanced risk and that cessation would diminish this risk. It was these people who thought that they would gain by stopping and the researchers therefore predicted that they would make more attempts to stop; this is what was found when smokers were followed up six months later. This evidence therefore supports a causal process from attitude to action.

Marsh and Matheson divided attitude into six domains:

Health: lung cancer, heart attacks, bronchitis, etc.
Affect control: tension, irritability, concentration.
Money: able to save, enough to spend.
Aesthetics: taste food, clothes, breath smells nice.
Self-esteem: pride, respect, achievement.
Social aspects: approval, avoid offence, example to children.

The last domain was not a subjective norm measure; it was a measure of social consequences rather than perceived normative pressure. Table 4.2 (Marsh and Matheson, 1983, p. 115) shows the correlations between these attitude domains and three other measures: 'desire' which was measured by whether the respondents wanted to stop, continue, etc., a measure that seems close to both A_B and intention; 'resolve' which was measured by a 'determined to try' item which is close to the normal intention measure; and 'confidence' which was measured by 'How sure are you that, if you tried you would give up smoking?' This last item measured the respondent's perceived freedom of action. The attitude measures were positively related to intention and, through intention, to the number of attempts to stop. Of those with the minimum score on the resolve scale, 15 per cent tried to stop whereas 60 per cent of those with the highest score tried. There were some people who said that they did not intend to stop but who did make an attempt nonetheless. Such people had more positive attitude scores than those who made no attempt. The researchers argued that this evidence suggested that changes in attitude may accumulate and eventually precipitate a change in intention. This in turn may lead to attempts to stop.

Table 4.2 *Correlations between attitude domains and measures of desire, resolve and confidence about giving up smoking (from Marsh and Matheson, 1983, p. 115)*

Attitude domain	Desire	Resolve (Intention)	Confidence
Health	0.42	0.36	0.05
Affect control	0.28	0.34	0.29
Money	0.30	0.28	0.01
Aesthetics	0.36	0.32	0.07
Self-esteem	0.44	0.40	0.10
Social aspects	0.36	0.31	0.11

The basic idea of reasoned action theory was justified in this study. Within the limits of such research it explained intention and action by reference to beliefs and supported a strategy of trying to persuade smokers to stop by influencing their beliefs so that they saw personal benefit from stopping. Furthermore the study showed where to place emphasis in health education, for example in explaining that the risk from cigarettes is related to the number smoked, that there is no threshold at which health hazards begin, and that there are health benefits for nearly all people who stop smoking.

Other determinants of smoking cessation

Marsh and Matheson found two variables that were related to intention but which fell outside the theory of reasoned action. These were: past experience of attempting to stop, and confidence. This is shown most clearly in a LISREL analysis of the data by Sutton, Marsh and Matheson (1987). Confidence and number of previous attempts to stop each had an influence on intention, only slightly weaker than the attitude factors combined. The analysis also showed that actual attempts to stop in the six months following the attitude measurements were strongly related to intention; previous attempts had marginal direct influence and confidence had no direct influence on this outcome (see Figure 4.3).

The Sutton, Marsh and Matheson (1987) analysis did not cover

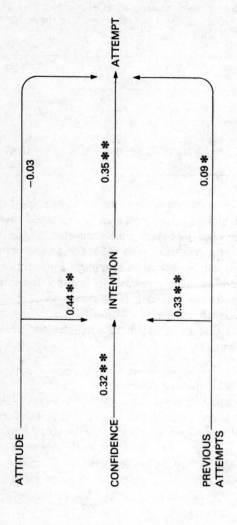

Figure 4.3 Standardized regression coefficients relating attitude, confidence and previous attempts to intention and later attempts to stop smoking (from Sutton, Marsh and Matheson, 1987). *, $p < 0.05$; **, $p < 0.01$.

the effect of attitude, previous attempts, confidence or intention on the success of the cessation attempts. In smoking cessation studies an adequate measure of success is abstinence from smoking for six months or, better, a year. In the six month period 35 per cent of the sample made one or more attempts to stop; about a third of these, over 10 per cent of the whole sample, were not smoking at the end of the period. These non-smoking 'succeeders' included some people who had just stopped and some who had not smoked for nearly the whole six months. Usually we find a preponderance of recent stoppers but in this case 57 out of the 108 'succeeders' had stopped in the first half of the six month period. Thus, although these 'succeeders' fall short of the clinical criterion of success, they do provide an indication of long term cessation. Table 4.3 shows those who tried and those who 'succeeded' in giving up by reference to intention and confidence and indicates a very strong relationship between confidence and 'success'. In fact the most confident were four times as likely to be non-smoking at the six month follow-up as the least confident. The confident people are more able to give up and this raises the question of the extent to which competence and opportunity to stop smoking can be increased through health education. For example a campaign might emphasize *method* rather than *motivation* and might address those who could help smokers by being more supportive. This strategy of raising the ability to stop has not been given much discussion; it is reviewed by East (1985a).

Table 4.3 *Subsequent smoking behaviour (percentage of their group) by typology of original smoking intentions (from Marsh and Matheson, 1983, p. 122)*

Subsequent smoking behaviour	*Intenders* Confidence		*Undecided*	*Non-intenders* Confidence	
	High	Low		High	Low
Making attempt	53	42	34	17	22
'Succeeding'	16	5	12	11	5

The relevance of confidence is explored further in Chapter 5. In the context of consumer behaviour, confidence focuses attention on the consumers' knowledge, ease of access, convenience in paying, assurance about finding the product, etc.; in other words on the factors that facilitate or obstruct action. In part this indicates the importance of distribution in the marketing process but notice that it is not actual opportunity but perceived opportunity that affects intention. To ensure that purchase takes place suppliers may need to advertise the accessibility of their wares just as much as their utility.

Student studies

You can experiment with reasoned action research with the help of PREACT, a computer program that assembles the questionnaire from inputs about the behaviour under investigation and the salient beliefs and referents. Table 4.4 contains summary data from some student studies; the first eight of these were made on small samples and serve merely as illustrations of the method. The last two studies were conducted on larger samples. The behaviours studied were:

1 Buying a Mars Bar this week.
2 Working in the library.
3 Taking exercise during the next week.
4 Drinking alcohol at lunchtime.
5 Giving blood when the transfusion service comes to the polytechnic.
6 Using the sports facilities at the polytechnic.
7 Having a building society account.
8 Keeping a bank account.
9 Watching Breakfast TV (East, Whittaker and Swift, 1984).
   (a) Naïve group before service started
   (b) Informed group before service started
   (c) Sample after service started
10 Getting married in the next five years (East, 1985b).
   (a) Whole sample
   (b) Women
   (c) Men

Prediction of intention

The adjusted R^2 figure in Table 4.4 describes the degree to which variance in intention is related to variance in A_B and SN. The beta weights show that one of these factors is usually dominant in the association with intention. The $A_B : \Sigma_1^i b_i e_i$ and the SN : $\Sigma_1^j NB_j MC_j$ correlations mainly support Fishbein's theory of attitude. In one of the examples the application was badly chosen; this was number 8, keeping a bank account, which was a necessity and not a voluntary activity for the students who were investigated. Giving blood (number 5) was poorly supported too; this may have been a feature of the particular study with its very small sample.

Table 4.4 *Summary data from student studies*

Study	Sample size	Adj R^2	A_B	SN	$\Sigma'_i b_i e_i$ and A_B	$\Sigma'_i NB_j MC_j$ and SN	A_B	SN	$\Sigma'_i b_i e_i$	$\Sigma'_i NB_j MC_j$
			Beta wts				Correlations			
1	21	0.51	0.77	0.15	0.51	0.23	0.73	0.02	0.52	0.52
2	22	0.21	0.53	−0.02	0.24	–	0.40	0.12	0.34	–
3	30	0.79	−0.09	0.95	0.60	0.57	0.60	0.89	0.55	0.50
4	29	0.24	0.56	−0.05	0.57	−0.17	0.55	−0.19	0.61	0.31
5	20	0.13	0.12	0.39	0.46	0.71	0.25	0.42	0.11	0.61
6	15	0.39	0.66	0.09	0.22	−0.31	0.59	0.13	0.09	0.30
7	21	0.49	0.56	0.23	0.59	0.80	0.61	0.51	0.68	0.56
8	18	−0.06	−0.21	−0.09	0.39	0.50	0.02	0.11	0.23	−0.24
9(a)	30	0.30	0.24	0.39	0.44	–	–	–	0.40	–
(b)	30	0.47	0.60	0.27	0.70	–	–	–	0.47	–
(c)	40	0.49	0.62	0.17	0.52	–	–	–	0.52	–
10(a)	75	0.57	0.63	0.22	0.36	0.78	0.74	0.53	0.22	0.58
(b)	38	–	0.69	0.15	0.28	0.74	0.76	0.46	0.18	0.60
(c)	37	–	0.52	0.35	0.44	0.80	0.69	0.61	0.22	0.55

The table columns are grouped: "Beta wts" covers A_B and SN; "Correlations" covers $\Sigma'_i b_i e_i$ and A_B, $\Sigma'_i NB_j MC_j$ and SN, and "Intention and" which covers A_B, SN, $\Sigma'_i b_i e_i$, $\Sigma'_i NB_j MC_j$.

Watching breakfast TV

Beside the bank account and blood transfusion studies there was one other group that gave a low beta weight for both paths in the theory. This was the group 9(a) (the naïve group) who were asked to complete a questionnaire on watching breakfast TV nine months before the service started in Britain. These people were given no information about the programmes they might see. When the expectancy-value products were correlated with intention it was found that only four out of the twelve had a strong positive relationship with intention. One interpretation of the low beta weights is that many of the items in the questionnaire had no salience for the uninformed respondents. The second group 9(b) (the informed group) was shown details of American and Australian breakfast TV services and informed about the nature of the service that they could anticipate in Britain. These people gave a much stronger beta weight to attitude, unlike the naïve group who gave strongest weight to subjective norm. This was predictable from theory. The information they were given was related to attitude and not to subjective norm factors and it was found, as expected, that the likelihood-evaluation products correlated more with intention.

In this study a further group (9(c)) was examined after the service had started; data from this group showed a pattern very similar to the experienced group and this suggests that the experience of new products can be simulated effectively by such experiments. This work indicates how advertising and new products may be tested by comparison of groups exposed and not exposed to the prospective advert/product. There is nothing new in this proposal but the greater sensitivity of the Ajzen and Fishbein questionnaire may make the procedure a more effective test. This is discussed further in Chapter 8.

Unpacking the beliefs

Even simple investigations such as these can bring unexpected results. One surprise was the dominant reason given for taking exercise. The preliminary evidence was that, among students, exercise was taken for the social contacts that it brought, not for health and fitness as might be supposed by health educators. Another investigation also indicated that drinking alcohol at lunchtime was controlled by perceived consequences such as expense and difficulty in working, not by normative control. The Mars Bar study also indicated some interesting reasons for consumption. Men were attracted to eating Mars Bars by their good value, and because they satisfied hunger; women gave taste as a reason for eating/not eating Mars Bars and they were worried about bad teeth. Table 4.5 shows these findings.

Table 4.5 *Salient beliefs about eating Mars Bars. Correlations between likelihood-evaluation products and intention*

If I buy a Mars Bar this week I will . . .	Correlation with intention Males	Females	Strongest factor
get good value	0.9**	0.2	b
enjoy the taste	0.6	0.7*	b
suffer from bad teeth	0.4	0.7*	e
get spots	−0.4	0.4	
put on weight	0.5	0.4	
get sticky fingers	0.4	0.0	
feel less hungry	0.8*	0.2	e

b = likelihood; e = evaluation
* $p < 0.05$ ** $p < 0.01$

Of particular interest are the findings of study 10. This shows that for both men and women students the intention to marry in the next five years was influenced more by A_B than by SN but despite this the aggregate of the expected utilities ($\Sigma_i^i b_i e_i$) had little relationship with either A_B or intention. One explanation for this lack of coherence in thought, feeling and intention (which some of the respondents spontaneously recognized) was that behaviour in this area is actually controlled by normative factors but that this was not well illustrated by the study because of weakness in the SN measure. An alternative view was that the respondents had no immediate need to make connections between marriage and its consequences and therefore had not given the matter much thought; impending marriage or actual experience of being married would probably change this. This lack of connection did not mean that the consequences were unrecognized or lacking in interest to the students. This suggests that recurrent, everyday activities are likely to be better justified in terms of their outcomes than actions about which respondents have had no experience. There was a marked similarity between the views of men and women about early marriage. There were no significant differences in evaluations and the only differences in belief probability were those that had an objective basis: women thought that they would have less money and reduced career prospects if they married in the next five years.

Exercise 4.2. Research by the student group

1 Select an action of mutual interest or commercial relevance for joint investigation by a group of students. The action must be individual and voluntary, e.g. watching Dallas, using second class post, carrying an organ donor card, buying a secondhand car, phoning one's parents every week, going to the dentist regularly, reading a newspaper every day, or applying for new share issues. Make sure that the action is appropriately specified, e.g. watching the next episode of *Dallas*, ringing one's parents once a week, buying a secondhand car through a newspaper advert.

2 Establish the target group. This is often other students because they are accessible but you may choose another segment, e.g. staff applying for new issues of shares.

3 From a sample of the target group elicit the salient beliefs and referents for the action. This is simply done if each member of the student group gathers one or two sets of salients which are then discussed and reduced to an agreed list by the student group. The elicitation procedure was described in Exercise 3.2.

4 Use the program PREACT to create an Ajzen and Fishbein questionnaire. The program asks for:

(a) A decision on the use of optional formats.
(b) The title of the questionnaire.
(c) The intention statement.
(d) The attitude statement.
(e) The first half of the outcome item, e.g. 'If I apply for new issues I will . . .'.
(f) The outcomes, e.g. '. . . make money'.
(g) The referents.

Mistakes can be rectified by editing the questionnaire file that is produced. Age, sex and occupational items are added automatically but may be deleted if inappropriate.

The program sets up the different scales for each item and works out the form of some of the items by parsing your input. The most useful format option is the choice of A_B scales. The best way to get used to this program and to these questionnaires is to try using the program on your own.

5 Print copies of the questionnaire. Try using PREPRI; this prints a slightly enhanced version of the questionnaire. If this program is unsuitable simply print the questionnaire file produced by PREACT.

6 An alternative to printing the questionnaire is to bring the respondents to the computer. The program ENACT presents the items on the screen and accumulates the user's inputs. The user must give the name of the questionnaire file and must use a switch which is explained on the screen if it is necessary to change the condition. The program automatically updates the respondent number and uses the last condition number when no switch is used.

7 The programs record files on the same drive as the one holding the programs. In practice this is less muddling than switching to another drive for output and it makes the software equally suitable for hard disk machines.

8 To analyse the data using SPSS, edit an existing analysis program such as CHAR.SPS which is on the diskette (see Exercise 4.1).

9 Examine your analysis and answer the following questions:

(a) Is the action most related to A_B or SN?
(b) Do A_B and SN correlate with their supposed determinants: $\Sigma_1^i b_i e_i$ and $\Sigma_1^i NB_j MC_j$?
(c) Which factors correlate most with the intention?
(d) Which factors might be used in advertising, if any?
(e) What are the shortcomings of this study and analysis?

This chapter has concentrated on the explanation of the theory of reasoned action. Chapter 5 examines the value of the reasoned action theory to those who seek to change behaviour, and the technical problems associated with the measurements used. One problem with reasoned action theory concerns what exactly it is explaining. It is not a moment-by-moment account of what goes on in people's heads, i.e. information processing. Instead it describes the outcomes, or possible outcomes, of such information processing. To really explain how people change we need the close up, moment-by-moment approach and this is presented in Chapter 7.

Summary

The theory of reasoned action is an extension of the SEU model. Care is needed in its choice of application and it has been more popular in academic than commercial research. A number of applications were reviewed. Established behaviours such as 'using the pill' and smoking do appear to be supported by reasons. Reasoned action research reveals these reasons and in this way explains behaviour and indicates where communications might be pitched to change action.

Further reading

Ajzen, I. and Fishbein, M. (1980) *Understanding Attitudes and Predicting Social Behaviour*. Englewood Cliffs, NJ, Prentice-Hall, chapters 5, 6, 7, 11 and 12

[5]
Further aspects of attitude–behaviour theory

This chapter is concerned with developments and criticisms of reasoned action theory.

The principle of sufficiency

In Fishbein and Ajzen's (1975) theory, evaluation is carried only on beliefs and therefore all attitude and behaviour change must come about through the acquisition of new beliefs or the modification of existing beliefs. Belief changes are a sufficient explanation for 'downstream' changes in attitude, intention and behaviour. Ajzen and Fishbein (1980) assert that variables *external* to the theory such as past experience, personality, age, sex, and other social classifications are associated with behaviour only because these factors are related to relevant beliefs. They state:

> Although we do not deny that 'external' variables of this kind may sometimes be related to behavior, from our point of view they can affect behavior only indirectly. That is, external variables will be related to behavior only if they are related to one or more of the variables specified by our theory. (Ajzen and Fishbein, 1980, p. 82)

Thus beliefs and the other components of reasoned action theory mediate the effect of external variables. This uncompromising cognitivism has been tested in a number of studies by the simple expedient of including external variables in the regression analysis to see whether this significantly improves the prediction of intention or behaviour compared with A_B and SN alone. For example, in the study on marriage intentions among students (Chapter 4), the addition of the respondents' sex to the regression analysis made no difference to the amount of variance explained. Similarly there were no *direct* effects of age or sex in the Marsh and Matheson (1983) study on smoking, i.e. any differences were related to differences of belief. Loken (1983) found no direct effect of external variables on television watching. But Crosby and Muehling (1983) did find that the inclusion of demographic variables improved the prediction of behaviour.

Another test of the sufficiency principle is to observe the effect of non-informative components of an advertisement. One study by Gorn (1982) did this by comparing the effects of advertisements with and without music. If music supplies no information the effect should be the same, but a difference was found. Clearly some influence does take place outside the cognitive paradigm specified by Ajzen and Fishbein.

The argument that external variables have no direct effect is a difficult position to maintain. Among the critical studies, Bentler and Speckart (1979) found that past drug use (or not) had a significant direct effect on subsequent use of drugs and that there was some direct effect of attitude on behaviour. Fredricks and Dossett (1983) compared Bentler and Speckart's model with Fishbein and Ajzen's in a study of class attendance among students. They found a direct effect of recent behaviour on subsequent behaviour but no direct effect of attitude which worked via intention. In 1981 Bentler and Speckart compared predictive models for taking exercise, dating and studying. The results mainly supported a model in which intention mediated attitude but there was some direct effect of prior behaviour on the subsequent behaviour. Bagozzi (1981) also showed some direct effect of prior behaviour. Ryan (1982) discusses some of the studies and points out that their relevance to Ajzen and Fishbein may be low because of the choice of measures used (e.g. Bentler and Speckart 1979, 1981; Bagozzi 1981). In the Marsh and Matheson (1983) study the previous experience of attempting to stop smoking had an independent effect on intention and a small direct effect on later attempts to stop smoking.

It seems clear that past experience often has an effect which is not mediated by the concepts of reasoned action theory. Through experience we learn to respond to stimuli and some of this learning may be unconscious and not affect stated intentions. Also, through experience people learn about their abilities and the opportunities that they have and these may not be fully measured by A_B and SN. However, modification of the theory of reasoned action is only worthwhile if adequately defined measures can be shown to work predictably across a range of actions.

Enlarging the determinants of intention

Two sorts of new determinant may affect intention and action. One is the external variable such as past experience that has been discussed. The second type of determinant is a subjective measure like A_B which covers a section of people's thought and feeling more effectively than A_B or SN. In this second category there have been two candidates: *personal subjective norm* and *perceived control*.

Personal subjective norm

If our behaviour is affected by salient persons and groups then it must also be affected by our own personal values; we can be a referent to ourselves. For this reason Ajzen and Fishbein included personal normative beliefs in their early theory (1969) but this factor was discarded on practical grounds when it was found that the correlation between personal norm and intention was so high that these measures were effectively equivalent. It appeared that the personal norm measure picked up both the A_B and SN effects and therefore failed to measure separately any effect of personal reference (Ajzen and Fishbein, 1980, p. 247). There is more scope for separately measuring personal norms when they have an effect opposite to that of A_B, e.g. giving blood (some people feel they should give blood but fear the effects of doing so).

It is possible that in some contexts personal norm captures more than intention. Moreton and East (1983) found that a personal norm measure of what a person thought 'they ought to do' gave a better prediction of behaviour (smoking cessation) than the standard intention measure.

Perceived control

This was introduced by Ajzen in 1985 in the theory of *planned behaviour*. In this theory perceived control (PC) is a determinant of intention together with A_B and SN. PC is measured as the perceived ability to do some action if the respondent should so wish. It is thus the same variable as the confidence measure used by Marsh and Matheson (1983). Being able to do something if you want to do it is a measure of freedom and this revision of reasoned action theory therefore quantifies the degree to which an action is voluntary. Ajzen also argues that there is often an overlap between past experience and PC. This is because past experience reveals the situational opportunities and the personal abilities upon which PC is based.

Moving from intention to action, Ajzen argues that the actual performance of the behaviour and its outcome depend on intention and the actual control that a person has over his or her behaviour. In most cases PC is an indicator of actual control and thus it has a second function in the theory of planned behaviour as a proxy for a measure of real control in predicting behaviour. Planned behaviour theory is shown in Figure 5.1; the proxy relationship is shown by the broken line.

Strictly speaking the inclusion of PC in the determination of intention lacks logical support. If, for example, someone was only 50 per cent sure that they could so something then all likelihoods and hence payoffs should be halved, thus taking this uncertainty into account. The fact that PC has a direct effect on intention may be linked to the effect of the availability heuristic which raises the perceived likelihood of more vivid outcomes (Chapter 7).

The theory of planned behaviour has received support in a limited number of studies. In three investigations Ajzen and Madden (1986) showed that the inclusion of PC raised the prediction of intention substantially. In one study PC also raised the prediction of the behaviour directly. This behaviour was 'getting an A grade' by students who, towards the end of their course, were relatively constrained by their past performance of which they were well aware. In these circumstances perceived control should have been close to actual control, the condition necessary to activate the link to action. The authors also found that the three determinants of intention operated independently, i.e. with no interaction effects. Another study by Schifter and Ajzen (1985)

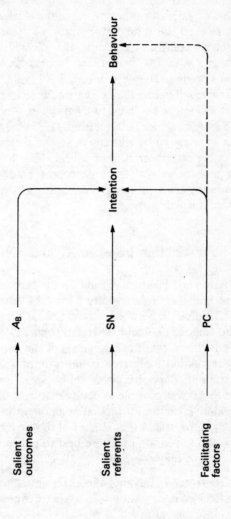

Figure 5.1 Theory of planned behaviour

again found that intention (to lose weight) was better predicted when PC was included. PC also raised the prediction of actual weight loss.

The role of perceived control in determining behaviour has also been shown in a number of studies based on the work of Bandura (1977). Bandura used the term 'self-efficacy' to mean much the same as perceived control. Condiotte and Lichtenstein (1981) found that people with low self-efficacy scores showed higher relapse back to smoking. They also found that smokers were able to predict their areas of vulnerability where relapse later occurred, suggesting that PC might be changed by training. Another study by McIntyre, Lichtenstein and Mermelstein (1983) found that self-efficacy scores were raised by training in smoking cessation skills but that this effect disappeared after a year. This has relevance to advertising and shows that there is scope for advertisements that explain *how* to get a product; the emphasis is normally on *why* the product is worth getting.

The distinction between A_B and SN

According to Ajzen and Fishbein A_B and SN are separate determinants of action and their relative effect must be determined by data analysis. The division between A_B and SN has been examined by Miniard and Cohen, 1979 and 1981; and Ryan, 1978 and 1982. Ajzen (1971) has shown that the change agent can use the weightings found by regression analysis as an indicator of where to pitch an influence attempt. Supporting this study Ajzen and Fishbein (1972) showed that it was possible to devise messages that affected either the normative or the attitudinal component but Fishbein and Ajzen (1981) have stated that studies of the existing basis for action give only an indication of where best to place emphasis in an influence attempt; they comment:

> it is impossible to tell in advance the exact extent to which
> . . . a given item of information will influence a person's
> attitude or subjective norm.

This reduces the value of attitude–behaviour theory for planning intervention but the measures used by the theory can serve in tests of persuasive effect.

A study by Ryan (1982) used the LISREL methodology of

Joreskog and Sorbom (1978) to trace the 'downstream' effects of information about a supposedly new toothpaste. This tested attitude formation rather than attitude change and Ryan concluded that there was interdependence between the attitude and normative beliefs in his study. This interdependence could lead to an underestimation of the effect of normative beliefs since their effect was passed to intention more via A_B than by SN. Ryan suggests that we should recognize more interdependence of normative and attitudinal variables and that influence attempts may be more effective when mutual implications of this sort are illustrated in the persuasive message. Ryan is careful to note the limits of one study; his findings are suggestive, not conclusive.

Fishbein and Ajzen (1975, pp. 304–7) discuss the nature of the normative component and the utility of distinguishing A_B from SN. They point out that a piece of information such as the effectiveness of a drug may lead to two separate effects along the two paths of the model and argue that this double process does not imply that the same effect is being counted twice. If a doctor prescribes a drug the medicine may be taken because the doctor is a referent *and* because inferences are made about the strong beneficial effects of the medicine. Under some circumstances the inferences could result in attitude changes that oppose the normative changes. For example a man who drinks a lot may be less inclined to use a drug when a doctor had convinced him of its potency for fear of amplifying the effect of alcohol. In support of the two path model Fishbein and Ajzen (1981) claim that usually A_B and SN correlate with intention more strongly than they correlate with each other.

Miniard and Cohen (1981) suggest that the theory would be more useful if all social determinants, normative and attitudinal, were grouped together in one concept. This would leave a residual A_B (A_B minus external social consequences). Such an arrangement might have practical merit for consumer research if a sharper separation was produced between the social factors concept and the residual A_B concept, but the evidence of one study is a poor basis for assuming that this would normally be obtained.

Measurement issues

Points of agreement

Much of the measurement in attitude–behaviour theory is now well accepted. There is little dissent over the *correspondence* principle that measures should be equivalently specified in terms of action, object of action, context, time and the personal nature of the action. A second point of agreement is that the correlation between behaviour and predictor variables will decline as the period elapsing between measures increases. Another distinction made by Ajzen and Fishbein (1980) is between behaviour (like dieting) and an outcome (like losing weight). An outcome is the product of a set of behaviours and is not reliably predicted on the basis of just one behaviour in the set.

In practice measurement considerations interlock with theory and cannot easily be considered in isolation. However, there are a number of problems that have affected measurement in this field and which stand relatively separate from issues of theory.

Salience

The methods for eliciting salient beliefs and referents are *ad hoc* and the use of modal salient beliefs inevitably means that some respondents have to answer questions that may not be salient for them. However, any vagueness in the measurement counts against the theory in empirical test; if the theory works using these methods the problems cannot be too great. One reason for this may be the effect of the neutral point which is scored at zero; neutral responses have zero effect on accumulated scores. If non-salient items tend to get neutral responses they will have less effect.

If salience is badly measured there is a danger that non-salient correlates of salient beliefs will be treated as salient. Thomas and Tuck (1975) show that this can occur. Non-salient beliefs may provide a prediction of intention and behaviour because of their correlation with salient beliefs but changes in non-salient factors would not have any direct causal effect on intention. Thus weakness in the measurement of salience might only appear when the theory was tested for causal effect.

One other problem with salience has been illustrated by Kristiansen (1987) who showed that users and non-users (of cigarettes) may have different salient beliefs. This effect could be found more generally and complicates the comparison of users and non-users.

The normative component

A number of theorists including Miniard and Cohen (1981) and Fishbein and Ajzen (1981) have expressed unease about the precision of the normative measures in attitude–behaviour research. The problem starts with the SN measure:

'Most people who are important to me think . . .'

which neglects the possibility that strong normative influence on an issue may come from a small number of important people. This measure also introduces social desirability effects. Certain behaviours (e.g. organ donation) show selflessness while other actions (e.g. yielding to pressure to do something of which one disapproves personally) may indicate weakness. A further problem with the SN measure is that the single scale measure usually used collects more error and less true measure than the multiscale measure which is usually used for A_B and this will diminish the weight of SN derived from the regression analysis.

These troubles have led researchers to use $\Sigma_i' NB_j MC_j$ in place of the SN measure and others have disputed the value of the MC measure and just used $\Sigma_i' NB_j$. Some of the problems with the MC measure arose when responses to it were treated as bipolar. Lutz (1976) and Loken and Fishbein (1980) have found that respondents interpret the MC measure in a unipolar fashion, i.e. compliance is always positive, and Fishbein and Ajzen (1981) now recommend that MC scores are treated as unipolar and not as -3 to $+3$. This help to make the MC measure count but it means that any counter-compliant tendency, i.e. to do the opposite of what a referent wants, cannot be measured.

One option (offered by PREACT) is to measure NB and MC in the same manner as the measures of outcome likelihood and evaluation, e.g.

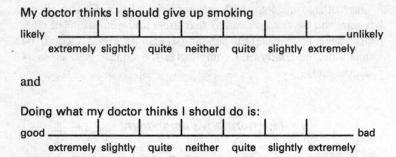

My doctor thinks I should give up smoking

likely |_____| unlikely

extremely slightly quite neither quite slightly extremely

and

Doing what my doctor thinks I should do is:

good |_____| bad

extremely slightly quite neither quite slightly extremely

This method was used alongside the conventional measures in the study of student marriage intentions (Chapter 4); predictions were slightly improved.

General versus specific measures of MC and evaluation

A further point of contention has been the general form of the MC measure. Respondents are asked for their general tendency to comply with the referent and not for their tendency to comply with respect to the specific action being investigated. Fishbein and Ajzen (1981) point out that the same argument can be levelled at their evaluation measure which is not behaviour specific. They argue that specification of these measures would increase correlation but would narrow understanding of the basis of behaviour.

Fishbein and Ajzen's argument assumes that there are generalized evaluations and motivations to comply and that these are tapped by the measures recommended, but it is possible that people implicitly specify the context when they asked general questions and give responses as though the question was more specified. Respondents could implicitly specify general measures in different ways than the corresponding belief measures. For example a respondent may think of compliance with his or her doctor in terms of adherence to rules of drug medication but this may be inappropriate when the doctor is seeking compliance on giving up cigarettes.

There is a compromise to this measurement dilemma. This is to use the general form but to juxtapose the likelihood and evaluation measures, and the NB and MC measures, in the questionnaire so that any implicit specification is likely to be that named in the previous item. This is done in the questionnaires produced using the PREACT program.

The relevance of reasoned action theory to inducing change

Table 4.1 shows a number of significant differences between users and non-users of the contraceptive pill. All the differences are relevant to explaining the use of oral contraceptives but some of these differences are of more use for influencing action. The relevance to influencing action in a population segment depends on three matters:

1 whether a change in a factor *will cause* a change in intention and action;
2 the extent to which the factor *can change*;
3 the *homogeneity* of beliefs and values within the target segment.

These three issues are discussed below.

Inferring causality

Cross-sectional studies comparing users and non-users do not show whether usage causes belief or belief causes usage or whether both have some other cause. Without experimental research, judgement is required to pick the beliefs that are most likely to have a causative role. For example the belief in the reliability of the pill may be a cause of its use whereas concern about morals, guilt feelings and sexual pleasure may be effects of use. We do not know the causal relationships but we can form a judgement. To add to the complication we have to acknowledge that something which was merely an effect may nevertheless become a cause in a persuasive communication.

The problem of causal direction is particularly acute when usage is continuous and covers the period of measurement, as in the case of Jaccard and Davidson's research on oral contraceptive usage. There is less ambiguity about cause and effect when the attitudinal measures are clearly prior to the potential action, e.g.

a prospective holiday, or in Marsh and Matheson's study of those who gave up cigarettes. Even when there is strong evidence of a causal relationship in a natural setting it still does not mean that this relationship can be used to good effect in persuasive communications. For this to be established an experimental test of alternative communications is required.

In a cross-sectional study the strength of any relationship between an outcome likelihood or evaluation and intention is likely to be indicated by the difference between the measures for users and non-users. When the use is prospective this becomes a comparison between those who intend and those who do not intend to perform the action. Another way of measuring this relationship is to correlate intention with its possible determinants. This avoids the need to dichotomize the intention measure. The observed relationship is part of a web of interrelationships which increase or reduce the measured correlation. This means that such correlations should be treated as suggestive, not conclusive, of a direct relationship.

Changeability

Some factors are more changeable than others. Variance within groups and between groups provides an indicator of changeability. Wide variation suggests that beliefs are not strongly anchored in common values. Another indicator is *headroom*, i.e. how much a measure can change in the required direction before it reaches the top or bottom of the scale. For example Table 4.1 shows that there is little headroom for changing non-users' beliefs about regulating their family size and the interval between pregnancies.

It is likely that some evaluation differences are fairly resistant to change. It is noticeable that users and non-users often have much the same evaluation of an outcome and differ more often on the likelihood of that outcome occurring (look at the figures in Table 4.1). Evaluations may reflect environmental circumstances that are beyond influence. For example the value of regulating the size of one's family partly depends upon how many children you have already. Evaluations are also likely to have more inertia than single belief likelihoods because they are based on several belief likelihoods. For example, by regulating family size a woman can avoid impacts on housing, family relationships and fatigue.

Belief changes do not necessarily produce behaviour changes. A belief change may be irrelevant, too small, or affect one path of the model, say A_B, when the influence passes mainly through the SN path. Even if intention is changed there may be no opportunity to change behaviour. Ajzen and Fishbein's theory is asymmetric: any behaviour change stems from belief change but belief change does not necessarily result in behaviour change.

Population homogeneity

For most people the reliability of birth control is an advantage but this is not necessarily so for everyone. Some women might want to become pregnant under circumstances that absolved them from blame by their partner. To these women a reliable method of contraception could be negatively evaluated. A consequence of this is that a general increase in the perceived reliability of the pill could increase the likelihood of most women using it but reduce the likelihood that a minority will use it. When there is value dissensus like this an increase in the perceived likelihood of an outcome throughout the population, e.g. that a party will win in an election, will produce greater polarization in attitudes within the population. Increasing the level of population dissensus may raise levels of discussion and antagonism and may have unpredictable effects in the population as a whole.

Dynamic effects of communications

It is clear that cross-sectional reasoned action research can give ideas but no proof about the best platform to use in persuasive communications. Much more useful would be a dynamic test of the proposed communiation. This takes the form of an experiment in which beliefs, evaluations, A_B, SN, intention and behaviour are compared between those exposed to the communication and those who are not.

Because reasoned action theory is not a true information processing theory it may not work so well at the dynamic level. It is possible that effects take time to appear since reasoned action deals with the outcome rather than the process. Lutz (1977), following Rosenberg (1968), suggested that there may be thresholds for change; 'stepped' changes might be assisted by messages that drew conclusions along the pathway of the attitude–behaviour model. Some evidence of delay in processing is found in the Marsh and Matheson (1983) research on smoking cessation. Their data suggested that slow belief based changes were at work so that it took some time for the higher attitude score to harden into a resolve to stop smoking.

There are a number of dynamic tests of reasoned action theory. Early support came from studies by Ajzen (1971) and Ajzen and Fishbein (1972). Lutz (1977, 1978) conducted a study in which belief change was manipulated and the flow of changes fitted reasoned action theory quite well but without much transmission from $\Sigma_i^i b_i e_i$ to A_B. Consistent with this Cowling (1972) noted that copy tests conducted by his company showed that advertisements often changed beliefs without changing intention. Ryan (1982) also found the $\Sigma_i^i b_i e_i \rightarrow A_B$ connection to be weak. Weak results do not refute the theory but neither do they give confidence in its utility. It is possible that these findings reflected the delayed change discussed above. In contrast to the studies above McArdle (1972) found a strong $\Sigma_i^i b_i e_i \rightarrow A_B$ correlation (0.63 and 0.77 in relevant conditions). McArdle used face-to-face persuasion on ten issues to persuade alcoholics to join a treatment unit and thus affected many more beliefs than the other studies.

Summary

In the theory of reasoned action a change in attitude, intention or behaviour starts with a change in salient beliefs. This position has been supported in some studies but past experience often has a direct effect on intention or behaviour. Ajzen's (1985) theory of planned behaviour takes some account of experience by introducing perceived freedom as a further determinant of intention. A number of measurement issues are discussed; some, like the measurement of subjective norm, remain problematic. Reasoned action theory gives only an indication of the factors that may be relevant to changing behaviour.

Further reading

Ajzen (1985) From intentions to actions: a theory of planned behaviour. In: Kuhl, J. and Beckmann, J. (eds) *Action-control: From Commitment to Behavior*. Heidelberg, Springer

Bagozzi, R. P. (1988) The rebirth of attitude research in marketing. *Journal of the Market Research Society* **30**, 2, 163–95

[6]

Attitude measurement in marketing

The purpose of this chapter is to look at the measurement practices which are conventionally used in marketing and to show
where these lack precision or theoretical support.

Quantitative and qualitative research

In marketing research the method of measurement and the theory
behind it are often relegated to a minor role and statistical procedures such as multi-dimensional analysis are given exaggerated
attention. Quantitative techniques of this sort certainly provide
an analysis but there is a need to validate the method in practice.
Do these techniques lead to more profitable new products or
product modifications?

Those who have avoided statistical methods and computing
have tended to use qualitative research. The discussion group
(called a focus group in the USA) is the most popular form of
qualitative research and is used to elicit the ideas that consumers
have about advertising, and about new and existing products. A
recruiter sets up the groups with a specified composition (e.g. by
product usage, sex, age, social class and region). A group leader
or moderator, skilled in ways of getting people to talk, then runs
the discussion for 1–2 hours, recording the whole procedure. The
participants are paid or receive gifts. The group leader listens to
the tapes and writes a report for the client. This procedure yields
imaginative ideas; it is quick, quite cheap and the results are
easily comprehended by most people. These factors have made
discussion groups very popular in marketing and advertising

research. However, the method is a form of elicitation rather than measurement. It is not suitable for quantifying the importance of different ideas in determining consumer choice, and it does not indicate how such ideas might change in response to advertising. Different qualitative researchers often produce quite different results, i.e. the method has poor reliability, and there has been little attempt to validate the decisions taken on the basis of qualitative research findings, i.e. to test them against decisions made using other methods.

Nonetheless qualitative research may have particular merits as a method of elicitation. The case histories of successful advertising campaigns reported by Broadbent (1981, 1983) and Channon, (1985, 1987) usually start with qualitative research reports on the brand image. These reports use descriptions such as: old-fashioned, individualistic, traditional, trendy, or bought by older people. Such descriptions are indicators of the social values and costs associated with purchase of the product and indicate the way in which consumption affects self-esteem and group membership. Respondents are implicitly saying: 'the brand is sound but only "wallies" buy it, so you won't find me buying it'; or 'it is the thing that trendy people are going for, it's for me.' Such attitudes are clearly important. If they are picked up best by qualitative research then it is a valuable method.

Exercise 6.1. Brand attributes

You are required to find out what attributes are related to the purchase of Mars, Twix, Wispa and KitKat chocolate bars. What questions would you ask and how would you do this? If you asked the same people the same questions three months later what proportion would change their minds?

Evaluative and descriptive beliefs

Barwise and Ehrenberg (1985) examined beliefs about cereals and detergent. The beliefs that are 'broadly evaluative' such as 'good value for money' are closely associated with brand usage and this supports previous findings by Bird and Ehrenberg (1970). 'More descriptive' measures such as 'stays crispy in milk' differentiate between brands such as Weetabix and Corn Flakes irrespective of usage.

Rossiter (1987) takes issue with Barwise and Ehrenberg over a number of aspects of their 1985 paper. One of Rossiter's concerns is about the classification of descriptive and evaluative beliefs *post facto*. Barwise and Ehrenberg (1987) responded by pointing out that most people can see the difference between attributes that describe the product such as 'stay crispy in milk' and attributes that describe the user's evaluative response such as 'fun to eat'; in this sense they say that the distinction between the beliefs can be *ex ante*. Barwise and Ehrenberg are fairly content to treat the evaluative/descriptive distinction as an empirical regularity that has appeared in a number of studies.

To my mind the main issue is missed in this debate. This is the weakness of the method of measurement of brand attributes which is used. Barwise and Ehrenberg use data collected by a method long used by British Market Research Bureau Ltd (BMRB) in the preparation of the Advertising Planning Index (API). In this procedure each respondent is shown a list of the 5 to 10 leading brands in a product field. The interviewer then asks, for each of 10 to 15 attributes, which brands have the attribute. Respondents are also asked about their frequency of brand use. This procedure seems to be fraught with problems which are explored under the following three headings.

What should be investigated?

Attributes of brands? Attributes of brand purchase? Attributes of brand usage? Advertising slogans? The target depends upon the purpose of the investigation. Profits are made because people *buy brands* so that this is normally the focus of research. But purchase attitudes may include the response to marketing features such as price, distribution and promotion and often it may be convenient to exclude these and to concentrate on product acceptability. When this is so the investigation may be on product consumption, i.e. eating, use, etc. So, depending on the purpose of the research, the attribute list should be about *purchase or use of the brand*. From this standpoint research focused on the brand object (rather than actions toward the brand) is misplaced though it may still be informative. In practice there is often substantial overlap between brand attitude and brand purchase attitude but this is not always so as Ajzen and Fishbein point out (1980, pp. 156–9).

How are the attributes chosen?
In commercial research the attributes are established by inspection of the product and its advertising, not by elicitation from consumers. Consider some of the detergent examples: 'gets things white' and 'gets stains out' are always obtained in an elicitation but 'makes whole wash easier', 'good in the washing machine' sound more like the manufacturers' claims than the consumers' judgement. An elicitation by marketing students gathered the salient beliefs about buying biological, normal or low-temperature washing machine detergent. The salient beliefs were:

- get my clothes clean
- get stains out
- make my clothes soft
- make my clothes smell nice
- get value for money
- avoid skin rash
- make my whites white

There may be a tendency to neglect the more negative aspects of products in commercial research, e.g. skin rash, despite the fact that these features are relevant to the success of a product. Other examples are: 'bad teeth' and 'spots' with regard to confectionery and the unpleasant smell of pet food. These factors may be very important in any explanation of why some consumers exclude themselves from certain markets.

Separation of evaluative and descriptive components
Are 'popular with the family', 'get things white', 'lots of food value', etc., evaluative or descriptive? The answer is *both*. Language is flexible and carries multiple meanings. Even the most evaluative term 'good' has a descriptive usage in statements such as 'this is a good knife' which might imply that it is sharp or easy to use. This means that a division of beliefs into evaluative and descriptive classes is not very satisfactory. People may agree on what category a belief falls into but this reflects a broad consensus on values which cannot be assumed in all cases.

The BMRB method

Inspection of the BMRB method shows that it is a crude measure of the likelihood that an attribute is possessed by a brand. Respondents have to use some implicit probability above which the brand is credited with the attribute. A scale could be used that would avoid the yes/no choice. Evaluation of attributes like 'getting things white' is not made in the BMRB research. Such values are assumed even though different attributes may have different values and several people may differ in their evaluation of a single attribute. For example, some people may regard 'lots of food value' negatively if they are trying to lose weight. But even when people agree that something is good there remains the matter of degree: how good is it? These problems suggest that considerable improvements could be made to research on attitudes to purchase or use by using scales for both the likelihood and the evaluation of attributes.

Expectancy-value method of measuring brand attitudes

Let us consider the attitudes to using brand X and brand Y washing detergents. An overall evaluation of brand use, A_B, can be made using an average of evaluative semantic differential scales, e.g.:

Using [brand] is:

good	3	2	1	0	−1	−2	−3	bad
kind	3	2	1	0	−1	−2	−3	harmful
nice	3	2	1	0	−1	−2	−3	nasty

Intention can be measured with a likelihood scale or by using the format:

Definitely will buy	[ ]5
Very likely will buy	[ ]4
Probably will buy	[ ]3
Might or might not buy	[ ]2
Definitely will not buy	[ ]1

Reported purchase may be measured by using different intervals appropriate for the product, e.g.:

Check one My most recent purchase of [brand] was:

In the last week	[ ]4
In the last month	[ ]3
In the last year	[ ]2
Not in the last year	[ ]1

The likelihood and evaluative aspects of the attributes can be measured separately by pairs of measures, e.g.:

If I use [brand] I will get clothes clean

likely	3	2	1	0	−1	−2	−3	unlikely

Getting clothes clean is

good	3	2	1	0	−1	−2	−3	bad

If I use [brand] I will get stains out

likely	3	2	1	0	−1	−2	−3	unlikely

Getting stains out is

good	3	2	1	0	−1	−2	−3	bad

Evaluations, being general, need be measured only once for all brands while likelihoods are measured for each brand. Using this procedure any brand differences should appear as a difference in attribute likelihoods.

Applying Fishbein's (1963) theory of attitude to these measures means that the sum of the products of likelihood and evaluation for each attribute should correlate with the overall attitude, i.e.

$$A_{\mathrm{B}} \propto \Sigma_1^i b_i e_i$$

For two brands X and Y:

$$A_{\mathrm{BX}} - A_{\mathrm{BY}} \propto \Sigma_1^i e_i (b_{i\mathrm{X}} - b_{i\mathrm{Y}})$$

When brand purchase is freely made and not controlled by the subjective norm the theory of reasoned action implies that purchase should be predicted by using such measures. However, Fishbein's theory may not be of much practical value in the case of detergents. Although there is freedom of choice many people see little difference between brands of detergent and this will show up in the results. Their brand choices are likely to be directed more by convenience (whether the brand is on the shelf) and by familiarity of name and pack design which are usually not elicited in an expectancy-value approach. The Fishbein approach works better for the choice between two brands that have different properties (e.g. in the confectionery field) or in distinguishing preference between sub-types of product, e.g. biological versus liquid versus normal detergent.

We may interpret Barwise and Ehrenberg's findings in relation to this system of measurement. They find that usage and evaluative beliefs go together. If expectancy-value theory applies then these evaluative beliefs should be those with large likelihood–evaluation products which thus exert a disproportionate effect on the total attitude-to-use score. The descriptive beliefs which differentiate between brands, but not usage, should be those with low value. For example I may differentiate between two detergents because they are different colours but if I attach no value to colour then this should not affect my usage. Thus, by measuring the evaluation component which was assumed in BMRB studies, it should be possible to show that evaluative and descriptive beliefs differ in magnitude of expectancy-value.

Constancy of brand attitudes

The BRMB method of measuring brand attributes has been used in another study by Barnard, Barwise and Ehrenberg (1986) which looked at the change in brand attributions over time. They found that the percentage of people stating that a brand had an attribute was constant but that only about half of those people who credited a brand with an attribute on one occasion did so again on a second occasion. The proportion reaffirming the attribute was larger when a larger percentage of the population believed that the brand possessed the attribute, thus indicating a double jeopardy effect similar to the way purchase frequency rates in a product field rise with penetration. The variation in responses is not well explained by the suggestion that people were steadily changing their preferences. Such respondent change would increase over time and although the data did show somewhat less change after one month there was no trend over longer periods.

Barnard, Barwise and Ehrenberg suggest that these data indicate a stochastic aspect to individual brand attributions similar to the stochastic pattern of purchasing. An alternative explanation is that the stochastic component is associated with imperfections in the measure. The latter view has been a feature of most treatments of measurement theory, e.g. Kish (1959). The first type of explanation assumes that the object of study is fluctuating so that a perfect measuring instrument would still show the fluctuation. The second assumes that the object is constant and would appear as such if the observing instrument was perfect. Both types of fluctuation may be at work; research using different methods of attribute measurement would clarify this matter.

Some further understanding of how brand attitudes change comes from an analysis by Barnard (1987). This supports the view that the stochastic element is in the person rather than the measure. Barnard found that people were more likely to associate positive attributes with a brand if they were currently using it and a large part of the change in brand attributions was associated with variations in usage. Barnard, Barwise and Ehrenberg argue that attitude follows purchase in fast-moving consumer goods (fmcg) markets. We know that purchase occasions have a stochastic form (Chapter 2) so that this would help to account for the stochastic form of brand attitudes. Bem's (1967) self-perception theory (explained in Chapter 7) could explain how attitudes change. People may perceive their own behaviour as current users and infer that they liked the brand ('It must be fun to eat otherwise I wouldn't be using it').

How does this work affect marketing practice? One conclusion is that too much attention may be given to brand attitudes, particularly as they are currently gathered.

Likert's method of summated ratings

Likert's (1932) method of attitude scale construction is best understood by following the procedure through, step by step. This is done in Exercise 6.2 below.

Exercise 6.2. Constructing a Likert scale

1 Choose a subject, e.g. shopping in supermarkets. Gather items expressed as propositions which can be agreed or disagreed with. Propositions can be favourable or unfavourable to the concept. For example favourable items might be:
'Being able to buy everything in one place is a great convenience.'
'Most supermarkets offer convenient parking.'
Unfavourable or negative items might be:
'Large shops are rather anonymous.'
'You often have to queue in supermarkets.'

2 Using several people as judges, check through the items to combine similar ones, to eliminate irrelevance and to clarify wording.

3 Set the items in a questionnaire with a fivefold response format:

strongly agree	[ ]5
agree	[ ]4
neither agree nor disagree	[ ]3
disagree	[ ]2
strongly disagree	[ ]1

The numbers are for favourable items. The number order should be reversed for negative items, i.e. 'strongly agree that large shops are rather anonymous' gets a 1. A respondent's score is the summation of the item response numbers.

4 Use this questionnaire with a sample drawn from the segment that you are interested in. Although most people use supermarkets you might be particularly interested in a sub-group such as young shoppers or women.

5 Conduct an *internal item analysis*. This assumes that the aggregate of responses to the questionnaire is a crude measure of the attitude to shopping in supermarkets and assesses each item against this aggregate. So, compute for each respondent the sum of their responses. A high score indicates that they are positive to shopping in supermarkets, a low score negative. Now compute the correlations between each item and the aggregate for all respondents. Keep the items that give a high correlation. Reject the items that show little correlation. Consider keeping any items with a high negative correlation after reversing the 5–1 scoring. How many items you keep depends on the size of the questionnaire that you want. Try to have approximately equal numbers of positive and negative items because this counterbalances tendencies to agree or disagree among respondents. Reconstruct the scale with the chosen items using the same fivefold response format.

6 Test the validity of the instrument. For example people who use supermarkets for most of their shopping should show higher scores than those who use corner shops.

Comments on Likert's method

1 It is best to gather items by elicitation from members of the segment to be studied. Unless this is done there may be gaps in the range of items. This would be a failure of *content validity*.

2 The item form suffers from the same problem discussed in the context of brand attributes, that evaluations are implicitly assumed to be the same across items and across the population. To assess the importance of a factor like 'convenient parking' it is necessary to know both the evaluation of the factor and its association with shopping in supermarkets. For example everyone may agree that out of town supermarkets offer convenient parking but it is only car users that attach high value to this attribute.

3 The Likert method assumes that one attitude dimension is being measured by a number of scales. The alternative possibility is that several dimensions are measured and the items contribute

differentially to these sub-attitudes. A correlation matrix of all the items may show up any sub-sets.

4 Sometimes negative features of brands are associated with use. This is probably because users are more familiar with such effects than non-users. For example the devotees of real ale know that sometimes the beer is cloudy. The internal item analysis is not designed to cope with such effects.

5 What do you do with a Likert scale? One use is to identify user groups. For example a scale on blood donation may successfully discriminate between those who gave blood and those who did not when they had the opportunity. When the scale is validated like this it is tempting to 'unpack' its components and try to find out the most discriminating factors. Such analysis supplies only correlations and the Likert measure does not show whether the evaluation or the likelihood is most related to usage. On these grounds the Ajzen and Fishbein method seems preferable to Likert's.

Scale referents in multi-attribute research

The last two decades have seen the emergence of methods based on *multi-attribute utility models* using semantic differential scales to measure the components. Fishbein and Ajzen's work belongs to this class and has been emphasized in this text because of its logical form and carefully specified procedures. There have, however, been many variants of this approach and some methodologically weak practices. The early review by Wilkie and Pessemier (1973) found no agreement between researchers on the appropriate referents to use on scales. In this chapter 'good–bad' and 'likely–unlikely' were used but a variety of alternatives are possible such as 'pleasant–unpleasant' and 'probable–improbable'. These alternatives reflect the two sorts of measurement that are required. One is the subjective value of an attribute, the other is a measure of likelihood or perceived association between the attribute and the concept. In market research there have been two scale referents that are difficult to fit into this pattern; these are measures of *importance* and *satisfaction*.

Fishbein and Ajzen (1976a) point out the problems with importance. These are:

(a) it may correlate with the likelihood measure;

(b) it may relate to the extremity of the evaluation measure, i.e. strong positive *or negative* feelings; for example food additives may be important to some people because they fear their effects while others may see them as important because of their good effects;

(c) there may be other attributes which are not seen as important but which are nonetheless highly valued and associated with the concept.

Thus, although measures of importance pick up something about an attribute, it is not clear in any particular case what this will be. Whatever it is, it is covered by the evaluation and likelihood measures so a measure of importance is not required.

Another claim about importance is that some attributes are more widely salient and hence more important in group application than others. This is true, but there have been no demonstrations that a third weighting factor improves the predictions obtained from evaluation and likelihood alone. Fishbein and Ajzen (1975, ch. 6) report that predictions are reduced by the inclusion of an importance measure.

Measures of satisfaction are also confused. Cohen, Fishbein and Ahtola (1972) deal with this in response to a paper by Bass and Talarzyk (1972). An attribute may be satisfactory because it is valued, or because it is reliably associated with a concept, or both. Satisfaction may be used as a short cut combination of likelihood and evaluation but this means that the separate contribution of these factors cannot be known.

Despite the arguments against importance and satisfactoriness they continue to be used in market research. Exercise 6.3 is designed to illustrate bad practice in this sort of measurement.

Exercise 6.3. Measuring the attributes of brands of chocolate bar

This exercise incorporates a number of bad practices. Identify what these are and work out a better procedure.

1 Ask people in the appropriate segment what the important characteristics of chocolate bars are. Copy these down and establish the attributes that recur.

2 Consider two brands of chocolate bar and for each attribute measure satisfaction with the scale:

extremely   3 | 2 | 1 | 0 | −1 | −2 | −3   extremely
satisfactory   unsatisfactory

3 Consider each brand and for each attribute measure the importance using the scale below:

extremely   3 | 2 | 1 | 0 | −1 | −2 | −3   extremely
important   unimportant

4 Set out the data for each brand as below:

Brand A:	Satisfaction	Importance	Satis. × Importance
Attribute: A			
B			
C			
etc.			
		Total:	

Brand B:	Satisfaction	Importance	Satis. × Importance
Attribute: A			
B			
C			
etc.			
		Total:	

5 Now measure the attitude to each brand using the average of responses to a set of semantic differential scales, e.g. good–bad, pleasant–unpleasant, beneficial–harmful, rewarding–unrewarding. Correlate these measures with the satisfaction/importance totals. The correlation is usually quite high but a stronger relationship should be obtained when the brand attributes are elicited and measured correctly.

Brand stimuli and brand benefits

In some fields the consumer may have little interest in the differences between brands but may have considerable interest in obtaining the product. Earlier this was noted with respect to detergents. Petrol is another example since very few people go out of their way to secure a particular brand of petrol though they may do so to secure some point-of-sale advantage. Again, the choice between Access and Visa credit cards is trivial to someone who carries both but is very important to the credit card company. Thus the choice between brands is often so unimportant to the consumer that it may be unconsciously performed or based on vague associations that have little rational basis. In this process the features of the brand and other aspects of the environment may operate as a stimulus to action.

Factors such as brand name, logo, pack design, colours, and other features that become associated with brands through usage or advertising are important as stimuli which may elicit the purchase or use of brands. Such stimuli help people to discriminate one brand from another and may speed recognition of a brand. Thus an important part of marketing effort may go into emphasizing brand features so that they are easily noticed and distinguished from the competition.

Sometimes, with 'me-too' products, a reverse strategy is used and the product is made to look like a well established brand by using similar packs and brand names. Here the representative heuristic may operate. The label and squared bottle of Larios Spanish gin looks like Gordon's (the taste is quite different but so, to be fair, is the price). In this case few customers are likely to mistake one for the other but once they have decided to buy cheap in the duty free shop they may well prefer a familiar looking Spanish gin like Larios to an unfamiliar alternative. The supermarkets also emulate the brand leaders with their own brands. For example, compare their concentrated washing up liquid packs with the brand leader, Fairy Liquid. Another example of package similarity is found in the bitter chocolate market. The designer, Robert Steward, produced a pack for Terry which used the same red and gold as the market leader Cadbury. Helped no doubt by the quality of their chocolate and some price promotions Terry took a substantial fraction of the market.

Exercise 6.4. Stimulus management

Focus on packs, logos, retail outlet design etc. and compile a list of examples where one supplier emulates another. How would you combat this practice if you were managing the leading brand of frequent-wash hair shampoo?

When stimulus factors have an influence on buying, manufacturers should try to establish strong stimulus features for their brand and to emphasize these in advertising. They would also be wise to choose features that are hard to copy, especially if they lead in the market. When brand attributes are very similar (e.g. petrol) suppliers must either differentiate their brand by a promotion that adds to the brand benefits (e.g. discounts and giveaways) or they can use the stimulus factors that have become associated with their brand (petrol station features, name, pack, music, colours, etc.) to cue buying behaviour. These aspects of brand identity need promotion but may add long-term value to the brand which more than justifies the investment. In recent years this same approach has been seen in a flood of corporate identity programmes.

Measuring the impact of stimulus features

Advertising may emphasize either stimulus or benefit features of the brand. Any explicit decision on emphasis should depend on measurement of these two different brand aspects. Consumer researchers have a role to play in advising between stimulus and benefit strategies. To do this effectively they need to elicit the perceived differences between brands and to determine the extent to which these differences are stimulus based, e.g. pack colour, or benefit related, e.g. value for money. A technique called *repertory grid analysis* elicits perceived brand differences but it must be said that there may be brand differences that affect behaviour which are not consciously apprehended; such differences will be missed by any question and answer procedure. Repertory grid analysis also produces a mix of stimulus and benefit features of brands and these are hard to disentangle.

Repertory grid analysis comes from a field of psychological research called *personal construct theory* which was developed by Kelly (1955). Kelly saw people as actively concerned to make sense of their environment by using frames of reference called *constructs*. The constructs are elicited using repertory grid analysis. The normal form of this elicitation is to take the brands in threes and to require respondents to state the ways in which two of the three are similar and different from the third. The relationship between the two which differentiates them from the third is the construct. This procedure is repeated with different threes to give new constructs to add to the list. This is a lengthy procedure, even with one person and is speeded up by using a computer program for presenting the alternatives and recording the constructs. (A PC package called Flexigrid is available from The Centre for Personal Construct Psychology, 132 Warwick Way, London SW1, tel. 071 834 8875.) Constructs may also be elicited by taking pairs of brands and asking for the differences. This might be a more parsimonious approach and emphasizes our particular concern, brand differentiation. Comparison between this construct list and the list of salients elicited for the purchase and use of the brands (see Exercise 3.2) should help in the judgement of stimulus and benefit features. Exercise 6.5 is intended to apply the thinking behind construct analysis.

Exercise 6.5. Constructs

1 Work individually. Go to a local supermarket which stocks wine. Look at the way in which the wine is grouped on the shelves by colour, sweetness, origin, strength, price etc. Try to determine which constructs are used to organize the display and whether there is some hierarchy of constructs embodied in the layout. How would you decide whether the display fitted the way people think about (a) wine and (b) buying wine? Are there any other considerations that you would have if you were in charge of a wine display?

2 Work as a group and pool the elicitations done individually on an agreed set of brands. Each person conducts two elicitations using different respondents, one to determine the perceived differences between the chosen brands (i.e. repertory grid analysis) and the second to determine the salient beliefs about buying/using the brands (i.e. Ajzen and Fishbein's method, Exercise 3.2). You might take the credit/charge card brands: Access, Visa, American Express, and store cards for study or you could compare *The Times, Financial Times, Independent, Guardian* and *Daily Telegraph* or you could examine beliefs about bar confectionery. Report which factors have a stimulus role and which factors are reinforcing (either increasing or decreasing action).

One problem about Kelly's approach is that it is a method for exploring the thinking of single individuals. In consumer behaviour we need to know how groups of people will behave and therefore the constructs of a sample of people have to be expressed in some aggregate form. This procedure introduces some distortion. As with Ajzen and Fishbein's method for producing modal salient beliefs, some constructs are going to be irrelevant to some people.

Another feature of construct analysis is the cognitive bias in the elicitation method. People tend to report how they think rather than how they feel about the alternative brands. This bias is acceptable if the method is regarded as a way of identifying the stimulus features of brands; it is a problem when people think that construct analysis will predict behaviour. Another reason why construct analysis is unsuitable for predicting behaviour is that it tends to leave out features that the brands have in common. Only differences are elicited but commonalities between all brands may have a bearing on purchase.

An early application of construct analysis to marketing was made by Frost and Braine (1967).

Conjoint analysis

The Fishbein and Ajzen model is *compositional*, i.e. the liking of an object is derived by composing together the separate measurements of its attributes. Conjoint analysis (Green and Srinivasan, 1978) is a reverse approach which measures groups of different attributes and infers the part-worths of each attribute by *decomposition* of these measures and in which the groups of attributes are either measured against scales or they are ranked. For example, what is your order of preference among cars having the following characteristics?

fast,	expensive,	uncomfortable
fast,	cheap,	uncomfortable
fast,	expensive,	comfortable
fast,	cheap,	comfortable
slow,	expensive,	uncomfortable
slow,	cheap,	uncomfortable
slow,	expensive,	comfortable
slow,	cheap,	comfortable

The order of preference tells us something about the relative attractions of each attribute. By using techniques such as regression analysis it is possible to obtain, for each respondent, the part-worths of the attributes and of any interactions between them. An interaction arises when two or more attributes together have a value that is more than or less than the addition of the part-worths. For instance, 'fast and uncomfortable' implies a sports car concept that can enhance the sum of the individual values for some people.

Conjoint analysis is used to answer problems in new product design, product modification and pricing. Essentially it is a means of sorting out a package of benefits that is attractive to the consumer. When many attributes can be offered it makes sense to find the combination which has the highest subjective value in relation to its objective cost. This idea was first defined by Haley (1968). When price is part of the product package it is possible to see how different prices affect the prospective return. An example of how conjoint analysis might have been used (I do not know whether it was) was the first Amstrad word processor. The suppliers chose a combination that was cheap, reliable, slow and which included software; the product was very successful in a market which many people thought was glutted.

Some of the thrust behind conjoint analysis seems to have come from those with a central interest in the techniques of analysing data rather than in the way in which people process it. It is true that, unlike compositional methods, it is possible to measure the interaction of benefits but nowhere in the definitive paper by Green and Srinivasan (1978) is there discussion of whether the aggregations of attributes and the comparisons required from respondents in conjoint analysis fit in with the way in which people think about choices. Critics can argue that attributes are not disembodied but related to particular objects and actions. This suggests that attributes are more accurately measured when they are related to the overall concept as in compositional methods. Conjoint analysis has not been evaluated against other methods and, since it is elaborate to apply, it is important that its exponents demonstrate its superiority.

Problems with the method are considerable. There is a tendency to use objective characteristics rather than those perceived by consumers. Even quite short lists of attributes lead to a very large number of combinations. In practice it is often easier to present attributes two at a time, called *trade off* analysis, rather than all of them which is called *full profile*. Even so, the large number of judgements required can create habitual responding and fatigue among respondents. There are also problems where characteristics are inferred when they are not given, e.g. a large and expensive car is assumed to do few miles per gallon. Unrealistic combinations have to be excluded. In contrast to conjoint analysis, compositional methods are economical and fairly easily computed.

Summary

The commercial application of attitude measurement reflects convenience, changing fashions, new computing technology and scientific advance. It may lack a theoretical rationale and may use methodologically unsound practices.

Simple measurements of brand attitude show that there are 'evaluative beliefs' that are associated with brand use. Attitudes measured in this way are highly changeable on repeat measure. Some of this change is related to fluctuations in brand use and the evidence indicates that brand attributions mainly follow brand use in fast-moving consumer goods (fmcg) markets. This limits the value of such brand attitude measurement.

One problem of conventional brand attitude measurement, which is shared with the Likert method of summated ratings, is that the evaluation of an attribute is not measured separately from the likelihood that a brand possesses this attribute. Expectancy-value methods do measure evaluation and will give a more complete picture of the correlates of voluntary brand consumption provided that brands differ in their benefits and that consumers give some thought to the brand purchase. Measures of satisfaction and importance are erratically related to attribute evaluation and likelihood and should be avoided.

Purchase may occur because it is stimulated or reinforced. Market researchers need to measure both stimulus and benefit associations of brands before deciding whether to emphasize one or the other in promotion.

In conjoint analysis attributes may be measured in bundles and the part-worths for each attribute extracted by regression analysis. There is no evidence to show that conjoint analysis is superior to methods which measure attributes singly.

Further reading

Aaker, D. A. and Day, G. S. (1986) *Marketing Research,* 3rd ed. New York, Wiley, chapters 5, 8 and 18

Barwise, T. P. and Ehrenberg, A. S. C. (1985) Consumer beliefs and brand usage. *Journal of the Market Research Society* **27**, 81–93

Green, P. E. and Srinivasan, V. (1978) Conjoint analysis in consumer research: issues and outlook. *Journal of Consumer Research* **5**, 103–23

[7]
Information processing and evaluative change

Exercise 7.1. How did you decide?

What did you have for lunch when you last went to the cafeteria?
How did you decide? What thoughts ran through your mind?
How did you resolve the choice between alternatives? How do you
think one of your friends made the same decisions?

Types of explanation

The theory of reasoned action is not a theory about how people
think. Its authors do not pretend that people actually assign likelihoods and evaluations, multiply them, and sum the products to
form their attitudes. Reasoned action theory works *as if* people
figure out their interests and rationally assess these when making
decisions. Similarly, NBD theory assumes that people's actions
can be treated in some respects as if they were random but its
authors do not assert that people actually work like dice.

From this standpoint reasoned action theory is concerned with
the outcomes of information processing, not its mechanisms. This
leaves a gap in our explanation of human behaviour. If people do
not do the cognitive algebra implied in reasoned action theory,
what do they do? It is important that these problems are recognized because they limit the inferences that we can make from
outcome theories about the changes in thought and action brought
about by advertising and other forms of persuasion. Though the
content of advertising may be chosen in part by reference to

theories like reasoned action its effect will depend on whether it activates appropriate mechanisms.

Despite the great sophistication of human beings we have limited attention and comprehension; we economize on thought by using habits which often guide us well but sometimes lead us astray. When we do reason out our problems our analysis is often flawed. The information processing that we use may serve a variety of purposes, some better than others. In short we should not assume that the mechanisms that underpin our actions are ideal. They may be deficient or sub-optimal and this is only revealed through research. This chapter focuses on the research that has been done on some of the mechanisms lying behind thought and action.

Mechanisms and meaning

Recognition

Advertisements have to compete for attention. Similarly brands on a supermarket shelf need the shopper's attention and some level of recognition if they are to be bought. The recognition may be minimal, perhaps just a sense of familiarity that takes no detailed account of the brand. But, whatever their form, the processes which draw attention and lead to recognition are important if we are to understand consumer responses to frequently purchased goods.

Recognition has also become important in a quite different sphere, in artificial intelligence, where it is a prerequisite for more discriminating exchanges between a computer and its environment. Reading characters, understanding speech, differentiating voices, and labelling different aspects of the environment all involve recognition, i.e. the identification of one stimulus from all those that are possible. The comparison with computers helps to show what is involved in human recognition. Interestingly, computers are not as good at recognition as they are at other tasks such as calculation. The problem seems to lie partly in the centralized structure of computers where memory and processing occupy discrete areas and the procedure for identifying a stimulus requires that large amounts of information are swapped between these two locations.

The brain is constructed on a different principle with memory and processing functions distributed throughout its structure. In a sense the structure of the brain is its program. The recognition problem 'is it X or is it Y?' can be represented as the activation of alternative pathways in the brain. These pathways arise between neurones as interconnections which have been built up from past learning. Such learning permits the brain to deal with a hierarchy of discriminations that end with a specific structure or identification.

Another difference between computers and brain operation is the extent to which processing takes place in parallel rather than series. Until recently computers have had little capacity to engage in different functions at the same time whereas this is normal in thinking. One stimulus has many aspects and can activate multiple pathways in the brain so that we can deal simultaneously with a range of questions generated by the same stimulus. For example: Is it a cat? What colour is it? Is it friendly? Parallel processing also implies integrating structures which keep the answers to these questions in one domain; we know that we are doing one thing, not three, when we are stroking a friendly black cat.

Psychologists use a different language for describing recognition and thinking which they see as a chain of internal responses, each stimulating the next. The alternative pathways are represented as alternative internal responses. The speed of recognition or behavioural response depends on the extent that one internal response path is clearly dominant over the others. This means that ambiguous stimuli, and more generally stimuli that are novel, changeable, surprising, incongruous, complex, or indistinct tend to be recognized more slowly and therefore get more attention. People have a need to resolve the response competition or *conceptual conflict* (Berlyne, 1954) created by ambiguous stimuli. By resolving the conflict and identifying the stimulus a person makes his or her environment easier to predict and control.

Arousal is high when people are over-stimulated *or* when they are deprived of stimulus (e.g. when they are bored). People prefer low levels of arousal and are therefore guided to intermediate degrees of stimulation. Conceptual conflicts may be welcome when people are inactive or bored because under these conditions more stimulation reduces arousal; at other times unusual stimuli may raise arousal (Berlyne, 1965; Berlyne and McDonnell, 1965) and this is probably their most common effect. It explains why

Harrison (1968) and Saegert and Jellison (1970) found that investigation was inversely related to liking, i.e. stimuli that create response competition are generally not much liked but are nonetheless given disproportionate attention time. This creates a problem in promotion: the stimulus that secures attention is often less attractive because it creates response competition. But people may appreciate such attention drawing stimuli more when they receive them under low stimulation conditions. This may support the influence of advertising in media such as television which are often received under low arousal conditions.

Mere exposure

The idea of response competition is used to explain an interesting phenomenon first reported by Zajonc (1968). Zajonc (his name is pronounced 'Zi-onse') observed that repeated exposure to a new stimulus made people like it more. This effect of *mere exposure* was so called because a change in the observer's evaluation occurs without any of the associations that are required in classical and operant conditioning (discussed in Chapter 1).

Zajonc observed this effect in both laboratory and field experiments using nonsense words, Chinese-like characters and photographs of men's faces. For example, in Zajonc and Rajecki's (1969) field experiment, nonsense words like NANSOMA were printed like advertisements with different frequencies in campus newspapers. Later the researchers got large numbers of students to rate the words on evaluative scales and there was unequivocal evidence that frequency of exposure correlated positively with evaluative rating. Zajonc's explanation for this was that the unfamiliar words created response competition in the minds of readers which was resolved, one way or another, with repeated exposure. Harrison (1968) measured response competition as the time delay before any free association with the stimulus was reported by a subject and found that the delay was reduced as the number of exposures increased. Because response competition is generally disagreeable, a reduction in competition should produce a more positive evaluation.

Rajecki (1982, ch. 4) reviews this issue and notes that two alternative explanations have been proposed. One is that subjects in experiments detect 'what was expected of them' in the experimental situation and comply by giving higher ratings to the more frequently presented stimuli. This sort of 'demand effect' has been found in experimental designs by Orne (1962). Another possible explanation is that mere exposure is classical conditioning after all, and that the novel stimulus was associated with positive aspects of the presentation situation in the experiments. It is not possible here to do justice to the detailed research that was used to examine these contentions and the reader is referred to Rajecki's excellent review. The outcome of this work indicated that the mere exposure effect could not be explained by the alternatives proposed and that reduction in response competition remains the front running explanation for increases in liking following repeated exposure.

The mere exposure research draws attention to the importance of choosing the right name for brands, i.e. one that has, or acquires, a strongly positive evaluation at the levels of exposure of the relevant consumer sub-groups.

Mere exposure is directly relevant to low involvement response to advertising. Batra and Ray (1983) have conducted a number of studies that simulate the rushed, noisy and irrelevant conditions under which most advertising is received. They found changes that supported Krugman's (1965) proposals on low involvement; specifically that awareness of the brand seemed to lead by a direct path to increased disposition to purchase and that attitude change followed later. The authors suggest that the attitude change was a delayed effect arising from mere exposure and that repetitive advertising works partly by reducing response competition and partly by keeping brands in memory.

The response to thought and feeling stimuli

We tend to think that recognition is a necessary precursor to any evaluation of a stimulus. This hierarchy is implicit in expectancy-value theory in the sense that the features of an action must be recognized before they can be evaluated. This hierarchy of response has been put in question by work done by Zajonc (1980) and Zajonc and Markus (1982).

Zajonc has assembled evidence showing that thought and feeling are, to a large extent, processed independently. The processing is assumed to follow an internal stimulus–response pattern.

According to Zajonc, the feeling aspect of thinking is processed earlier and faster than the knowledge component and the processing mechanisms are different. Much of the processing of feeling occurs below the level of awareness. Zajonc argues that people react to two classes of stimulus: preferenda (feeling) and discriminanda (cognition); he points to the survival value attaching to a fast response to dangerous stimuli. It is better to jump out of the way without knowing why, than to recognize that it is a car that hits you.

Zajonc presents a number of experimental findings. Two are described here. They concern the relative speed with which evaluative and cognitive judgements are made. Firstly, Kunst-Wilson and Zajonc (1980) found that preference judgements (feeling) were made marginally more quickly than recognition judgements (cognitive) despite the fact that conventional thinking suggests that recognition is a precondition of preference.

The second study was more startling still. Marcel (1976) used an instrument called a tachistoscope to present words or blank space to subjects at very short durations. On half the occasions there were words and these were either short or long, and either pleasant or unpleasant. If the subjects thought they saw a word they were asked to judge its length against comparison words and to say whether the word was evaluated as 'good' or 'bad'. A positive word might be 'friend' or 'food' while a negative word might be 'enemy' or 'cruel'. The duration of exposure was reduced until the subjects were guessing the presence of words at chance level and could not therefore have been recognizing anything; at this duration Marcel found that word length judgements were also at chance level. However, at this point the subjects were still scoring at above chance rates on their evaluative judgements when words were present, thus indicating that the feeling response proceeded more rapidly than the recognition response and could occur without it.

This work may have relevance to the recognition of goods in shops. It shows that the response may be partial and that an evaluative response may occur below the threshold of awareness. There is no direct implication of this work for the theory of reasoned action. Fast recognition judgements of the sort studied by Zajonc are quite different from the complex reflective choices typically faced by subjects choosing between multi-attributed alternatives. However, these studies do show the sort of mechanisms that underly thinking and changes in preference and confirm the view that expectancy-value theories are more properly seen as end-of-process models that have little to say about the basic mechanisms in information processing.

Schemata

Ideas have form. Schemata are these forms and they act like moulds for cognitive content. A schema is, according to Crocker, Fiske and Taylor (1984):

> an abstract or generic knowledge structure, stored in memory, that specifies the defining features and relevant attributes of some stimulus domain, and the interrelationships among those attributes. . . . They help us to structure, organize and interpret new information; they facilitate encoding, storage and retrieval of relevant information; they can affect the time it takes to process information. . . . Schemas also serve interpretive or inferential functions. For example they may fill in data that are missing or unavailable in a stimulus configuration. (p. 197)

The notion of the schema was implicit in Bartlett's (1932) work on remembering. Bartlett wrote of the 'strain after meaning' and showed how unusual structures that fell short of representing any object were interpreted by reference to more familiar and available ideas (Figure 7.1). The term 'schema' covers notions like *cognitive category*, and *stereotype* (assumptions about persons or groups); as a *script* the schema may be extended to behaviour sequences. In their most abstract form schemata may cover *relationships* like logical validity and causality, or hierarchy, transitivity and symmetry (described by De Soto and Albrecht, 1957).

Miller (1959) noted how information was more readily remembered if it came in 'chunks' and schemata provide an explanation of why this is so; the chunk has 'shape' and can be recognized by reference to a schema that fits that 'shape'.

New information, if accepted, usually modifies how we think about a concept. Usually we revise our judgement by incorporating the new information alongside existing information. For instance new information on the reliability of a brand of computer

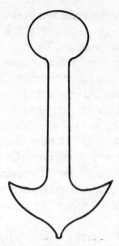

Figure 7.1 Bartlett's battle axe. People see this object as an axe, turf cutter or key because these are similar (from Bartlett, 1932)

may be added to our knowledge of the brand and cause us to update our 'value for money' assessment. But sometimes the new information may radically alter our views so that a concept is interpreted by reference to a different schema. On a mundane level the notion of product positioning may reflect this. We might, for example, see Cadbury's Bourneville plain chocolate quite differently when it is presented as a culinary ingredient in chocolate mousse. Category shifting advertising may be a high risk strategy compared to revision advertising because there is less likelihood that the more substantial change will be accepted.

Some amusing examples of category shifting were achieved by an Australian activist group which tried to counter the advertising of the tobacco and drink companies. The group was called the Billboard Utilizing Graffitiists Against Unhealthy Promotion and since they lacked finance themselves they 'refaced' the posters of their adversaries. When a cigarette company offered a car as a prize their poster was given the caption 'From the people who put the "car" in carcinogen'. The acronym (BUGA UP), the adjustments to the posters and the speeches in court when members of the group were prosecuted gave entertainment to the people of New South Wales and this group's activities have been emulated occasionally in Britain.

Many of BUGA UP's more successful enterprises were legitimate. One was to counteract the free distribution of cigarettes in shopping malls. To most people a gift is a kindness and the giver is regarded as well meaning. To counteract such promotions BUGA UP distributed free pieces of apple and arranged for children to parade around the mall with a banner saying DANGER – DRUG PUSHERS AT WORK. This apparently transformed the perception of the tobacco companies representatives from benign kindliness to malign self-interest. Tobacco companies have a squalid history of refusal to admit to the hazards of their products; they *are* licensed drug sellers and an important part of their public relations is to counteract such facts by sponsoring concerts, sport and research. BUGA UP's achievement was to reassert the drug seller schema as the one by which the tobacco company's actions were judged.

A second BUGA UP enterprise sabotaged a Marlboro 'Man of the Year' competition in Australia. BUGA UP proposed their own candidate. Their choice was a man disabled by smoking, confined to a wheelchair, and smoking through a hole in his throat provided by a tracheotomy. The man himself was a willing accomplice and starred in a poster which was printed and sold in large numbers. The idea of the strong heroic figure that Marlboro had tried to cultivate was ridiculed. In its place were put the schemata of disease and disability which are more accurately related to smoking cigarettes. Marlboro eventually awarded the prize in private; it had acquired a negative news value.

Heuristics

Thought and recognition will proceed more easily if the schema is more 'available', i.e. can be easily accessed; this introduces the idea of heuristics. The term *heuristic* was used by Kahneman and Tversky (1972, 1973) and Tversky and Kahneman (1974) to cover inexact or rule-of-thumb processes which may be used unconsciously in thinking. Heuristics make certain ideas more prominent and may make people think that certain happenings occur more frequently than they do. Though in general heuristics may facilitate information processing, they may also lead people to make errors under particular conditions.

Exercise 7.2. Availability effects

In Britain approximately 600,000 people die each year from all causes. How many people die prematurely each year from the following causes? Enter the figures that you think apply:

Smoking:

Road accidents:

Industrial diseases:

Industrial accidents:

Asbestos:

Nuclear industry:

Markus and Zajonc (1985) provide a nice example of the way in which heuristic reasoning may support the prestige of the medical profession quite unjustifiably. They point out that the control condition of *no treatment* is absent from our experience of medical intervention. Most people would get better without treatment but, when treatment has been given, there is a tendency to assume that it has helped recovery. This may be seen as an example of the *availability* heuristic at work. This is the judgement of increased probability to events that are more easily brought to mind. When therapy has been given it is more cognitively available as a cause of recovery than ideas about the natural processes counteracting disease that occur within the body.

The judgement of risk is notoriously erratic. Much of the reason for this may lie in the poor information about actual risks in the media but judgement may also be distorted by the action of heuristics. Lichtenstein *et al.* (1978) have suggested that some risks are exaggerated by people because they hear about them more often in the media. Those who completed Exercise 7.2 are likely to have over-estimated the risk of death from road accidents, asbestos and nuclear emissions. The approximate answers are given overleaf.

Other popular examples of risk misjudgement might be the reluctance of Americans to come to Europe in 1986 following the attack on Libya by the USA. They were fearful of reprisals but, by staying in the United States, they probably ran a higher risk of being killed by gun-proud fellow-Americans. Similarly oral contraceptive scares have caused women to abandon the pill even

---

Approximate annual numbers of deaths in Britain by cause

All causes:	600,000
Smoking:	88,000
Road accidents:	5,000
Industrial diseases:	8,000
Industrial accidents:	600
Asbestos:	20
Nuclear industry:	10

---

when the identified risk was very small in absolute terms. The idea of 'availability' is fairly loose and it is not easy to specify quite which topics will claim disproportionate attention. Despite this, the possibility that policy may be distorted away from important but less obvious outcomes raises concern. Good management anticipates problems so that they do not happen; preventive medicine stops diseases before they occur. By contrast crisis management and remedial medicine have immediateness and impact; do they get too much credit and detract from the effort that is put into pro-active control?

Availability will operate in favour of the visible, concrete happening and against intangibles and 'non-events'. This suggests that people may give too much support to the status quo and may draw too easily on hindsight to support a case. Very successful 'anti' programmes such as the anti-racist policy in London schools may lose support because their success ensures that there are few examples of racism to jog thinking.

Another heuristic mechanism is *representativeness*. This is the tendency to judge likelihood from similarity between the case in hand and assumptions about the class to which the case belongs. For example a person may be seen as a barrister because of features of dress and delivery of speech. In this case the judgement draws on the stereotype of a barrister but such a judgement takes no account of the low number of barristers in our society which makes it unlikely that the person belongs to this group.

Heuristics are relevant to the content of persuasive messages which must draw on the more easily accessed ideas so that the message is more readily understood and given high likelihood. When the subject is obscure a more familiar analogy may help in the presentation.

Exercise 7.3. Who was to blame? (abridged from Tversky and Kahneman, 1980, p. 62)

Solve the following problem:
A cab was involved in a hit-and-run accident at night. Two cab companies, the Green and the Blue operate in the city. You are given the following data:

(i) 85 per cent of the cabs in the city are Green and 15 per cent are Blue.

(ii) A witness identified the cab as a Blue cab. The court tested his ability to identify cabs under appropriate visibility conditions. When presented with a sample of cabs (half of which were Blue and half of which were Green) the witness made correct identifications in 80 per cent of the cases.

Question
What is the probability that the cab involved in the accident was Blue rather than Green?
Decide on your answer before reading on.

What is your judgement in Exercise 7.3? Tversky and Kahneman put this problem to several hundred subjects; the median response was 80 per cent. Thus subjects tended to take note of the witness credibility and to ignore the market shares of the two cab companies. The correct answer is quite different. The cab can be identified as Blue either correctly when it was Blue or incorrectly when it was Green. The chance that the cab was Blue (0.15) and was recognized (0.8) is 0.15 × 0.8 and the chance that the cab present was Green (0.85) and was recognized wrongly as Blue (0.2) is 0.85 × 0.2. The answer requires the ratio of probabilities of Blue to either Blue or Green:

$$\frac{(0.15)\,(0.8)}{(0.15)\,(0.8) + (0.85)\,(0.2)} = 0.41$$

The basic explanation for this effect is the resort to heuristics when problems are hard to understand. Happenings, cause and effect, etc. are discontinuities and are more available than continuing states. This means that more weight is given to the witness test than the market shares of the cab companies. Tversky and Kahneman's work is laden with examples like this; for most readers the problems point to one sort of solution which then turns out to be false. In particular, people give disproportionate weight to the causal data and neglect *diagnostic data* that may be equally informative. Another example helps here:

Which of the following events is more probable:
(a) that a girl has blue eyes if her mother has blue eyes.
(b) that the mother has blue eyes, if her daughter has blue eyes.
(c) that the two events are equally probable.

The correct answer is (c) but among those who did not choose (c) three times as many people preferred (a) to (b). The mother to daughter inheritance is causal, the daughter to mother inference is diagnostic.

It appears that we have a mechanism for paying particular attention to the more active aspects of our situation; we are tuned to change and intervention. By contrast data dealing with the unchanging background appear to be pallid and uninteresting. This mechanism probably serves a useful purpose in general by directing attention to aspects of the environment that require response but it can cause mistakes in particular cases.

The availability of causal data has a particular relevance to marketing. Marketing interventions are attempts to cause changes in a context which is relatively unchanging. In particular the brand market share and the system of distribution do not change much in the medium term. These conditions limit the effects of an intervention like advertising but may get less attention than they deserve because of their constancy. It also seems quite likely that work which focuses on market stasis (much of Chapter 2) may be harder for people to accept and attach importance to.

Processing value and probability

Value

Objective value, expressed in money or other units, and probability, measured or given, are information which is processed by

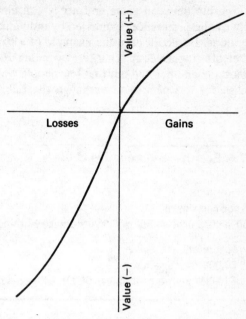

Figure 7.2 The value–utility relationship

human beings. The internal representations, utility and subjective probability, do not bear an exact correspondence with the objective forms. There is some sense in this. Two Mars Bars are not twice as attractive as one to most people. The relationship between value and utility has a long history going back to Bernoulli (1738) who described how the curve of utility against value flattens as value increases giving a concave shape, and marginal utility therefore diminishes as value rises. This can be seen in Figure 7.2.

One obvious interest to economists of this sort of effect is the justification that it gives for exchanges. The marginal utility of additional supplies of a good to someone who already possesses a lot of that good is low in comparison to someone who possesses few of the good. If the latter has a surplus of some other good then exchanges may be possible whereby each party gains utility. Another aspect of the non-linear relationship between utility and value is that it gives sense to redistribution of wealth through political action; the poor person's gain in utility is greater than the disutility incurred by the rich loser.

The relationship between value and utility can also be shown most clearly by the preferences expressed by individuals between different options. Bernoulli gave the example of a pauper with a lottery ticket offering an equal chance of winning 20,000 ducats or getting nothing and pointed out that few people would say that it was foolish for the pauper to exchange the ticket for 9,000 ducats.

Exercise 7.4. Positive and negative choices

Which do you prefer?
A: £9,000 for certain, or
B: £10,000 with a probability of 0.9; otherwise nothing.

Which do you prefer?
C: Losing £9,000 for certain, or
D: Losing £10,000 with a probability of 0.9; otherwise nothing.

The concavity of the value–utility relationship for gains explains why people are risk averse for positive utilities. What about the avoidance of losses? On the available evidence there is a point of inflection in the utility function as it passes through the origin; below zero, utility falls faster in relation to value and then curves back toward the x-axis as shown in Figure 7.2. This produces a risk preference for losses because, for example, a 0.9 chance of losing £10,000 has a smaller disutility than a certain loss of £9,000. In Exercise 7.4 most respondents prefer A and D.

Probability

Exercise 7.5. The Allais Paradox (Allais, 1953)

Allais asked one group of subjects to choose between the two options:
A: $4,000 with a probability of 0.8; otherwise nothing.
B: $3,000 for certain.
Which do you prefer?

Another group were asked to choose between:
C: $4,000 with a probability of 0.2; otherwise nothing.
D: $3,000 with a probability of 0.25; otherwise nothing.
Which do you prefer?

Faced with the choices in Exercise 7.5, 80 per cent of subjects preferred option B to A but 65 per cent preferred option C to D. This is paradoxical because the ratio of the values and the ratio of the probabilities is the same in each choice pair yet the preference order reverses for most subjects. One explanation for this is that probability is weighted as it is converted to subjective probability. Figure 7.3 shows the proposed form of subjective probability in relation to objective probability. Kahneman and Tverksy (1979) suggest that the weighting diminishes the subjective likelihood of most probabilities so that B is preferred to A. In the choice between C and D, C is the better risk on average outcome and Figure 7.3 shows that any weighting effects on the subjective likelihoods also tend to support that choice.

No mathematical expression has been given for the probability weighting function but its effect at the lower end of probability

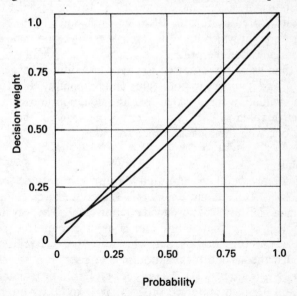

Figure 7.3 The probability relationship

could explain why people take out insurance and take high odds gambles. Above about 0.15 the weighting depresses subjective probability so that chances of ½ and ⅔ have effects closer to ⅓ and ½.

Prospect theory

Kahneman and Tversky (1979, 1984) incorporate the conversion of value and probability in *prospect theory* and propose that utility is given by:

$$\Sigma_1^i w(p_i)v(x_i)$$

This is a sum of products formulation where $v(x_i)$ is the utility of an outcome and $w(p_i)$ is the decision weight for the occurrence of the outcome. Tversky and Kahneman use the term 'decision weight' rather than subjective probability because the weights do not sum to unity and therefore do not follow the exact rules of probability.

Prospect theory is not just an equation. Kahneman and Tversky suggest that decisions have two stages. In the first the choices are restructured by turning them into outcomes based on some reference point which is in the mind of the decision maker. Thus a person may see the price for a car, not as £7,000 but as £2,000 more than he or she expected to pay. This editing phase is called *framing* and it applies to both value and probability. It is followed by an evaluation stage which uses the equation above to give a subjective value to each prospect and this leads to the selection of the one with the highest subjective value.

Framing
The reference point concept used in prospect theory is familiar in psychology. Thibaut and Kelley (1959) used the term 'comparison level' and Helson (1964) used 'adaptation level'. The way in which a problem is presented has impact on the preferred solution because the presentation sets the frame or reference point. Although the second formulation in Exercise 7.6 is the same as the first (A = C, B = D), 72 per cent preferred programme A to B and 78 per cent preferred programme D to C. By framing the problem in terms of the gains (i.e. lives saved) it is possible to

steer preference to the risk averse option A in the first choice. In the second choice the framing in terms of losses (lives lost) makes people risk prone and steers them to option D. Using the appropriate frame is clearly a lesson for anyone in the field of persuasive communication.

Exercise 7.6. Life and death (Tversky and Kahneman, 1981, p. 453)

An unusual disease is expected to kill 600 people. Two interventions are proposed; which do you prefer on the basis of the following information:
If programme A is adopted, 200 people will be saved.
If programme B is adopted, there is ⅓ probability that 600 people will be saved and ⅔ probability that no people will be saved.

When you have decided consider how you would react to this alternative formulation:
If programme C is adopted, 400 people will die.
If programme D is adopted, there is ⅓ probability that no one will die and ⅔ probability that 600 people will die.

Thaler (1985) suggests some interesting implications of framing for presenting gains and losses. Framing suggests that losses have less impact when presented in aggregate whereas gains have more impact if each positive aspect is presented separately. Another application of framing is to present costs as an increment to another large expenditure, e.g. the cost of carpeting in a house that has just been bought. In these circumstances the extra cost is treated as a small increment in disutility because it is framed on the flattened part of the utility curve. In general people assess costs in proportional terms and will take more trouble to save £5 off a £20 item than £5 off a £100 item.

Problems with prospect theory
The possibility of using framing in persuasive communication has seized the imagination of researchers but it has yet to result in major applications. In principle prospect theory has application to bargaining, advertising and the stabilization of commodity and

share markets where risk proneness on loss may prevent mass selling. In practice the deficiencies in the evidence supporting prospect theory limit its scope. One problem is that reference points differ between people and may change over time. It is not easy therefore to establish the reference points that will affect the decision. The studies of subjective probability and utility are done using rather artificial and often hypothetical examples. There is no check that the gains and losses presented in the problems are accepted without additional assumptions by the respondents. In betting problems results are affected by size of stake and the opportunity to repeat a play may affect the choice made. There is also concern about using 'majority verdicts' for each problem; a distribution of responses should be used for any prediction of group effect. Prospect theory has not been well demonstrated in field conditions. One worry here is that distortions of objective probability and value may be related to the medium of communication. For example matters conveyed in conversation may be weighted more than the same statements in print. In prospect theory the weighting of probabilities gives rise to *subcertainty*, i.e. the subjective probabilities of A and not-A add up to less than unity for much of the range and this is intuitively odd.

Dissonance theory

Leon Festinger introduced the theory of cognitive dissonance in 1957. His ideas were tested extensively in the following years and this led to modifications in both the form of the theory and in its predictions. Over this period competitive theories rose and fell but it is not my purpose to spend too long on the more abstract arguments that were generated. The reader is referred to Rajecki (1982, ch. 6) or Eiser (1986, ch. 4) for careful reviews of the main issues.

Festinger's original statement described a condition of arousal, called cognitive dissonance, that arose in people when their beliefs did not 'fit together'. This condition led them to change their thought, feeling or action in such a way that the fit was improved. The imprecision of the 'ill fitting' description led to attempts to clarify this aspect of the theory. Brehm and Cohen (1962) suggested that dissonance was felt when people committed themselves to an action which was inconsistent with their other behaviour or beliefs, or which later turned out to have undesirable consequences that might have been foreseen. Another way of putting this point is to say that dissonance is aroused when there is *insufficient justification* for an action. It is this version of the theory that made it attractive to consumer researchers since it implied that people may experience dissonance when they commit themselves to a high involvement purchase. If purchase does give rise to dissonance it will be followed by behaviour that bolsters the purchase choice, e.g. attitude change in favour of the brand selected, recommendation of the brand to others and an interest in any information that justifies the purchase. Such effects shift interest from before to after the point of purchase and suggest that advertisements may have most impact *after* purchase in consolidating the reputation of a brand.

Evidence of post-purchase re-evaluation was obtained by Brehm (1956) who offered undergraduate women a choice between durables which they had either valued at much the same level (high dissonance, since it is hard to justify preference for one) or which they had valued quite differently (low dissonance). Brehm's hypothesis was that after they had made their choice the women in the high dissonance condition would up-value their chosen alternative and down-value the product that they had rejected and that they would do this more than the women in the low dissonance condition. Brehm's findings supported his hypothesis.

More generally the evidence was mixed and was open to alternative explanation. I conducted a study similar to Brehm's and like him I obtained a re-evaluation effect (East, 1973). However when the alternatives were put back into the range from which they had been extracted for the choice, and were then rated again by the subjects, the re-evaluation effect disappeared. It seemed likely that re-evaluation in this case arose from attempts to emphasize the choice just made. A person who has just chosen A and rejected B makes this clear by rating the chosen alternative above the rejected one.

Another failure of the theory concerned the information that was sought after a choice. According to the theory there should have been preference for facts that justified the choice but Sears (1968) found that people were generally open to any evidence relevant to their choice. Facts about the malfunctions of a brand do not give support to purchase but they are useful and people do not discriminate against such evidence.

Much of the research on dissonance theory was conducted with a design that was called 'forced compliance' in which subjects, usually students, were persuaded to do something that they did not approve of. The classic study in this mould was done by Festinger and Carlsmith (1959). They persuaded the student subjects, who had just completed a boring task, to lie about it to a new subject. They were to tell the new subject (actually an accomplice of the experimenters) that the task was interesting; for this they were paid one dollar in one condition and 20 dollars in the other. The researchers argued that 20 dollars was sufficient justification for lying and would cause little dissonance whereas the one dollar payment was insufficient. This meant that the researchers predicted that the less the payment the more the dissonance and, supporting this, they were able to show that there was more attitude change in the low payment condition. Those paid one dollar tended to see the task as less boring than $20 subjects and this shift of attitude had the effect of diminishing the lie.

Many of the studies in the forced compliance design failed to show most effect under low payment conditions but instead showed an incentive effect, i.e. the more the payment, the more the attitude change. Researchers such as Linder *et al.* (1967) and Collins *et al.* (1970) suggested that the degree of commitment and freedom of choice were relevant to whether dissonance was aroused or not. Obviously a variety of situational variables can affect a person's response but this line of inquiry is potentially very confusing.

Much of the confusion was resolved by Nuttin (1975). Part of Nuttin's explanation was that previous researchers had failed to show which condition was most arousing. Instead they had made assumptions that were never tested in the experiment. Nuttin suggested that the highest arousal could sometimes occur with no reward, sometimes with low reward and sometimes with high reward and that this explained why the experimental findings had become so haphazard. In a series of experiments Nuttin was able to corroborate this argument and show that high dissonance could not always be expected under low reward.

The dominant counter theory to dissonance was a form of attribution theory (Chapter 1) which was proposed by Bem (1967);

he called it *self-perception theory*. Bem argued that attitudes were verbal reports based on observed behaviour. Just as we infer the attitude of another person by noting what they do and say, so also, according to Bem, do we infer our own attitudes from observations of our own behaviour, e.g. we say we like it because we know we did it. Bem was able to point to a seminal study by Schachter and Singer (1962) where the experimenters used a drug to induce arousal but managed to get subjects, who were ignorant of the effects of the drug, to report widely different emotions from anger to euphoria by varying the cues available to subjects.

Following this argument, Bem reasoned that people who were given details of the experience of subjects in the Festinger and Carlsmith experiment would be able to say how those subjects eventually rated the boring task. When Bem 'ghosted' people through this experimental procedure and got them to complete the ratings of the boring task as they thought the subjects in the original study would have completed them he was able to confirm that these ratings corresponded with those obtained in the conditions of the original experiment. Bem reasoned that if observers could do this it was reasonable to propose that the original subjects acted in the same way, observing their own behaviour and inferring their attitude to the task from these observations, i.e. 'I said it was interesting and since I did this for only one dollar it probably wasn't that boring.' A consequence of this argument is that arousal may be unnecessary for attitude change; it might not occur or, if it does occur, it may play no part in the attitude change.

There is evidence that arousal does occur in dissonance studies. Gerard (1967) conducted a study on choice in which the blood in the capillaries was monitored using a device called a photoplethysmograph. When a person is aroused their capillaries constrict and the amount of blood in the tissue diminishes. The photoplethysmograph measures light reflected by the tissues which increases when there is less blood present. Gerard measured arousal in this way at the point of decision and found that more subjects were aroused in the high dissonance condition. Other studies have employed different measures of arousal and have confirmed that it is associated with dissonance.

But there remains the possibility that the arousal is unrelated to any dissonance reduction effects. This issue was resolved by a clever experiment designed by Cooper, Zanna and Taves (1978). In their study they used drugs to modify arousal under three conditions. Amphetamine raised arousal in one, phenobarbital reduced it in another, while in a third condition the subjects received a placebo (milk powder) which had no effect. All subjects were told that they were being given the placebo so that they did not attribute any state of arousal to drugs. The subjects were then put through a forced compliance procedure in which they wrote an essay favouring a free pardon for Nixon (something which students were generally against). After this they were asked to give their ratings in favour of a pardon for Nixon on a 31 point rating scale. The results are shown in Table 7.1.

Table 7.1 *Average ratings of subjects in favour of a pardon for Nixon under different conditions of arousal (31 point scale, higher scores favour pardon) (Cooper, Zanna and Taves, 1978)*

Control sample (no drug, no essay)	Arousal modification		
	Tranquillizer	Placebo	Stimulant
7.9	8.6	14.7	20.2

This evidence shows that arousal is necessary for change in attitude; when it was eliminated by the tranquillizer there was no effect. Under normal circumstances with the placebo there was a shift and this was increased when arousal was increased by the amphetamine. In this study the inferences that the subjects could make were held constant by telling them all that they had the same placebo. What about the reverse situation when subjects are aroused by dissonance but are led to attribute their arousal to a drug? Do they show dissonance reduction shifts of attitude under these conditions?

This was explored in an earlier study by Zanna and Cooper (1974). In this experiment subjects were told that the purpose of the research was to investigate drug action. All subjects actually received a placebo but one group was told that it was a tranquillizer, one that it was a placebo and one that it was a stimulant. Dissonance was aroused by requiring the subjects to write an essay against their beliefs, this time in favour of banning inflammatory speakers from the campus which was generally opposed by American students. After the essays the students' ratings were obtained. Table 7.2 shows these ratings.

This time most effect occurred when subjects thought that they had been given a tranquillizer, presumably the dissonance arousal was all the more evident when subjects expected to feel sedated

Table 7.2 *Ratings in favour of a ban on inflammatory speakers on the campus under different believed conditions of arousal (31 point scale, higher ratings favour ban) (from Zanna and Cooper, 1974)*

Control sample (no drug, no essay)	Arousal modification believed by subjects		
	Tranquillizer	Placebo	Stimulant
2.3	13.4	9.1	3.4

and it thus produced more attitude change. By contrast those subjects who attributed their arousal to a stimulant showed virtually no dissonance reduction effect.

These two experiments show very clearly that arousal is necessary for attitude change but that no change will occur if the arousal is not related by the subject to the attitude object.

This stream of research has a number of applications to consumer behaviour. In the first instance it defines the limits of dissonance effects following purchase. Effects will only occur when the purchaser is aroused and attributes that arousal to the purchase process. This effectively excludes minor purchases which are unlikely to create arousal. It should also be noted that dissonance arousal is greater when the purchase is hard to justify but this may arise for a variety of reasons: the purchaser may feel that the brand is too expensive, may worry about quality or after sales service, and may have doubts about the appropriateness of the brand etc. Such arousal will activate post-purchase behaviour but, as noted, there is little evidence that people are selective and that they pick information and activities that will justify their purchase. It should also be noted that there are other forms of arousal engendered by purchase which may be more important than dissonance. Some people are elated by a new possession and are receptive to information because of this arousal which owes nothing to dissonance.

Dissonance research helps us to understand how to produce effective persuasion. It suggests that we must create a disturbance in the recipient by using the issues on which change is desired. Very often the poster or commercial will create a disturbance by using ideas that are extraneous to the issue and when this occurs it is unlikely that any attitude or behaviour change will be focused on the object of the advertisement. I can illustrate this point with one health education poster which was shown by research to be associated with a major change in behaviour in 1974. This poster was produced by Saatchi and Saatchi for the Health Education Council and showed a naked, substantially pregnant woman who was smoking. The nakedness made the pregnancy manifest; the poster was shocking to many people, a response that was amplified by the incongruous smoking. The poster carried a series of points about the risks to the foetus if a woman smoked during pregnancy. I like to think (I cannot prove it) that the effectiveness of this poster came partly from its disturbing nature and partly from the tight relationship between the source of the disturbance and the message.

Researching the sequence of decision making

Self-awareness in thinking

You may think that introspection will reveal the *processes* used in judgement and decision making. This is doubtful. Nisbett and Wilson (1977) and Evans (1980) have presented evidence showing that the subject's reports of his or her own strategy in solving problems cannot be relied upon. We may know our beliefs and feelings but not how we came to think and feel them. From the previous section we can see that heuristic processes can affect judgements without our being aware of the process. However the issue has drawn counter arguments. For example, Smith and Miller (1978) claim that Nisbett and Wilson rely too much on a simple distinction between content and process in thought and that people can have privileged access to some of the processes that they use. This literature has been reviewed by White (1988). In this context you can now consider your responses to Exercise 7.1.

These problems are discussed in relation to consumer behaviour by Rip (1980) and by Wright and Rip (1980). This issue raises considerable doubts about consumer investigations that rely on the subjects' reports of their own thinking processes.

Decision rules

Nisbett and Wilson's work shows that objective studies are required to establish how people process information when they choose between products. Much of the marketing research on the processes of choice has been designed to establish a decision rule which will explain which alternative people choose. Investigations have been conducted to see whether the full compensatory multi-attribute model works best or whether predictions are improved by abandoning compensation and assuming that the decision is reached by evaluating alternatives in a more limited way. For example by ignoring attributes below a threshold value (conjunctive), by choosing the alternative with the most attributes above an arbitrary threshold (disjunctive) or by processing by reference to the most important attribute first and moving to the next only in the event of a tie (lexicographic). Tversky (1972) proposed a variation of the lexicographic procedure in a rule called 'elimination by aspects' (EBA). Here attributes are weighted; the most important is considered first and all alternatives that fall below the threshold for this attribute are eliminated. Attention then shifts to the next most important attribute and this process continues until one alternative remains. A problem with this method is that it implies a large amount of processing when there are many alternatives.

This type of research always produces a 'winner' since one model is of necessity going to give better results than the others in any contest but, undermining such research, is the way in which the winner varies from study to study. One reason for the variety of findings lies in the sensitivity of the decision process to environmental factors. Some of these factors arise from the method of investigation itself; for example, decisions are studied by real time reports (protocols), eye movement studies and other methods that are likely to affect the subject. Other factors involve the layout of the alternatives. Svenson (1974), using booklets on each brand, found that this induced processing by brand rather than attribute. This was hardly surprising. Park (1976) found that the decision process was affected by product complexity and familiarity, and van Raaij (1977) found effects from distraction, information availability and time pressure.

In the face of this chaotic range of effects Bettman (1977), Bettman and Zins (1977) and Bettman and Park (1980) suggest that people construct a tailor-made decision procedure, when faced with a particular choice, using fragments of different decision rules. This requires a general rule that explains how the fragments are put together. This is surely a blind alley; the decision rule approach has failed to show order and we should be trying other approaches. One approach is to look for mechanisms that direct attention when people choose.

The attention mechanism in choice

This section reviews work on the time spent on the different alternatives before choice and proposes a mechanism that could account for the findings. Despite the relevance to consumer behaviour there has been little work done in this area.

A central problem for decision researchers who seek to study our thought is the lack of any behaviour that can be observed. To discover how people learn to use a computer we can observe their actions. These actions may be corroborated by subjective reports but generally actions speak louder than words. In decision making the observable action is often restricted to the overt choice. However, when the alternatives are physically present, it is possible to observe the direction of gaze and to infer which alternative a subject is thinking about. Gerard (1967) first used this method of investigation.

My own work in this area began with a small study of option choice among students (East, 1972). On their course the students could choose two options out of five and talks were arranged on each option so that the students could form some idea about what the content of each option was. These talks occurred at different times during the week. Each student was asked to put the options in order of preference before and after the talks and was asked to state which talks had been attended. A rational analysis of the choice suggests that the talks on the options ranked second and third would be the most important to attend. Often the student would be sure about his or her first preference and doubt would centre on whether to do one or other of the next two. Was this reflected in the attendance? Student attendance at the talks was recorded against the preference for the options which they expressed before and after the talks. Both before and after the talks the students attended their first preference most frequently; this was followed by the attendance at the talk on their third preference, then the second, fourth and fifth. Table 7.3 shows this.

Table 7.3 *Number of students at option talks (from East, 1972)*

Preference order	Before talks	After talks
1	26	31
2	19	25
3	21	26
4	17	16
5	11	15

The results suggested two effects. The high attendance at talks on the third option seems to reflect the strategic requirement to sort out the choice between the options ranked second and third but the findings also show that either the preference order or the evaluation of an option has a strong direct effect on attendance.

Following this study an apparatus was designed to measure the durations of time spent on alternatives before a decision is made. The apparatus used slide viewers connected to a hidden timing mechanism. As in the earlier study by Gerard (1967) the choice was made between French Impressionist paintings and the subjects were led to believe that they would get a poster of the picture that they chose. Control of the viewers was left entirely in the hands of the subjects so that the time spent on the different alternatives was unconstrained. Two experiments were conducted (East, 1973). The first experiment presented subjects with two alternatives and the second with three, and both experiments had two levels of choice difficulty: *high*, between alternatives that had previously been rated equally by the subject, and *low*, between alternatives that had been rated unequally.

This sort of study allows subjects to change their order of preference and several of those in the high choice difficulty condition did so. These subjects were asked at what stage they changed their minds and the attention data were reallocated to the contemporaneous preference order. With or without this correction, the results showed that the subjects spent more time looking at the alternatives that they liked more, i.e. that the ratio of attention times was a function of the ratio of the evaluations. Choice difficulty raised the time taken to decide, a finding that has been consistently found. Contrary to assumptions often made in psychology, more alternatives under high choice difficulty did not raise the decision time. This may indicate that simpler mechanisms come into play when decisions become too elaborate or difficult.

Table 7.4 shows the results. It must be noted here that Gerard himself found that more time was given to the alternative that was *not* chosen. Gerard explained this as an attempt to come to terms with not having this alternative. There is no obvious explanation for this difference in findings but Gerard, who reported only one study on a two-alternative choice, used a complicated apparatus for recording attention and it is possible that measurements were attributed to the wrong channels, thus reversing the results.

Table 7.4 *Duration of attention (seconds) to the alternatives in choice experiments (from East, 1973)*

Choice difficulty	Order of preference	Two alternatives	Three alternatives
High	1	46	25
	2	37	23
	3	–	21
Totals		83	69
Low	1	24	24
	2	18	16
	3	–	9
Totals		42	49

The evidence of how attention is distributed suggests a simple controlling mechanism with evaluation guiding thinking. In natural settings people have to allocate time to parts of their environment and good adaptation requires that they attend to aspects offering the most potential gain. Their evaluations of the objects around them provide one indicator of potential gain. (They also need to avoid loss so that people are also likely to attend to noxious and uncertain features but these were not varied in the experiments.)

If evaluation guides attention it means that second and third preferences will get proportionately less attention and their worthwhile attributes are less likely to be discovered. Thus the attention mechanism tends to confirm our existing preferences when new observation supports what is already known. However if negative findings force a derating of the first preference then more total time will be allocated as the alternatives are evaluated more equally and a larger proportion of this time will be spent on the second preference. This mechanism carries a bias in favour of existing preferences but it is an efficient way of allocating the scarce resource of time. It ensures that little time is wasted on low rated prospects.

It is quite difficult to see how to use the attention mechanism to persuade people to change their minds. One possible strategy is to bury information about the less attractive alternative within a message on the preferred alternative. In this way it is more likely to receive attention. The mechanism also suggests that negative information about a first preference is more likely to get attention than positive information about a second preference.

Summary

This chapter is about the mechanisms involved in recognizing, thinking, evaluating and investigating. Recognition is performed well by humans but is delayed by competing responses. Stimuli creating response competition draw attention but are less liked; liking grows with frequent exposure. The evaluative response to stimuli is often faster than the cognitive response and these mechanisms seem to involve relatively independent processing.

Interpretation, recall and understanding are affected by the way information fits cognitive structures called schemata. These schemata range from familiar concepts like product types to abstract relationships such as causality. Influence may cause people to revise their thinking within a schema or to transform their understanding by relocating their ideas in a different schema.

In making judgements people use simplifying processes called heuristics. They call upon information more if it seems *representative* of a category and if it is *available* (because it is discrete, eventful, vivid, recent or part of direct experience). Such processes affect judgement of risk and cause people to neglect information that is relevant but 'pallid'.

We convert the objective forms of value and probability into internal forms of utility and subjective probability. The utility function is concave to the x-axis as value increases in magnitude. There is evidence that subjective probability is enhanced when it is low but that it is underweighted above about 0.15. These effects are incorporated in *prospect theory* and help to explain some common preferences between risks, e.g. that most people are risk averse for gains and risk seeking for losses.

The search for decision rules has produced much variety and little order. A rather different way of understanding decision making is to find out what drives attention and investigation during the pre-decision period. Some work is reported in this area.

Further reading

Eiser, J. R. (1986) *Social Psychology: Attitudes, Cognition and Social Behaviour*. Cambridge, Cambridge University Press, chapters 4 and 7

Lindzey, G. and Aronson, E. (1985) *Handbook of Social Psychology*, Vol. 1, 3rd ed. New York, Random House; chapter 4 by Markus, H. and Zajonc, R. B. The cognitive perspective in social psychology, pp. 137–230; ch. 5 by Abelson, R. P. and Levi, A. Decision making and decision theory, pp. 231–310

Kahneman, D. and Tversky, A. (1984) Choices, values and frames. *American Psychologist* **39**, 4, 341–50

Thaler, R. (1985) Mental accounting and consumer choice. *Marketing Science* **4**, summer, 199–214

[8]
Media advertising and sales promotions

Introduction

The first four sections of this chapter are concerned with the ways in which people react to advertising and to sales promotions such as discounts, special displays and redeemable coupons. The first section places advertising and sales promotions in context as components of the promotional mix. The second section introduces the new scanner-based methods of research into promotion and reports on some of the findings that have been obtained using these methods. The third section on sales promotions and the fourth section on advertising develop some of the issues first raised in Chapter 2 and are focused on the question: 'How *much* do people respond to promotion?' The fifth section explores the different ways in which advertising is seen by practitioners and the possible explanations for its effects, and the last section examines the scope for pre-testing advertising copy at an early stage in its development.

At this point I must forewarn any reader who expects a grand synthesis in which the effects of promotion are explained in detail by the psychological processes reported in the previous chapters. Promotion has great variety and its effects are measured in aggregate; this is difficult to relate to research on individual processes reported by psychologists. The explanation of promotional effects has also been held up by lack of good evidence. Academic researchers have to rely on information supplied by market research and advertising agencies which are concerned on the one hand to preserve confidentiality and on the other to present a positive image of themselves. This leads to selection in the

173

material that is available. For example the articles in the *Advertising Works* series (Broadbent, 1981, 1983; Channon, 1985, 1987) are reports of *successful* campaigns and we lack information about cases where advertising did not work. In these circumstances there is great value to be attached to the dispassionate review of the insider and Broadbent (1989) draws on both academic and agency research and contains a wealth of information on the effects of advertising; this is a work of great circumspection and I commend it to the reader.

In the last few years we have begun to get rather better information on the effects of advertising and sales promotions because of the introduction of scanner panels in the USA. I have devoted most space to this evidence but explanations in these fields are necessarily tentative. Despite my caution I am sure that the reader will find the material in this chapter of great interest. The results of scientific investigation are placing doubt on some widely held assumptions and have implications for marketing practice.

There are a number of technical terms used in advertising and I have defined these in a glossary at the end of this chapter.

The promotional mix

Brands should be marketed according to a plan covering product development, packaging, pricing, market research, distribution and promotional expenditure. Within the amount allocated to promotion there is a mix of expenditures on publicity, sales representation, sales promotions and media advertising; promotion is further sub-divided and may be directed to either trade or consumers and it may support specific brands or more general targets such as the family brand name or the manufacturing company. Ideally the size and division of the budget should depend upon the consumer responses to different forms of promotion but these responses are difficult to measure, particularly in a natural setting where several influences on sales may operate at the same time.

Synergy

It is generally believed that the different components of promotion and marketing are mutually supportive, an effect called *synergy*. It is easy to see why this might be so; advertising helps to explain what a sales representative is offering and informs people about special offers that are available in local stores and this makes the representative more effective and the discount more used. Advertising also encourages retailers to give space to brands. This was well illustrated in the case of Manger's Sugar Soap (Broadbent, 1983) where the advertising increased the stocking in shops. Advertising may help consumers to accept the price of the brand.

If there is synergy there should be an optimum mix, a distribution of the budget that maximizes the return on expenditure in a given set of circumstances. It would be fine if the optimum mix could be calculated from theory but this is not realistic. Different products, advertisements and promotions produce different effects and the competition varies. In practice managers focus on the different parts of the budget and usually start with rules of thumb such as maintaining the advertising to sales ratio, matching the competition or following the previous year's practice.

Advertising and pricing

In markets where supply is limited, the effect of advertising may be to raise price by raising demand. This applies to auctions and to share markets where corporate advertising may create increased demand and raise the share price or the premium on new offers.

Advertising may also affect the acceptability of product prices. Broadbent (1989) illustrates this with a case where improved advertising increased the proportion of purchasers who were tolerant of the brand's higher price. Adding value to a brand often amounts to this: increasing the number of people who think the price is fair. King (1984) noted that over two decades the market share of Andrex had scarcely changed yet the price premium had risen from 10 per cent to 35 per cent, indicating that steady advertising had contributed lasting added value. Gabor (1988) has reviewed the research on consumer responses to price levels. This shows that people tend to have upper and lower levels of price acceptability and that one factor that determines these levels is the perception of quality. Too low a price indicates poor quality and Gabor quotes several studies where a higher price produced more sales. On the other hand a very high price indicates quality that costs too much and which the customer cannot necessarily afford.

The upper and lower limits of acceptable price may vary from brand to brand in a product field and it is likely that advertising will help brands to secure the higher range by assuring the consumer about brand quality. This process may also operate at store level and may, for example, help to explain how Tesco has raised both its quality image and its margins in recent years. More generally, price, brand, store and other factors can all operate as cues to quality and advertising may add to this process.

Gabor's description of how consumers respond to price depends upon their ability to recall the prices that they paid for the brands that they use and Gabor found that this recall was high for common products at a time when resale price maintenance existed and most prices were therefore controlled. Such recall may be lower now that shops can charge what they wish but even when exact prices are not recalled by consumers they may still use some internal reference price to judge the acceptability of a brand. The use of internal references is reviewed by Klein and Oglethorpe (1987).

Media advertising versus sales promotions

In Britain and America more emphasis is now placed on sales promotions than media advertising. Schultz (1987) reported that many US companies devote as much as 70 per cent of expenditure to sales promotion. It should be noted that the size of sales promotion expenditure depends upon the discount from a 'normal' price which may be rather artificial. However the trend is more discernible and Broadbent (1989) quotes trade sources showing that from 1976 to 1986 there was an increase in consumer sales promotions and a reduction in the proportion of media advertising. This has worried the advertising industry and the value of sales promotions in relation to advertising has been hotly debated.

Fulgoni (1987) thinks that the shift to sales promotions has come about partly through retailer demands for point-of-sale support as a condition for stocking a brand. He notes that manufacturers who accede to such pressure weaken their control over the brand and enhance the retailers' power. By comparison media advertising sustains and may build demand for a brand so that retailers need to stock it if they are to meet consumer needs. Manufacturers' discounts suit retailers. They reduce prices at the supplier's expense and the retailer may be able to stockpile brands at trade discount for later sale at a higher price. Discounts may build traffic when they are a regular feature but Walters and Rinne (1986) found no evidence that the short-term sales of non-promoted items were affected by promotions of other goods in the store.

Schultz, writing about the US market, suggested that short-term thinking favoured promotions because they delivered rapid increases in sales, albeit at reduced margins. He also noted that the difficulty of demonstrating the effect of advertising made it less attractive to managers. Ogilvy (1987), in characteristically trenchant style, castigates the same short-term thinking and argues that the reduction in media advertising means that brand image will languish to the long-term detriment of sales and market control. Broadbent (1989) develops this issue which depends upon the long term effects of both discount and advertising. Since price is associated with quality in the eyes of consumers there is a danger that repeated price promotions will diminish the perceived value of the brand and eventually reduce market share. By contrast the long-term effect of advertising is thought to create added value and therefore to increase sales. This argument can be supported with examples but systematic studies are rare.

Supporting the use of sales promotions is the widely held view that they give 'more bang for your buck', i.e. money spent on sales promotion has more profit impact than the same amount spent on advertising, even after allowing for the lower price of the brand on deal. A study which specifically compared discounts with advertising would be very difficult to mount but the recent evidence on long-term effects suggests that media advertising has been undervalued. Notice, however, that sales promotions do help managers to fine tune sales in the short term and thus have considerable value in avoiding overstocking and layoffs.

Research developments

BehaviorScan

In the USA it is now possible to measure the effects of television advertising and store promotions very accurately using cable TV, checkout scanners and computing. The most advanced form of this research method is called BehaviorScan and has been developed by Information Resources Inc., a high technology market research firm based in Chicago. The methods used by IRI have been described by Malec in 1982 and Fulgoni and Eskin (1981). By 1987 IRI had established research panels in ten communities in the USA. Isolated communities are used where off-air TV reception is poor and people therefore rely on cable TV. About 70 per cent of households in the community join IRI's panel (Fulgoni, 1988) and in 1988 the total television panel size reached 15,000. IRI controls the cable system; it can switch the advertisements received in designated homes and can monitor the TV channel that the household set is tuned to. This means that one group of households can receive one advertisement while another equivalent group receives a quite different version. Alternatively different weights of advertising can be compared.

Scanner panels

The other half of the system is based in the local stores and records purchase. All stores are equipped with IRI's checkout scanners which accumulate the purchases per household from the bar codes on the products purchased. Each household has an identification card which members of the household show to the checkout operator. Customer compliance is increased by prizes based on the household number. The whole system depends upon computer control of advertising transmissions and computer analysis of scanner data. The data analysis can show how much of a particular brand was purchased by households receiving particular advertising schedules.

IRI also uses the scanner system to monitor the effects of store promotions. As a result of this technology (and IRI's openness in disclosing general findings) we now understand much better how consumers respond to promotions. A great advantage of IRI's method is that it is panel based so that a customer's purchasing history can be explored; this means that we can see how a sales response to a discount comes about, i.e. we can find out how many people bring forward their usual purchase, stockpile, consume more, or switch brands.

The accuracy of scanner and diary panels

Any system of measurement has errors associated with it. Malec (1982) noted early problems with scanner measurement because some goods were uncoded and because the UPC did not specify brand varieties. The BehaviorScan system does not pick up out-of-town sales but these are rare with the packaged goods studied by IRI. There is also some question about whether the rather isolated communities studied by IRI are representative of the rest of the USA, particularly when these communities are used as test markets. The reliability of the scanner panels is supported by a comparison between store sales and panel sales. Eskin (1985) reports that there is little discrepancy when panel figures were compared with store sales; by brand, 91 per cent of panel measures are within 10 per cent of store sale measures. This comparison shows that panel sales are typical of the locality. Furthermore the aggregated scanner data correspond with nationwide sales showing that IRI can monitor the national pattern.

The main alternative to scanner panels are diary panels but these show a number of deficiencies. The following deficiencies of diary panels in the USA have been noted by Fulgoni and Eskin (1981).

1 *Low recruitment*. Only 8–10 per cent of households agree to join and half of these no longer participate by the end of a year. The British experience is rather better than this, but in the USA IRI's scanner panels can secure 70 per cent of the community and the retention level is high.
2 *Poor recording of purchases*, particularly when more than one member of the household shops regularly. Shopping trips where few items are purchased often go unrecorded. There is bias in favour of stores with a high share of the market and against those with a small share. Lower income groups and minority groups are less likely to report patronage.
3 *Distortion of responses*. Some people are affected by their membership of diary panels; they become more price sensitive

and purchase more own brands though this effect lessens over time.

The result of these biases can produce misrecordings that are shown up by comparisons with scanner data. There are more serious deficiencies in the data that are obtained by ad hoc surveys based on consumer recall. Generally the effect of erroneous recall is to exaggerate purchase, sometimes by as much as three times (Fulgoni, 1988).

Scanner research in Britain

Britain (in 1989) has no scanner panels based on store purchase. AGB Ltd and Nielsen Marketing Research are developing panels which use the bar codes to record purchase but this measurement will be done by the panel member at home, not in the store. This procedure places the burden of accuracy (and any recording of price and promotional features) on the panel member and is likely to generate a number of errors. Nielsen now run an in-store scanner based market survey called Scantrack which provides fast and accurate reports of sales through a large number of stores. This service can track promotion effects but it cannot follow the impact of promotions at an individual level because it is a survey and not a panel. Morris (1987) reports on Scantrack applications. Examples of Scantrack research are shown in Figure 8.1 (pp. 182–3).

In Britain TV advertising is often compared using area tests. Different weights of advertisement versions may be used on, say, Tyne Tees Television and Yorkshire Television, and the area sales of the brand compared. There are problems of sales lag, defining area boundaries and non-equivalences between areas that reduce the efficiency of such research. Furthermore the deficiencies in the advertising are discovered after a large amount has been spent on development and air time. Nielsen Marketing Research and Harlech Television are partners in a new British service called Stats Scan which uses the transmitters at Bristol and Cardiff to compare different advertisements that are scheduled at the same times. The comparison of sales response uses two matched house-wife panels whose household TV is monitored and who record their purchases at home using bar code readers. The panels can both be drawn in the Newport/Cardiff area so this procedure is more controlled than an area test using aggregate sales in two different regions as the basis of comparison. On the debit side the panel numbers (2000 in total) are rather small for detecting advertisement effects.

There are difficulties about establishing a BehaviorScan system in Britain. Towns are less isolated. People may be less willing to participate in measurements that reach into the home. Cable television is essential for a BehaviorScan type of service and TV aerial reception in Britain is generally good so there is little scope for providing cable to all the inhabitants of an area. There are also legal problems about interference with television advertisements. IRI have no plans to introduce a BehaviorScan service in Britain.

Some findings from panel research

IRI's targetable TV and scanner data have thrown light on a number of issues which are discussed below.

Timescale effects in consumption research

Scanner recordings permit very rapid analysis of sales so that panel data can easily be produced on a weekly basis and may be presented by store. Diary panels can, in principle, give results for short periods and may also be based on single sources but usually their findings are reported at a higher level of aggregation. Thus scanner research has narrowed the focus and has helped to reveal the impact of short duration interventions in the market. Figure 8.2 shows the differences between bimonthly, monthly, weekly and weekly single store data. Price changes in the store show little effect on sales when averaged over two months. As the period is reduced and then shown at store level the large response to price changes become visible.

How much do people switch away from commercials?

In Britain, Kitchen (1986) found that 54 per cent of a sample of people with a remote control said they were likely or highly likely to flick to other channels when the commercials came on. During the programme the proportion was 23 per cent. The IRI system monitors the viewing channel every five seconds and thus provides an accurate measure of channel changing. Eskin (1985) found that net audience loss rarely exceeded 4 per cent during the commer-

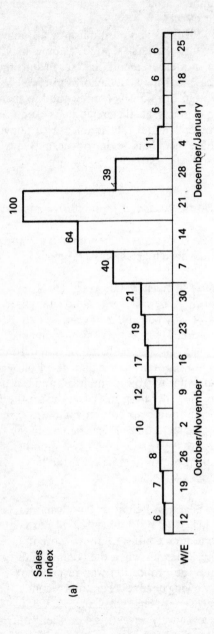

(a)

Sales index

W/E	12	19	26	2	9	16	23	30	7	14	21	28	4	11	18	25
	6	7	8	10	12	17	19	21	40	64	100	39	11	6	6	6

October/November   December/January

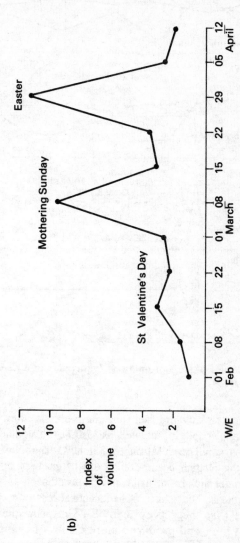

Figure 8.1 Weekly demand from Scantrack research for two product categories: (a) port, showing the build up of weekly sales over the Christmas period; and (b) confectionery, showing the sales peaks for special days (Nielsen Marketing Research)

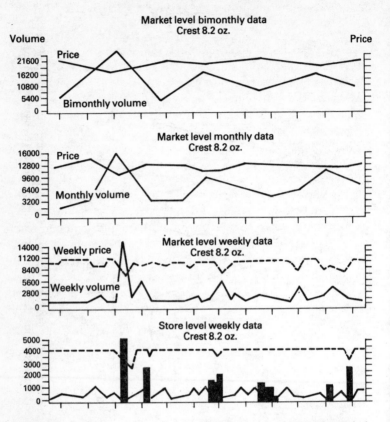

Figure 8.2 Effects of sales promotions averaged over different periods (from Eskin, 1985)

cial; this figure reflects the fact that commercials often gain audience by channel changing as well as losing it. Even so the USA finding seems small in relation to Kitchen's data, all the more so because the British commercials are often very entertaining. Possibly channel flickers return almost immediately to their starting programme so that there is little actual loss of viewers. It is also possible that the survey method of measurement used by Kitchen is at fault and produced more claims of channel flicking than actually occur; this would be consistent with other evidence of over-claiming on recall.

Segmenting the audience

Audiences can be divided on t

product type. Using such audie

improve the targeting of comr

exposures to a user segment for

illustrated how this type of me

showed that a higher proportion

television in the daytime perioc

programmes to others. Better tin

cials would have improved the a

ment. This is illustrated in Figure

how audience size varies. It is likely that the high proportion of instant coffee drinkers in the afternoon occurs when the audience is low. Media planners take account of reach and price per viewer as well as accurate targeting when they buy time for mass consumption products like instant coffee. (Refer to the glossary for an explanation of advertising terms like 'reach'.)

The audiences for different programmes can be grouped demographically but generally the variation in audience composition between programmes is small. An alternative segmentation is based on advertising exposure which can be measured directly by the BehaviorScan technology. Those with high exposures to TV advertisements are heavy viewers who give a poor response to commercials. Habituation may cause them to switch off psychologically when advertisements are screened. Heavy viewers who are more often the unemployed also tend to have less disposable income. Light viewers are therefore an attractive target group.

Garrick (1986a) argues that companies could spend their advertising dollars far more efficiently if they used exposure analysis. There are clearly gains to be made but these may not be large in Britain. Goodhardt, Ehrenberg and Collins (1987) found that the majority of light viewer's TV time is spent on the high-rating programmes and only 23 per cent is devoted to programmes with lower ratings of less than 10 per cent of households. This pattern is much the same for heavy viewers. Lighter viewers do differ from heavy viewers in respect of the time of day when they watch, viewing little before 6.00 pm. Goodhardt, Ehrenberg and Collins conclude that the main characteristic of light viewers is that they tend to watch mainly at peak time and they note that this is what makes it peak time, the audience is swelled by both light and

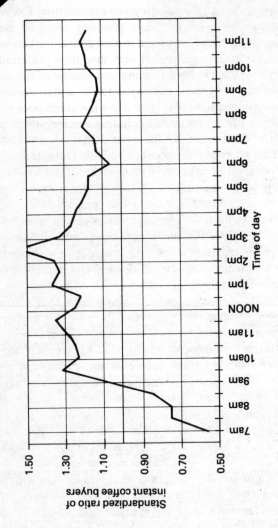

Figure 8.3 The ratio of instant coffee drinkers in the TV audience to instant coffee drinkers in the population by time of day (adapted from Eskin, 1985)

heavy viewers. Depending on the cost per viewer, there may be some advantage in going for the after 6.00 pm peak viewing period to secure a higher proportion of light viewers.

The response to combined promotions

Fulgoni (1987) has aggregated the IRI scanner data from a large number of studies to produce the mean effects shown in Figure 8.4. This shows relatively little effect from a price cut on its own; a 10 per cent cut leads on average to a 20 per cent gain in sales, an elasticity of −2. However, when the deal is complemented by either an advertising feature in local newspapers or by a temporary special display (bins, free-standing product and end aisle stacks) the effects are much greater, rising to 78 per cent and 105 per cent respectively. When price cut, advertisement and display are combined it might be expected that the total effect is:

$$78 + 105 - 20 = 163 \text{ per cent}$$

but there is an extra effect of 40 per cent which Fulgoni attributes to the synergy of the different forms of promotion. Totten's (1986) study also found that feature and display interacted to produce a greater effect and that this phenomenon was very strong when the line was also discounted.

Unfortunately this sort of data can be ambiguous. It appears that the different combinations of promotions occur in different stores for different products and at different times; like is not compared with like. It could be that the stores that use the three-fold promotion of discount, display and advertisement feature devote more time and space to each component and Totten (1986) notes this possibility. If this is so, the extra effect may not be due to synergy but to the fact that the promotional components were better managed. This problem, that unmeasured variables may be responsible for an effect, is always present when the data are derived from non-experimental designs. An ideal experimental design randomizes the influence of variables not investigated.

Management implications of IRI's research

Garrick (1986a, 1986b) has suggested that advertisers could make better use of IRI's research facilities. He notes that the research commissioned with IRI is predominantly concerned with weight increases but that the results show that only in about 20 per cent of the cases will increased advertising weights pay for themselves.

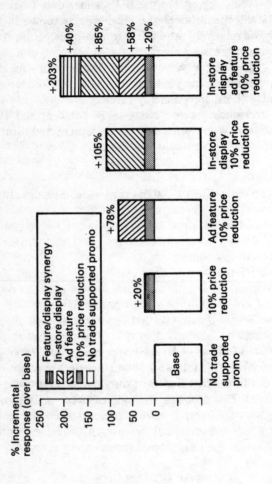

Figure 8.4 Average response to trade promotions (from Fulgoni, 1987)

By contrast the copy tests conducted by IRI (about 20 per cent of their commissions) often show the clear superiority of one advertisement over another and this is evidence which can be acted upon without extra expense.

Garrick suggests that BehaviorScan copy tests could be used more extensively. Although a full copy test can take up to a year Garrick notes that most of the tests that show differences over a year also show an effect at three months which managements can act on. Copy tests can also be used to evaluate different length advertisements, 15 second spots rather than 30 second spots for example. Tests can also evaluate the effects of different sequences of advertising, e.g. continuous versus burst and drip. Finally tests can evaluate the effect of alternative media plans based on the exposure analysis discussed above.

However, copy tests via BehaviorScan are very expensive and may delay the start of a campaign. It may be better to run area tests of alternative advertisements using the different TV regions. To be fully convincing the BehaviorScan copy testing procedure should itself be validated by comparing the field performances of the tested advertisements to see whether these square with prediction. Normally the advertisement showing the weaker sales response in the test is dropped so that a field comparison cannot be made. It would also be interesting to have a no advertisement control condition in copy tests. The procedure used must reflect commercial requirements but it prevents an assessment of how much each condition affects sales. There may be some biases associated with the BehaviorScan procedure. One possible problem is if viewers think a new advertisement is being tested and this affects their sales response more than the advertisement itself. Such an effect would particularly afflict comparisons of new against old advertisements. It should also be noted that IRI's commissions are not representative of all TV advertisements. Agencies and clients are more likely to propose tests when they think that a difference will emerge.

Sales promotion research

What are the effects of a sales promotion? Consider the possibilities. Some regular consumers may stockpile and buy less later, some may buy more and increase consumption, some may be induced to switch brands to the promoted item and some may try the brand even though they never normally buy that type of product. The trialists may or may not continue to purchase the brand after the promotion is over. A clearer view of these outcomes is now emerging.

Duration of effect

Cotton and Babb (1978) did find higher post-promotion purchase rates for some dairy products but this effect was small; most of the purchase gain occurred during the promotion. Shoemaker and Shoaf (1977) found a drop in the repurchase rate after a promotion, suggesting some stockpiling. McAlister (1986) found no stockpiling in instant coffee promotions and there was no evidence of carry over effects in the England and Ehrenberg tray experiments (1986, 1988). Totten and Block (1987), using IRI data, report little post-promotion sales decline. They illustrate this with the sales of Pepsi Cola (Figure 8.5) which continue in the non-promotion periods as though the promotions had not occurred. Totten and Block also look beyond the immediate post-promotion period to see whether there are any longer-term effects on base level but found no evidence with three products. This last finding provides some reassurance to those who fear that sales promotions erode long term customer support.

The conclusion of these findings is that the impact of a sales promotion is generally confined to the period during which it occurs. There will be some exceptions to this: new products, which have no previous base level, can only show a gain from promotions. Also the type of promotion may affect the duration of effect. Most sales promotions are price discounts or extra product for the money but packet coupons and proof of purchase schemes may show longer-term effects.

Small incentive promotions

The evidence that the sales effect of deals usually stops when the deal stops is a challenge. The better deal is the one that lasts and this has led Scott (1976) to suggest that small incentives, or ones that require the purchaser to expend effort, could be more

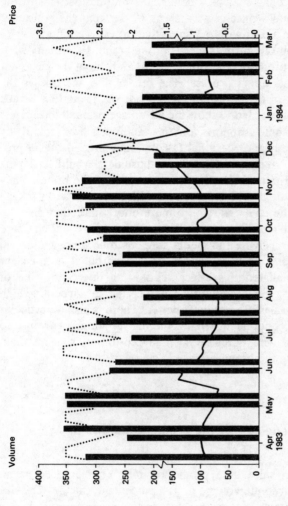

Figure 8.5 Sales of Pepsi Cola show no relationship between promotional sales and base rate sales (from the *Marketing Fact Book* Scanner Data Base, Information Resources Inc.)

cost effective than large ones. Scott applies Bem's (1967) idea of self-perception and argues that a large discount, say 25 per cent, or a 'two for one' promotion, will increase sales but will lead new purchasers to think that they bought the product because of the deal. With smaller incentives such as 10 per cent the consumer may forget the incentive and assume that previous purchases were connected with the intrinsic merits of the brand. Essentially what is needed is a promotion that increases sales without the customer recognizing this direct process. The reader may see this as the five-card trick of marketing and it was not surprising that Scott's (1976) own study failed to show the advantage of small incentives.

However, some support for this approach was found by Dodson, Tybout and Sternthal (1978). They argued that a promotion which required effort from consumers would lead purchasers to attribute their effort to the merits of the brand. They compared media distributed coupons with discounts and package coupons. Media coupons require more effort since they have to be cut out. The researchers found a higher level of repeat purchase among those receiving the media coupons than among those in the discount and package coupon conditions but it is not clear that effort mediated this effect. This is an interesting line of inquiry but it remains doubtful whether the low incentive/high effort type of sales promotion is better. There is also a particular problem with coupons in Britain: the big supermarkets refuse to match coupon with purchase so many customers redeem them without buying the brand.

The size of the promotional bump

The effect on sales of a promotion may be measured as an increment in absolute volume or as a percentage change. The size of the percentage change in sales during promotions is highly variable. Eskin (1985) and Fulgoni (1986) both show that promotions can multiply turnover dramatically, sometimes even ten-fold, during the period of the promotion. Garrick (1986a) found that a promotion plus advertisement feature produced the following increases by category:

Frozen dinners	43%
Soup	45%
Mayonnaise	86%
Cat food	150%
Coffee	210%
Margarine	360%
Potato chips	600%

Cotton and Babb (1978) also showed wide variation in the effects of promotions ranging from about 20 per cent to 400 per cent. However, this evidence is of limited value if the base is not reported; a tenfold increase in a brand that has less than 1 per cent of the market is not a large total sale whereas a tenfold increase in a brand leader would be remarkable.

The impact on competitors

In the economy as a whole, short-term market competition approximates to a zero sum game in which one brand's gain is at the expense of a buyer's other potential purchases or savings. In some fields like toilet paper, petrol and detergent the total consumption of the category is relatively fixed and therefore the gain is likely to be at the expense of other brands in the category. The consumption of other products such as confectionery, canned tuna and biscuits is more flexible and promotional gains need not be at the expense of competitors in the same product field. What does the evidence show?

Totten and Block (1987) state:

the actual data, however, show that competitive brands seldom have major sales declines during the promotional periods of other brands. On the contrary, sometimes competitive brands enjoy sales increases.

It should be noted that the examples that Totten and Block quote are of groceries where total consumption is flexible and they report the evidence per store. (It is possible that other stores suffer reduced sales.) They are also referring to the base line sales of competitors, not the total sales over a period. Even so this evidence is surprising to those who implicitly assume that one brand's gain is achieved via the loss of share of other brands in the same field. However, the relative independence of competitor sales fits the idea discussed in Chapter 2 that consumers form stable dispositions to buy brands that are little affected by promotions for other brands.

An important consequence of the evidence that competitor base sales are little affected by another brand's promotion is that sales volume is preferable to market share as a measure of promotion effect. The market share for brand A changes when a competitor has a successful promotion even though the sales volume for brand A remains constant. This makes sales volume a more reliable indicator of how a brand is performing.

Where do the extra sales come from?

Totten and Block argue that over 80 per cent of the incremental volume produced by a promotion comes from *discount switchers*; only a little comes from those who are loyal to other brands, new buyers of the product type or from existing loyal buyers. Since these switchers normally buy on deal they do not show up in base levels which are permanently depressed by the availability of goods on promotion. It must be remembered that American promotions are so frequent that consumers can adopt a strategy of buying only on promotion (for example more canned tuna is bought on deal than at regular prices). So, according to the discount switcher theory, promotions mainly service a large free-wheeling group of consumers who rarely buy at normal prices. This theory could be consistent with the multi-brand portfolio evidence described in Chapter 2 which showed that consumers in general have a portfolio of brands which they buy in much the same ratio over the longer period. In the American market people could keep to a portfolio of brands which they buy only on promotion.

At present the switcher theory lacks detailed support. Totten and Block (1987) and McAlister and Totten (1985) define a switcher as a purchaser who is less than 80 per cent loyal to the brand under review. Those familiar with multi-brand purchase would regard this as a high level of loyalty; the 'promotional bump' would be differently distributed if loyalty were defined at a lower level. However, the crucial question concerns the purchasing history of the switcher, defined in this way. If the switcher conscientiously buys only on deal then Totten and Block will have made their case. In the USA the extra sales caused by a promotion will be explained by the operations of the promotions-only buyer. But if the switcher buys much the same proportions of deal and no-deal brands as others then the case falls and we lack a full explanation of where the extra sales come from.

Totten and Block note that promotions do increase total product type sales but this claim remains relatively unquantified. What is required here is evidence that a shift in the general level of promotions for a category has an effect on total sales of the category, both in the store and in the community, and this has not been documented for different categories.

Totten and Block also investigate stockpiling. This does occur and is most frequent among heavy users when promotions are rare. When the promotions are very frequent there is no need to stockpile. This finding is of relevance to Britain. It is likely that British consumers do stockpile more than their counterparts in the USA because promotions are less common in Britain.

Small brand advantage

High penetration brands have less headroom for growth so that promotions cannot produce spectacular *percentage* increases. McAlister (1985) found that lower penetration brands benefit proportionately more from price promotions. This is to be expected if the more extensive media advertising for large brands generally makes them less price sensitive. A further advantage of sales promotions to the small brand is that they lose a smaller proportion on the extra sales to regular customers who take advantage of a price promotion by buying at a reduced rate. Totten (1986) confirmed that small brands fare proportionately better than large brands in promotions in a major study of 116 categories using IRI data. 'Small brand advantage' has become widely accepted in marketing. The supporting evidence is in terms of percentage increases and the advantage may be less certain when profit is used as a criterion.

It is worth noting that when branding is weak the effect of media advertising may generalize from the advertised brand to the product class. Any generalization will provide more sales for the large brands since gains are likely to be proportional to market share. This potential effect of media advertising makes it an unattractive method of promotion for the small and little known brand. This problem is solved when the advertising is via direct mail and the supplier controls the market.

There is some value in designing promotions that appeal particularly to the new customer. This is because profit is lost when regular buyers take advantage of a promotion and buy more cheaply than normal. Shoemaker and Tibewala (1985) found that regular purchasers claimed to redeem coupons whatever their value whereas non-users stated that they were more likely to use a coupon with a high value. This suggests that there is an optimum discount value for coupons which may be calculated if the take-up rates per unit discount are known for users and non-users. In general this thinking favours large discounts and works against Scott's (1976) theory, discussed above, that suggests that small discounts are better. The same concern about take-up by regular users led Neslin and Clarke (1987) to try to identify the type of promotion that appealed more to non-users.

Price elasticities and promotion

Elasticities are relevant to decisions on pricing, and to the choice between price promotions and media advertising. For example Cadbury's Fudge bars are found to have an exceptionally low price elasticity of -0.5 per cent and a very high elasticity in response to advertising (see Channon, 1985, p. 134). This implies that discounts would lose money and the best strategy is to maintain or raise the price while supporting the brand with media advertising; this is what the manufacturer did. By contrast Mars Bars, which are bought on value for money (see Chapter 4), are often promoted by discounts or extra product.

A serious problem with price elasticities is their non-linearity. Gabor (1988) argued that the variability of elasticity over a price range made the concept of little value to business. The value of elasticity measures would be enhanced by evidence of a consistent pattern across different products and recent IRI research suggests that there is one important pattern. Totten and Block (1987) found that for many groceries the sales response to price discounts was kinked when the brand was also supported by additional promotional action, such as displays. This can be explained by reference to Figure 8.6. The lower curve shows the relationship between sales and price and here discounts always increase sales. The higher curve shows the relationship between sales and price when there is additional promotion. At about $3.20 the curve kinks and flattens showing that small price discounts in the $3.20 to $3.35 range bring no extra sales and reduce profit when there is extra promotion. In this situation the marketer should either offer substantial discounts or none at all. This interaction between discount and display has not been demonstrated in Britain. If it is connected with the way in which information about promotions is processed by individuals then it is likely that the same effect will be found outside the USA.

Effects of media advertising on sales

Short- and long-term effects

Often media advertising has no measurable effect. When sales are influenced the effect is spread over a longer period than a sales promotion. After a campaign has stopped there is a decay in the effect on sales which fall back towards a base level which may be different from the pre-campaign level. Thus the sales effect of advertising splits into two components, the short-term effect covering the campaign period and the decay period following it, and the longer-term effect, if any, which is the change in base level. This is shown in Figure 8.7. Broadbent (1989) notes that advertising can rarely be shown to be profitable in the short term; profit comes more from long term effects but these are hard to measure.

We tend to think of the growth and decay of advertising effect as a change that occurs in the dispositions of the individual and this assumption is encouraged by the similarity between the curve for forgetting information and the decay in advertising effect. However, as Broadbent (1988) commented, some of the effect of advertising is produced by changes in the environment, particularly in the distribution system.

The reader is reminded that evidence on advertising effect is difficult to obtain and may be selective but there is little doubt

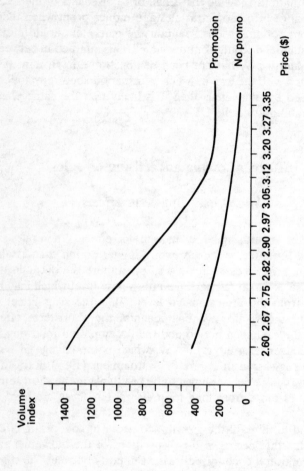

Figure 8.6 The price/promotion response model (from the *Marketing Fact Book Scanner Data Base*, Information Resources Inc.)

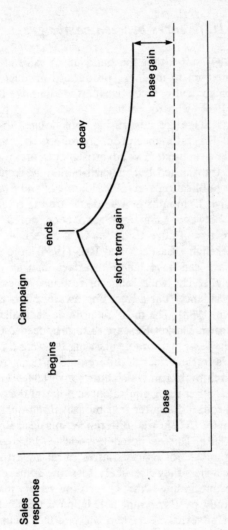

Figure 8.7 Two effects of advertising

that Figure 8.7 indicates the form of effective advertising even though this may be obscured by other market influences.

Differences between campaigns

Broadbent (1984) states that the build up of sales effect differs widely from medium to medium, product to product, and campaign to campaign. Differences between media have been noted by Speetzen (1984) who found that TV advertising had a rapid impact whereas magazine advertising took longer to show any effect on sales. This difference probably reflects the way in which different media are used. TV advertisements are usually seen when they are transmitted but magazines may be kept and read long after their publication and some, like *Field* and *Country Life*, can easily survive 12 months in a dentist's waiting room!

Differences between campaigns have been noted by Brown (1985) in his review of advertising for Cadbury's Dairy Milk and Fry's Turkish Delight. Eastlack and Rao (1986) note that a new creative approach can have far more effect than an increase in advertising weight. The wide range of response to campaigns is supported by evidence that advertising awareness is also widely variable (Brown, 1985). The most memorable campaign recorded by Millward Brown Market Research Ltd produced 290 times the awareness of the least memorable allowing for weight of advertising. Some guide to the effect of different advertising comes from TV copy research by IRI in which alternative advertisements are run against each other using equivalent samples of the population. Fulgoni (1987) found that after four months three-quarters of the copy tests done by IRI showed differences in sales response of at least 10 per cent. (But as noted previously this research was commissioned and is not representative of all advertising. Copy tests are made when they are likely to show some difference.) One other relevant finding is that advertising variety may increase response. A study by Burnkrant and Unnava (1987) found that three different advertisements had more effect than the same advertisement presented three times.

Although different media, copy and products influence the sales effect of a campaign there are a number of generalizations that can be made about most campaign effects. O'Herlihy (1976) notes the following points.

1   Although products do affect the duration of the sales response the variation is not great and in most cases the short-term effect of a campaign is over in four months.
2   The advertising is particularly influential on infrequent buyers.
3   Sustained advertising results in a saturation effect. When the advertising is pulsed the successive campaigns will have less effect unless time is allowed for sales to fall away from the saturation level. In this respect advertising campaigns differ from sales promotions which show little mutual interference. More recently O'Herlihy (1983) reported that diversifying the adspend across media helps to reduce the saturation effect.

Campaign effectiveness also depends upon market factors. Broadbent (1989) suggests that campaign effectiveness is likely to be greater when:

1   adspend on other brands in the category is low so that the campaign secures a high share of voice;
2   the product is new and the advertising promotes trial;
3   the brand is well supported by the trade.

Three other market factors are likely to indicate responsiveness to advertising. The first is where the penetration is below the norm derived from the double jeopardy calculation. This occurs when brand popularity is based on high purchase frequency rather than high penetration and advertising may be expected to widen the user base. The second market factor is the purchase frequency itself. When products are bought infrequently, e.g. cars, it is likely that most people will have forgotten the advertising when the time comes for purchase though Corlett (1985) does report some delayed effect of holiday advertising. This does not mean that the advertising is unprofitable; the value of the market may justify the advertising expenditure. Low purchase frequency has the effect of shrinking the effective target group to the few people who are in the market at the time of the campaign. The third market factor is the flexibility of purchase. As previously noted some categories like petrol and toilet paper have a fairly constant total volume so that gains occur at the expense of other brands whereas in other markets, such as confectionery, the gains are unconstrained by total market size.

Measuring the sales effect

Companies spending large amounts of money on advertising want
to measure whether their money is being wisely spent. It is particularly hard to extract the effect of advertising on sales. The effect
is small, spread over time and is confounded with market trends,
seasonal effects and the influence of promotions for all brands in
the category.

Advertising awareness

One proposed proxy for sales effectiveness is the measure of
advertising awareness. Unfortunately this measure does not necessarily relate to sales impact. For example the advertising of Cadbury's Fudge seemed very effective on sales but it did not have
much effect on awareness (Channon, 1985). Broadbent and
Colman (1986) found little relationship between advertisement
awareness and sales effectiveness in a study of eighteen campaigns
in the confectionery market. Another problem with the awareness
measure is that people become more aware of advertising when
they buy brands on promotion. This seems consistent with evidence reported in Chapters 2 and 3 that attitudes follow usage in
the frequently purchased goods sector.

Modelling and adstock

These problems have led individual companies to design mathematical models to try to disentangle the effects of promotions,
competitor activity, distribution, trend and seasonality. In order
to do this they need a measure of accumulated advertising presence which can be set alongside the other determinants of sales
and Broadbent's (1984) *adstock* measure is usually employed in
such models. Following Broadbent's (1988) exposition the sales
response can be represented by the equation:

$$R_t = b + sA_t + \ldots$$

where R_t is the sales response in period t, b is a base level of
sales without advertising, s is a slope coefficient for the particular
campaign, A_t is adstock and the dots signify that there are other
determinants of sales.

   To compute the adstock figure the contribution of each TVR
is discounted in relation to the time elapsed since it was shown.
On the basis of experience the discounting assumes a geometric

decay, i.e. the rate of decay is constant but, because it applies to a dwindling quantity, the change becomes less and less as it approaches the base level. Such processes are usually measured by their half-life, the time taken for a displacement to decay to half its value. Broadbent (1984) found that half-lives vary between three and ten weeks for different products with most being between four and six weeks. The more successful campaigns are distinguished, as far as short-term effects go, by larger slopes rather than by longer half-lives; in other words the better campaign produces a bigger initial shift in sales response.

Once obtained, adstock can be used alongside other measures in a mathematical model of sales. Some marketing departments go to considerable trouble to construct such models but the value of the exercise is open to doubt. Francis Bacon thought that mathematics made men subtle, wisdom he reserved for history. Mathematical modelling is certainly subtle but it requires the identification of the factors affecting sales. The model will fail if substantial determinants are omitted or if determinants change their degree of influence. Any model applies to the past and is an uncertain guide to the future where new and unmeasured determinants may appear and changes in the campaign, media schedule or competitor activity can play havoc with predictions. Barnard and Smith (1989) have written a useful guide to mathematical modelling.

Measuring long-term effects of advertising

The long-term sales gains produced by advertising are crucial to its profitability. If modest gains can be extended over a period of years then the advertising is more likely to pay for itself and may be much more attractive as an investment than sales promotions. For this reason the measurement of long-term effect is central to the debate on promotional expenditure and whether sales promotions really do give 'more bang for your buck'.

Some evidence (as yet unpublished) on long-term effects of advertising in the USA is now to hand. IRI looked at eight different products in a controlled experiment in which a test group received a higher weight of advertising than a control group for a year. Sales in the test group were raised to a mean of 25 per cent above the control group for the year. In the following year with no difference in advertising between the two groups the test group showed sales that were 29 per cent above the control group.

Five of the products could be followed into a further year and for these the figures were:

Test year   22% mean increase
1st year after test   28% mean increase
2nd year after test   8% mean increase

The value of this evidence lies in the clear demonstration that the effect of advertising can extend for over a year after the campaign has stopped, something that cannot be claimed for sales promotions. The study showed considerable differences between the brands studied and further research is needed to explain how longer-term advertising effects vary with market factors.

Advertising weight and sales response

Is there a threshold effect with increasing advertising weight? Krugman focused attention on this issue in a famous paper (Krugman, 1972). McDonald (1970, 1986) made a similar claim that two exposures of an advertisement in the inter-purchase interval was the optimal level but a detailed analysis by Broadbent (1986) did not. A threshold assumption could apply when the advertising *converts* people, i.e. gets people to try the product for the first time or gets people who were previously loyal to another brand to switch. Following this line of thought several exposures might be necessary to overcome habit. Support for a threshold effect can be found in studies of learning where behaviour changes pick up after the first few trials. Learning is required with new products but most advertising is for established brands where there is little switching and people generally have fairly constant dispositions to buy several brands in a product field. On this argument there need be no threshold for repetitively purchased goods.

A second process which may enhance the effect of a few exposures is the way a campaign may gather momentum from word of mouth and editorial comment. Particularly striking advertisements may cause people to discuss them. Others who have not seen the advertising but are involved in the discussion may be alerted to the advertisement so that it has more effect when they do see it. This is one of the effects of widely publicized complaints

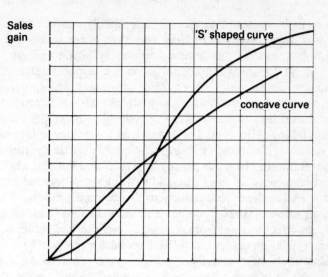

Figure 8.8 Possible relationships between sales gain and advertising weight

about an advertisement which may benefit the advertiser by making the public take notice of the offending advertisement.

Figure 8.8 illustrates two possible relationships between sales response and advertising weight. Three mechanisms can affect the shape of the 'S'-shaped curve. The first is the effect of threshold which causes the acceleration in the lower part of the curve; too few exposures would not get people over the threshold, hence the slow pick-up. The second mechanism is an aggregate effect. With more exposures the proportion of the population left below the threshold gets smaller and so the effect of advertising falls off at higher exposure levels. The third mechanism is a satiation effect. It is found that advertising, like reinforcement, loses some of its force as exposures become more frequent so that diminishing marginal effects are found (O'Herlihy, 1976). This mechanism is also responsible for the shape of the concave sales response curve.

Support for the 'S'-shaped curve is modest. O'Herlihy (1976) thought that it applied to new products. An 'S'-shaped curve was obtained for Swan Vestas matches (Broadbent, 1981, p. 115). Eastlack and Rao (1986) found that the advertising effect was 'S'-shaped for campaigns supporting V–8 vegetable juice. However

Steiner (1987) reports that the curve is usually concave toward the x-axis from the origin or from very near to the origin and a formidable review of one hundred studies by Simon and Arndt (1980) found dominant support for a concave response function.

Evidence on the sales response to advertising exposure also comes from weight tests. One might think that an increase in weight would lead to more sales and reductions in weight would lead to a falling off in sales. The research on advertising reductions does not always confirm these expectations. A classic controlled study of Budweiser beer advertising by Ackoff and Emshoff (1975) showed an increase in sales when advertising spend was reduced. There is also evidence that reductions in advertising may have no effect on sales. Aykac, Corstjens and Gauschi (1984) found no significant effect on sales from reduced advertising and Aaker and Carman (1982) report that no effects on sales were found for six products when their advertising budgets were reduced. At issue here is the long-term effect; usually studies do not follow the product long enough to see whether sales start to decline eventually.

Fulgoni (1987) looked at the proportion of BehaviorScan weight tests in the USA where significant increases in sales resulted from increases in advertising spend. Table 8.1 shows that a substantial proportion of tests give no statistically significant gain despite the fact that IRI's clients might be expected to pick cases where they expected an effect. Fulgoni (1987) points out that sometimes the increase in weight is confounded with a change in the media plan. If the new consumers reached are not buyers in the product field there will be no sales gain from the increase in advertising but this is a failure in media planning rather than weight. Fulgoni also suggests that weight test failures may be the result of indifferent copy; advertising which is ineffective will still be ineffective when its weight is doubled.

Table 8.1 *Percentage of BehaviorScan weight tests showing significant sales increases*

	1982	1984	1985
Established brands	41	41	55
New brands	54	64	77

The concavity of the advertising response function explains why advertisers try to achieve a wide reach and avoid high exposures per person. The diminished returns from extra exposures mean that it is better to have high cover rather than high levels of exposure. TV programmes that secure large audiences command higher rates per viewer because it is easier to secure a flat profile of exposures by using such programmes.

Ideas about advertising

Practitioner theories

Advertising practitioners have theories about how the advertisement should be constructed which they base on ideas about how consumers choose. Tuck (1977, ch. 2), who was herself a copy writer, provides an interesting account of these theories. Much of the early copy writing was based on the idea that, within limits, people responded rationally to an advertisement. The 'main promise' of the product was the basis of the copy platform. Reeves (1961) was the best-known exponent of this approach with his idea of the 'unique selling proposition' (USP), i.e. that feature of the brand, real or constructed, that differentiated it from the opposition.

Later, doubt set in about the changeability of preference by rational argument and a psychoanalytic approach developed. In the psychoanalytic account products were associated with unconscious desires in consumers and copy writers accepted the task of building on these hidden motives. In this they were aided in Britain by the expansion of commercial television; the visual medium is believed to be better for the direct transmission of such ideas. Another approach, developed by Ogilvy (1963), concentrated on the brand image which he treated as the set of associations and evaluations that placed the brand in relation to a person's life style. Ogilvy tended to give an up-market image; he liked to give his brands a 'first class ticket'.

Other practitioner ideas have been reviewed in Chapter 2, particularly the concepts of sole brand loyalty, conversion and the leaky bucket theory which are discredited by evidence that most people form stable dispositions to buy a portfolio of brands.

More recently Lannon and Cooper (1983) have promoted the idea that advertising is culturally situated and that it makes sense and influences people because it reflects the shared meanings in social groups and societies. They ask 'What do people do with advertising?' rather than 'What does advertising do to people?' and they argue that a person-centred anthropology of advertising is much more use to the creative staff who make advertisements. Lannon and Cooper argue that much British advertising draws heavily on shared cultural experience. They state: 'After Eight uses the myth of the upper class, an enduring archetype; Hovis uses the myth of the industrial working class sentimentalities combined with Yorkshire stubbornness; Mr. Kipling Cakes are made by an imaginary prototypical bespoke master baker living in a bespoke calendar art cottage; Courage recreates the pub of the 1920s/1930s as the preserve of the working class male; Campari uses a modern Eliza Doolittle figure.' The fact that this quotation still makes sense, years after it was made, further supports the idea that advertising draws on culturally shared meanings. Lannon and Cooper think that British television advertising has gained in popularity because it reflects well accepted archetypes.

The Lannon and Cooper approach has raised the importance of qualitative research in Britain because this type of investigation explores the ways in which brands are used and thought about by different social groups. It also bodes ill for attempts to produce advertisements that work well across several cultures. However, because Lannon and Cooper's approach to advertising is essentially qualitative, it demands a case-by-case treatment and does not provide us with substantive generalizations. One point of contact should be noted between Lannon and Cooper's ideas and the research reported in Chapter 7. The 'culturally shared archetype' is a schema which aids recognition and thought.

Practitioners have also developed theories about the stages whereby influence comes about. One of the earliest was 'AIDA': Awareness, Interest, Desire, Action. Such theories rest on an analysis of what is necessary if influence is to be achieved. It is supposed that a communication must gain attention, then comprehension, acceptance, and modification of beliefs before finally securing action. A benefit of this linear sequential model is that it suggests a programme of copy testing for the agency. Colley (1961) developed this approach with 'DAGMAR' (Defining Advertising Goals for Measured Advertising Results) which is still an influence in copy design and testing, particularly in the USA. DAGMAR assumes that effective advertising follows a path: awareness, comprehension, conviction and action and this leads to advertising objectives and tests for each one of these stages. Another similar model was proposed by Lavidge and Steiner (1961).

Lannon (1985) and Lannon and Cooper (1983) argue that models like DAGMAR fail in two respects. Firstly they imply that people are passive receivers and thus present a partial account of purchasing and consumer experience, and secondly they ignore how people behave as consumers. I think that they overstate their case here; effective advertising must leave traces in some of the individual recipients and a sensible programme of research sets out to detect these traces which must exist whether the consumer is active or passive. There are other criticisms that may be made of sequential models. They ignore the repetitive nature of most buying by making conversion rather than reinforcement the object of advertising effort. They also fail on the evidence since the connection between the stages of the sequence is poor. This is examined in greater detail below.

The Yale research

The development of models like DAGMAR is associated with the work of Hovland, Rosenberg, McGuire, Abelson, Brehm, Janis and Festinger in the Yale Communication and Attitude Change Program. Their work is designed to answer the questions: 'Who said what? Via which media? To whom? With what effect?' It led to research on the credibility of sources, attention to and comprehension of messages, acceptance by recipients of messages, and the design of persuasive communications. Some of the results were unsurprising, for example that people believe someone who is expert more readily than someone who is not, but the research produced a stream of empirical findings some of which have a bearing on the construction of advertising.

There were early critics of the Yale approach. Krugman (1965) suggested that a sequential model was less suited to the shallow information processing initiated by low involvement purchase. He proposed that information might directly affect behaviour and attitude change might follow later. Festinger (1964) found few cases of attitude change where the sequence was followed through to 'action'.

In the sequence of effect model the link from attention to

understanding and recall has not been well substantiated in advertising research. Pomerance (1977) reviewed a large number of agency studies and found no correlation between attention to an advertisement (i.e. whether respondents stopped a display for closer inspection of the advertisement) and later tests of advertisement recall. Further doubts have been expressed about the relevance of comprehension in advertisement tests. It may be useful to pick up misunderstandings of the copy using checklists or focus groups. But are the points which are remembered relevant to eventual purchase? Comprehension tests probably help to eliminate some bad copy but may not help much in pinpointing the version with the strongest effect on sales. The link between recall and purchasing is badly supported. Gibson (1983) found little support for recall as an indication of eventual behavioural effect. Ross (1982) found that recall did give some prediction of purchase but brand preference changes predicted purchase better. A survey by Ostlund, Clancy and Sapra (1980) cited a number of studies giving poor support to recognition and recall methods for assessing advertising but noted that these methods retained their popularity despite this.

Exercise 8.1. Advertisement recall and product use

1 In class make a list of advertisements that you can recall from the last week's television viewing.

2 What are the aspects of the advertisement that make it memorable? Are these advertisements for products that you use?

Correspondence

One deficiency in the Yale School approach has been analysed by Fishbein and Ajzen (1975, ch. 11). Their theory of reasoned action embodies a sequence of effect among corresponding measures (as discussed in Chapter 3). A problem with the Yale approach is that measures are not corresponding. Measures of attention, reception and recall of a message are unlikely to correlate well with the quite different measure of purchase. The measures that relate to purchase will be beliefs about purchase, attitude to purchase and intention to purchase. Ajzen and Fishbein suggest that correspondence is the key to understanding whether the sequence of effect is found. Without correspondence advertisements may be understood and accepted by consumers without affecting their motivations to purchase. Occasionally an advertisement may be misunderstood but produce belief changes that do affect purchase. Another failure of the sequential model occurs when people receive the intended message but make inferences from it that counteract purchase.

An example of correspondence in persuasive communication is provided by a study by McArdle in 1972 which is summarized by Ajzen and Fishbein (1980). McArdle tried to persuade alcoholics to join an alcoholic treatment unit (ATU) using three experimental methods and a control condition. In a traditional fear appeal the dire consequences of continued drinking were spelled out. In a second negative condition these same consequences were related to not signing for the ATU. In the third positive condition these conditions were presented as costs avoided by signing for the ATU. In the fourth control condition there was no message. In all conditions the alcoholics were invited 'to sign up for the ATU now'.

The results appear in Table 8.2 which shows subsequent signing up for those who were initially willing and those who were initially unwilling to take this action. Signing up was significantly lower in the traditional fear appeal group, lower even than the control. Analysis of beliefs showed that the traditional fear group had accepted the message in the form presented as the consequences of continued drinking but had failed to make inferences to signing up for the ATU. The other two experimental groups had received a message which bore directly on the consequences of signing or not signing for the ATU. In these conditions many accepted and changed relevant beliefs, increasing their support for signing for the ATU. In these groups signing up was significantly above control level. In the traditional fear appeal the sequence of effect did not occur because the message was off-target.

McArdle's data have a parallel in consumer advertising that concentrates on the product rather than the purchase. For example a consumer may accept a message about the prospective return from share investments but not buy because of fears about the procedures for purchase; a message that dealt with purchase would

Table 8.2 *Percentage of participants signing up for an alcoholic treatment unit*

Appeal	Initially	
	Unwilling (%)	Willing (%)
Traditional	5	50
Not signing	30	100
Signing	20	95
Control	14	82

be more appropriate. Lack of correspondence is thus one reason for the low correlations between measures drawn up on the basis of DAGMAR. The correlations are also low because the influence of advertising is quite weak so that even relevant changes may have little impact. Beyond this is the problem that much advertising may work by associative mechanisms that do not fit the theory of reasoned action or similar models. When the choice lies between brands that scarcely differ from each other there is little scope for a reasoned argument.

Awareness, trial and reinforcement

Ehrenberg's (1974) awareness, trial and reinforcement (ATR) model of advertising shifts the emphasis to the post-purchase period. Since most brands are familiar to consumers it is important to get people to repeat their purchases. Awareness and trial apply only to unfamiliar products. Since people do not usually switch but retain split loyalties to several brands, the need is to maintain and, if possible, enhance these loyalties, and since this happens after experience with the brand the process is partly retrospective and not just prospective. The idea that most advertising takes people along a road to Damascus and converts them to the brand is absurd in many cases and yet it remains the assumption of many people including some advertising professionals.

One reason for this reluctance to accept any other paradigm is the fact that conversion fits the easily accessed causal schema described in Chapter 7. Even in situations where conversion seems to make sense there may be better reinforcement approaches that are not so obvious. Does party political advertising convert the opposition or retain existing supporters? Should advertising against smoking try to convert existing smokers or support recent ex-smokers who will mostly return to cigarettes? If you are promoting a new car do you convert people to the car or work on getting them into the showroom as Mazda did (Channon, 1987)? Most people have been in a car showroom before.

The ATR model emphasizes the importance of existing users and it focuses attention on points in the purchasing process where reinforcement advertising may be effective. For these reasons it is important in the definition of advertising strategy but it does not seem to me that there has been a clear specification of the psychological processes that are implied by a reinforcement concept of advertising. Two processes that might be favoured by a reinforcement approach but seem less appropriate on close scrutiny are psychological reinforcement and cognitive dissonance. Reinforcement in the sense that Skinner used the term is not practicable in media advertising. In Skinner's research on conditioning the reinforcement was effective because it took place at the same time and in the same place as the response that it was designed to modify and neither of these conditions applies to media advertising.

Important purchases may arouse post-purchase dissonance and make the buyer more aware of brand related information and more keen to justify the purchase to others. Ehrenberg mentions that process but dissonance cannot apply to minor purchases which produce no arousal. Dissonance occurs when the purchase decision was difficult to make and remains hard to justify and these conditions do not apply to most repetitive purchasing.

One process that is relevant to the ATR model is selective perception. Past experience with a product increases the accessibility of attitudes used to interpret advertising so that information and advertising relevant to a past purchase is more readily perceived.

Classifying advertising

Advertising has to achieve its limited effect by the use of symbols: words and images and their associated beliefs and evaluations. It is these symbols that mobilize corresponding symbolic forms in the minds of recipients, a process which may make people more alert to certain brands and think more (or sometimes less) favourably about buying and using them. Some of these processes may have an inferential or logical form while others may be simple associations that take place with little awareness.

In this process the skills of the creative designer are of enormous importance and Alesandrini (1983) lists some of the more definable techniques that should be used (and which rest on the use of available schemata): giving information form and relevance, using pictures and incorporating these in the message form, chunking data for easier recall, agenda setting and trading on existing learning with analogy and metaphor. Advertisements may also reveal an influence strategy. They may:

- be informative about the price and the benefits of using the brand;
- reposition the brand;
- differentiate the brand from others;
- emphasize the brand name, pack and other visual features so that the brand is recognized when it is seen;
- use disturbing images to secure attention;
- employ well-known people;
- be entertaining or startlingly creative;
- use associations with existing values and images;
- seek to reassure purchasers;
- seek to convert non-purchasers;
- encourage people to commend the brand;
- imply that many people already use the brand;
- imply that few are discriminating enough to use it;
- tell the audience how to obtain the brand;
- sell the corporate image or the family brand name.

Are there any methods which help us to choose which sort of advertising tactic to use? One approach is to look for copy or execution features that differentiate the good advertisements from the bad. For example, Stewart and Furse (1984) found that brand differentiating factors were most important to successful advertising while Moldovan (1984) found that credibility was most important followed by stimulation, taste, empathy and clarity. Brown (1986) found from many studies that the advertisement that produced more awareness was the one that was more arresting, and therefore attended to, but he argued that the creative features must embrace the brand name. Brown thinks that the advertisement must convey the idea that many others buy the brand and that experience with the brand will justify the claims in the advertisement.

Such judgements about what makes an effective advertisement are made with hindsight and may treat chance differences as though they were real causes. They neglect the fact that advertising has many different forms and that this may prohibit generalizations about effectiveness. Thus, we need classifications of advertising, buyer decision making and purchasing behaviour that reduces these heterogeneous concepts to more precise ideas that might be explained.

One approach is based on the assumption that advertising should fit the consumer decision-making process found for the product advertised. An example of this is the Foote, Cone, Belding (FCB) Grid reviewed by Vaughn (1980, 1986) and Ratchford (1987). The grid uses an x-axis that divides thinking-centred decisions from feeling-centred ones and a y-axis that expresses high and low involvement. The two axes produce four quadrants. The model is illustrated in Figure 8.9. Confectionery purchases might be feeling-related and low involving while the purchase of a new television set will appear diagonally opposite as high involving and thoughtful.

Typologies like this have limited value for classifying advertising. Thought and feeling are not necessarily antithetical and just because a purchase is low involving and feeling based does not mean that the advertising must have this pattern. The advertising is not usually received at the time of purchase so why should it fit the purchase process? Thus the nature of the purchase decision does not lead to any clear rules on the type of advertising used; in any case advertising frequently uses several different modes of influence at once. To compound the problem further, different people may decide in different ways and be influenced by advertising in different ways.

The value of purchase decision classifications which guess at the thinking of the consumer seems low and the FCB grid is simplistic. It is better to look for more visible aspects of purchase and here my original dimensions introduced in Chapter 1 of frequency, importance and freedom of purchase have merit because they imply different sets of human response and suggest different emphases in advertising. Different processes associated with frequency and importance have been shown in work done at Stanford

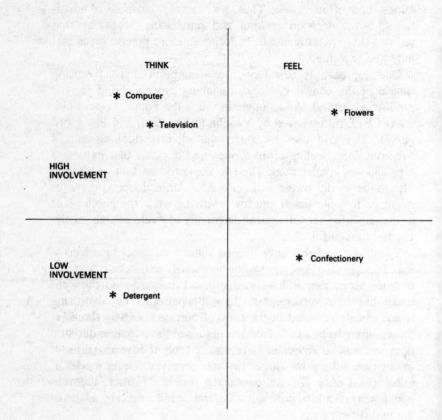

Figure 8.9 The FCB grid

University by Batra and Ray (1983). They found evidence for three different sequences of response in subjects:

1 A low-involvement process, consistent with Krugman's (1965) ideas about how people respond to television advertising, where the advertisement affected ideas and increased purchase disposition without any direct change in attitude. When attitude was changed it followed changes in purchase disposition and probably arose from a reduction in response competition (see Mere Exposure, Chapter 7). Batra and Ray thought that such advertising worked by counteracting tendencies to forget the brand and through the reduction in response competition. According to Batra and Ray, most advertising has this form.

2 A high-involvement sequence, following the Ajzen and Fishbein theory, in which changes occurred in the order: thought, attitude, intention. This was found in a study of political advertising and was most often conveyed through the print medium.

3 A high-involvement sequence which they called *dissonance-attribution* in which the behaviour occurred first and was followed by changes in attitude and then belief. This sequence occurred when there were few apparent differences between important alternatives, e.g. cars. It was more common when personal influence was the factor that precipitated purchase.

Batra and Ray find that repetition has little effect under high involvement. There is a threshold and people 'get the point' so that further exposures produce no more change. Thus for this sort of influence a wide-reach and low-exposure strategy is required. By contrast low-involvement learning is facilitated by repetition.

One other approach to the way in which advertising works is simply to list the processes that may be found. When advertising does have an effect it may:

– raise evaluation and recognition by mere exposure;
– increase brand recognition and brand name recall through classical conditioning (i.e. by associating the brand with pleasant stimuli);
– control attention and arousal;
– frame the choice differently;
– use schemata to modify or transform the way in which the brand is perceived (repositioning involves this process);

- use heuristic mechanisms such as representativeness and availability so that the brand is recognized or recalled more easily;
- provide information which reduces arousal and helps people
  to interpret their experience of the brand;
- get people to use word-of-mouth influence on prospective
  purchasers.

It is inevitable with such complexity that we are not going to be
able to explain 'how advertising works'. We may, however, be
able to explain how some particular advertisements work, given
time and research.

Pre-testing copy

Exercise 8.2. Two hypothetical campaigns

How would you assess whether the two hypothetical campaigns
described below would be successful? What would improve the
design of advertisements? List *all* the psychological processes that
might be involved.

Campaign A is for Black and Decker smoke alarms and supplies
authoritative details about how people would be saved from fires
if a smoke alarm woke them up before they were asphyxiated. It
mentions the low cost of the alarm, and its ease of purchase and
fixing. In this way the motivation to buy the product class is
harnessed and directed to a particular brand using plausible
claims about that brand's particular benefits. The product and the
advertising campaign lend themselves to a rational campaign for
which reasoned action theory provides an explanative structure.
Psychological processes of fear avoidance, self-defence and belief
revision can be brought into play.

Campaign B is more creative. It is for Andrex toilet paper and here
there are considerable constraints on any rational approach. It is
not that people lack reasons for using toilet paper; they are all
fully convinced and there are few non-users to be recruited.
Telling users of a brand that the paper is soft, strong and very
long (Channon, 1987, p. 179) merely repeats what they already
know through experience, and more detailed explanations about
the way the tissue performs its functions are socially

unacceptable. Andrex is one of several similar soft toilet papers so the campaign must use marginal differences between the brands.

One feature of Andrex is that it is packed in a paper cover, unlike most other brands which are sold in plastic covers. The campaign makes a virtue of this difference. On television the theme is 'How long does it take to load a roll of Andrex?' The starting point is a two-roll pack. Assorted individuals are seen to split the pack with greater or lesser skill, remove the paper on one of the rolls and mount it on a toilet roll holder. Champions emerge who split the pack across their knee, toss one roll aside, impale the paper cover of the remaining roll on their finger, draw it off, and load the roll in a few seconds. Disasters happen (e.g. the discarded roll falls into the lavatory bowl), rules are announced, a new four-pack competition starts, children demand Andrex and parents complain about the broken packs that litter their houses. The plastic-covered competition is powerless to respond.

Stages in copy development

The development of advertising begins with ideas for the copy. After this copy is designed and modified, the advertisement is constructed, used, and eventually it is discarded. Alongside the development of advertising is a research process. Which theme should be chosen? Does the chosen theme have any impact in its draft form? Which completed advertisements should be used with what weighting? Should the completed advertisement be used in a limited campaign first before going national? Is the advertisement worn out and due for replacement? Tests before the launch of a campaign are called pre-tests; those that follow the progress of an advertisement in use are called post-tests.

Diagnosis and comparison

It is important to recognize that there are two different requirements in pre-testing. One is *diagnostic* and is concerned with the themes that are more suitable for a campaign. Here the research must produce information about which features of a product should be given most emphasis. This sort of work can also lead to product modifications. The second requirement is *comparative*, to show how effective different advertisements are. As the advertisement passes from idea through to the completed version the emphasis shifts from diagnosis to comparsion.

A large amount of money must be spent to develop advertising. Print advertisements require costly artwork and TV advertisements cost much more per minute than ordinary television programmes. Thus early diagnoses of the better theme and better copy avoid wasted expenditure. There are two major problems facing those seeking to test advertisements at an early stage. Firstly the primitive versions of the advertisement, e.g. the storyboard or video animatic, lack the details of execution which may be crucial to its success; actors, graphics, voices and music all add to the effect of the advertisement but are absent from the pretests. This problem is particularly acute for television advertisements. The second problem is that it is difficult at this stage to test the effects of the advertisement on real purchase without artificiality.

A variety of methods are used for evaluating the early form of advertisements. The discussion group is popular in Britain both for establishing possible campaign themes and for assessing the initial copy. As a copy test the discussion group can be effective in eliminating vagueness, ambiguity and negative effects but it has not been shown to be effective at picking the best version from several alternatives. One problem about the discussion group is that the members influence each other and the whole process is filtered through the perceptions of the group leader who writes the report. With one group leader and often only four groups the scope for bias is large.

Some research has cast doubt on the ability of people to judge advertisement effectiveness. Bogart, Tolley and Orenstein (1970) found that 83 advertising professionals could give some prediction of the recall and recognition effects of advertisements (correlations 0.64 and 0.55 respectively) but they were unable to predict which advertisements had the most effect on sales. Similarly Mackie and Valentine (1975) found that judges of eight leaflets designed to encourage seatbelt usage rated two leaflets first and second which turned out to be fourth and fifth in effectiveness when driver behaviour was observed.

An advertisement must be *received* in some sense. At the very least it must secure attention if it is to have any effect. Thus a persisting line of investigation has been into the activating effect of the advertisement. One approach is physiological: when the subject observes the advertisement, measures are made of pupil size and direction of gaze, skin conductance, and the activity in the two hemispheres of the brain. Although such methods disclose arousal there is some difficulty in interpreting this. People can be aroused by unpleasant as well as by pleasant stimuli so that the behavioural implication of arousal is uncertain. Arousal is also measured psychologically using verbal enquiries about the advertisement: was it amusing, interesting, etc.? The use of such tests is plausible. Ray and Batra (1983) have pointed out that an advertisement that excites may direct attention and start people thinking, and a study by Mehrotra, van Auken and Lonial (1981) showed small but significant correlations between a measure of advertisement interest using an adjective checklist and measures of intention change. However Sullivan and O'Connor (1983) found little relationship between an evaluative checklist measure of response to advertising and a behavioural intention measure. These studies suggest that measures of emotional response to advertisements are weak predictors of sales effect. Other tests have used day-after-recall and recognition. Earlier it was reported that these measures show poor correlation with 'downstream' measures of brand preference, purchase intention and actual sales.

Intention to buy

When the sales impact of copy cannot be used as a test criterion there is a strong case for using intention as a proxy for actual purchase. At the end of Chapter 3 and in Chapters 4 and 5 considerable research was presented showing how intention was related to action.

The case is particularly strong in the case of consumer durables because intention is more likely to be a cause of action when purchase is infrequent. Intention is also used as a post-testing criterion in such markets because the long interpurchase intervals make any sales response slow to appear (e.g. the Ford Granada case in Channon, 1987, p. 213).

Turning to frequently purchased goods we know from Bird

and Ehrenberg (1966) that there is a close relationship between intention and purchase/usage and that their evidence suggested that usage led to intention. But given the evidence in Chapter 3 it is likely that an intention formed by product experience can be modified by advertising and that when this occurs there is some impact on consumption.

How could intention to buy fail as a criterion of advertising effect? Firstly, it fails when the advertising serves some purpose other than sales promotion, e.g. to support a higher price. In this case a measure of brand appeal that offsets the effect of price may be more suitable. When advertising stimulates distribution it may have little effect on the intentions of purchasers though it may affect the intentions of sales staff and retailers. In non-profit contexts advertising is designed to induce some action other than purchase. For example to drive carefully or eat less fatty foods. A different intention criterion is required in these cases. Rather less obvious is the type of advertising that induces the recipient to influence others to buy; this requires an 'intention to recommend the brand' criterion.

Secondly, the intention criterion will fail when advertising influences buying by some route that avoids intention. The review of the sufficiency principle in Chapter 5 showed that this does occur. In some cases there is a direct path from past experience to later behaviour, possibly because cues to action are learned unconsciously. Advertising could set up purchase cues of which the respondent is unaware. Recognition tests might be useful in detecting such an effect. The theory of planned behaviour also indicated that perceived control relates directly to action as well as through intention so that the intention measure may understate the sales gains that are induced by a change in the perceived opportunity to purchase. This suggests that a measure of 'ease of purchase' may have a place for testing some advertising. Finally, when the copy is evaluated in artificial circumstances, there is a need to establish its power to secure attention under the circumstances in which it will be used. There is thus some case for measuring the attention drawing effect of advertising.

Intention is thus an imperfect guide to advertising effect but is probably the best single proxy for actual sales that is available. It follows that, in general, advertisements are best pre-tested by measuring their impact on intention. When the change of intention has a basis in changes of belief it may be possible to diagnose these belief changes. This is useful at the early stage in developing advertisements when a decision on copy theme is required. This rational line of enquiry makes sense with some brands and many product types and would be suitable in the Black and Decker smoke alarm case.

When actions can be traced back to beliefs and evaluations there are two sorts of research that are required. As explained in Chapter 5 it is necessary to find out which beliefs are related to intention and also whether these beliefs are changeable. This is the basis of *key belief analysis* which is described by East (1984).

Frequently purchased goods like Andrex are consciously bought. If asked, people can indicate their propensity to purchase as an intention and can divide their likelihood of purchase across a range of brands. Thus intention may serve as a criterion of advertisement effectiveness in this market too.

The case for using intention is enhanced by evidence that the current practice in copy research is inadequate. A survey by Jobber and Kilbride in 1986 showed continuing support for assessing advertising copy by using brand and copy attitudes, comprehension and interest. The intention criterion is not going to revolutionize the pre-testing of copy. Nothing will do this because the early stage of copy development is too remote from actual purchase for any test to be very effective. However the available evidence suggests that the best hope lies in using the intention criterion for the pre-testing of advertisements.

Summary

Advertising and sales promotions form part of a mix of marketing activity. It is generally believed that parts of this mix act synergistically to help other parts. In particular advertising can support price and distribution as well as sales.

The use of sales promotions has risen in the last decade and media advertising has fallen as a proportion of promotional spending. Some practitioners claim better returns from sales promotions but business pressures provide another reason for their use. Advertising agencies argue that media advertising can have a long term effect that is hard to measure.

Scanner panels and surveys provide data on store sales for short periods. This type of research is very accurate and has revealed serious deficiencies in USA diary panel data. Scanner panel research has shown how much sales promotions increase sales, how there is little carry over of effect into the post-promotion period and that sales promotions often have little effect on competitors' sales. The research indicates some mutual support between price cut, display and local advertising and also suggests that, in the USA, some people base their grocery purchases on promotions and rarely buy at normal prices.

In the USA techniques for swapping the TV advertisements received by households have made it possible to run experimental tests on copy, weight and media schedule alternatives and to use the scanner record of purchase as the criterion of advertisement effectiveness.

The effect of media advertisements on sales varies with product, copy, medium and market factors. An advertising campaign normally produces a much smaller effect on buying rate than a sales promotion but the response to advertising persists over a longer time and may have some long-term effect on base levels. Advertising influence over a period should be measured using the adstock model which allows for the decay of effect of an exposure over time. The shape of the sales response to advertising weight remains a matter of debate but it seems likely that it is concave for many repetitively purchased goods. For new products and in some other cases sales may show an 'S'-shaped relationship with exposure level, indicating threshold effects. A better understanding of the relationship between advertisement weight and response will help in decisions about media buying.

Ideas about the nature of advertising have been expressed by the practitioners themselves, by social psychologists and by marketing researchers. There has been an over-emphasis on the 'conversion' role of advertisements and an under-emphasis on the 'reinforcement' role of maintaining repeat purchase. A continuing interest is in classifications that will help to define the sort of advertisement that is effective for particular types of purchase. Dividing purchases by frequency, importance and voluntariness helps us to distinguish the sorts of process involved in the purchase decision but it is readily admitted that the explanation of advertising effect is in its infancy.

There are major cost savings to be achieved by early testing of advertising copy but this is hindered by the initially incomplete form of the advertisement and by the artificiality of the testing situation. On the evidence available advertisements may be pre-tested using an 'intention to buy' criterion but this may need to be supplemented by other tests.

Further reading

Gabor, A. (1988) *Pricing, Concepts and Methods for Effective Marketing*, 2nd ed. Vermont, Gower

Totten, J. C. and Block, M. P. (1987) *Analyzing Sales Promotion: Text and Cases*. Chicago, Commerce Communications Inc., ch. 3

Broadbent, S. (1984) *20 Advertising Case Histories*. London, Holt, Rinehart and Winston

Broadbent, S. (1989) *The Advertising Budget: The Advertiser's Guide to Budget Determination*. Henley, NTC Publications

Glossary

Adstock is a transformation of the TVR schedule. It is a weighted sum of TVRs for a period. The weights allow for the decay in the effect of the advertisement on the viewer from the time when the advertisement was seen.

Average Frequency is the mean number of times the target population is exposed to a given advertisement in a period.

Bar codes are the line markings on product packs which can be read by scanners at supermarket checkouts. In the USA the bar code is called the *Universal Product Code (UPC)*.

Copy is the material presented in the advertisement.

Copy test is a technique to evaluate the impact of the copy on recall, comprehension, attention, arousal, interest, intention to buy or actual purchase.

Coverage, *see* Reach.

Creative is used to describe both the advertisement and the people who design it.

Effectiveness. In the commercial context an effective advertise-ment is one that raises the profit trend. This may occur through increased sales, by holding back sales decline, by supporting price levels and by ensuring that the brand is stocked by stores. In non-profit contexts the effectiveness of an advertisement has to be measured by the change in behaviour that it produces, for example by the reduction in road accidents for a given adspend.

Elasticity of advertising is the percent gain in sales for a 1 per cent increase in advertising spend.

Execution is the way in which the copy is presented using actors, intonations, emphasis, etc.

Opportunities to See (OTS) is also used to describe level of exposure. Usually the measure is used to show the fraction of the population reaching a given OTS.

Period is the time unit in which an advertising measurement is expressed, e.g. exposures per quarter.

Reach is the proportion of a target population exposed to the advertisement at least once in a period.

Television Rating (TVR) is the proportion of the potential audience exposed to the commercial. It is therefore the reach of a television advertisement but it is also used to accumulate total television exposure in a period. For example a campaign may be credited with 200 TVRs derived from 20 different showings of the advertisement at an average rating of 10.

Weight of advertising is the number of exposures in a period.

Weight test measures the impact on sales of changes in the weight of advertising.

References

Aaker, D. and Carman, J. (1982) Are you overadvertising? *Journal of Advertising Research* **22**, 4, 57–70

Aaker, D. A. and Day, G. S. (1986) *Marketing Research*, 3rd ed., New York, Wiley

Abelson, R. P. (1972) Are attitudes necessary? In: King, B. T. and McGinnies, E. (eds) *Attitudes, Conflict and Social Change*. New York, Academic Press, pp. 19–32

Ackoff, R. L. and Emshoff, J. R. (1975) Advertising research at Anheuser-Busch Inc. 1963–68. *Sloan Management Review*, Winter, 1–15. Also in: Enis, B. M. and Cox, K. K. (1985) *Marketing Classics: a Selection of Influential Articles*. 5th ed., London, Allyn & Bacon, pp. 413–24

Ajzen, I. (1971) Attitude vs. normative messages: an investigation of the differential effects of persuasive communications on behavior. *Sociometry* **34**, 263–80

Ajzen, I. (1985) From intentions to actions: a theory of planned behavior. In: Kuhl, J. and Beckmann, J. (eds) *Action-control: From Commitment to Behavior*. Heidelberg, Springer

Ajzen, I. and Fishbein, M. (1969) The prediction of behavioral intentions in a choice situation. *Journal of Experimental Social Psychology* **5**, 400–16

Ajzen, I. and Fishbein, M. (1972) Attitudinal and normative variables as factors influencing behavioral intentions. *Journal of Personality and Social Psychology* **27**, 41–57

Ajzen, I. and Fishbein, M. (1977) Attitude–behavior relations: a theoretical analysis and review of empirical research. *Psychological Bulletin* **84**, 888–918

Ajzen, I. and Fishbein, M. (1980) *Understanding Attitudes and Predicting Social Behavior*. Englewood Cliffs, NJ, Prentice-Hall

Ajzen, I. and Madden, T. J. (1986) Prediction of goal directed behavior: attitudes, intentions and perceived behavioral control. *Journal of Experimental Social Psychology* **22**, 453–74

Alesandrini, K. L. (1983) Strategies that influence memory for advertising communications. In: Harris, R. L. (ed.) *Information Processing*

Research in Advertising. London, Lawrence Erlbaum Associates, pp. 65–82

Allais, M. (1953) Le comportement de l'homme rationel devant le risque: critique des postulats et axiomes de l'école américaine. *Econometrica* **21**, 503–46

Allport, G. W. (1935) Attitudes. In: Murchison, C. (ed.) *A Handbook of Social Psychology*. Worcester, MA, Clark University Press, pp. 798–844.

Aykac, A., Corstjens, M. and Gautschi, D. (1984) Is there a kink in your advertising? *Journal of Advertising Research* **24**, 3, 27–36

Bagozzi, R. P. (1981) Attitudes, intentions and behavior: a test of some key hypotheses. *Journal of Personality and Social Psychology* **41**, 607–27

Bagozzi, R. P. (1988) The rebirth of attitude research in marketing. *Journal of the Market Research Society* **30**, 2, 163–95

Bales, R. F. and Strodtbeck, F. L. (1951) Phases in group problem solving. *Journal Abnormal and Social Psychology* **46**, 485–95

Bandura, A. (1977) Self-efficacy: toward a unifying theory of behavioral change. *Psychological Review* **84**, 191–215

Barker, R. G., Dembo, T. and Lewin, K. (1941) Frustration and regression: an experiment with young children. *University of Iowa Studies in Child Welfare* **18**, 1

Barnard, N. R. (1987) Lecture to Centre for Marketing and Communication, London Business School

Barnard, N. R., Barwise, T. P. and Ehrenberg, A. S. C. (1986) Reinterviews in attitude research. MRS Conference, Brighton

Barnard, N. R. and Smith, G. (1989) *Advertising and Modelling: An Introductory Guide*. London, Institute of Practitioners in Advertising

Bartlett, F. C. (1932) *Remembering*. Cambridge, UK, Cambridge University Press

Barwise, T. P. (1986) Repeat-viewing of prime time TV series. *Journal of Advertising Research*, August/September 9–14

Barwise, T. P. and Ehrenberg, A. S. C. (1985) Consumer beliefs and brand usage. *Journal of the Market Research Society* **27**, 81–93

Barwise, T. P. and Ehrenberg, A. S. C. (1987) Consumer beliefs and awareness. *Journal of the Market Research Society* **29**, 1, 88–94

Bass, F. M., Givon, M. M., Kalwani, M. U., Reibstein, D. and Wright, G. P. (1984) An investigation into the order of the brand choice process. *Marketing Science* **3**, 4, 267–87

Bass, F. M. and Talarzyk, W. W. (1972) An attitude model for the study of brand preference. *Journal of Marketing Research* **IX**, 93–6

Batra, R. and Ray, M. L. (1983) Advertising situations: the implications of differential involvement and accompanying affect responses. In: Harris, R. L. (ed.) *Information Processing Research in Advertising*, London, Lawrence Erlbaum Associates, pp. 127–51

Beales, H., Mazis, M. B., Salop, S. C. and Staelin, R. (1981) Consumer search and public policy. *Journal of Consumer Research* **8**, June, 11–22

Belson, W. (1988) Major error from two commonly used methods of market and social research. *Market Research Society Newsletter*, August, p. 33

Bem, D. J. (1967) Self-perception: an alternative explanation of cognitive dissonance phenomena. *Psychological Review* **74**, 183–200

Bentler, P. M. and Speckart, G. (1979) Models of attitude–behavior relations. *Psychological Review* **86**, 5, 452–64

Bentler, P. M. and Speckart, G. (1981) Attitudes 'cause' behaviors: a structural equation analysis. *Journal of Personality and Social Psychology* **40**, 226–38

Berlyne, D. E. (1954) A theory of human curiosity. *British Journal of Psychology* **45**, 180–91

Berlyne, D. E. (1965) *Structure and Direction in Thinking*. London, Wiley.

Berlyne, D. E. and McDonnell, P. (1965) Effects of stimulus complexity and incongruity on duration of EEG desynchonisation. *Electroencephalography and Clinical Neurophysiology* **18**, 156–61

Bernoulli, D. (1738) Specimen Theoriae novae de mensura sortis. *Comentarii Academiae Scientiarum Imperiales Petropolitanae* **5**, 175–92. Translated by L. Sommer in *Econometrica* (1954) **22**, 23–36

Bettman, J. R. (1977) Data collection and analysis approaches for studying consumer information processing. In: Perreault, W. D., Jr (ed.) *Advances in Consumer Research*, vol. 4. Atlanta, Association for Consumer Research, pp. 342–8

Bettman, J. R. and Park, C. W. (1980) Implications of a constructive view of choice for analysis of protocol data: a coding scheme for elements of choice processes. In: Olson, J. C. (ed.) *Advances in Consumer Research*, vol. VII. Ann Arbor, MI, Association for Consumer Research, pp. 148–53

Bettman, J. R. and Zins, M. A. (1977) Constructive processes in consumer choice. *Journal of Consumer Research* **4**, 75–85

Bird, M. and Ehrenberg, A. S. C. (1966) Intentions-to-buy and claimed brand usage. *Operational Research Quarterly* **17**, 27–46

Bird, M. and Ehrenberg, A. S. C. (1970) Consumer attitudes and brand usage. *Journal of the Market Research Society* **12**, 233–47; **13**, 100–1; **14**, 57–8

Bogart, L., Tolley, S. and Orenstein, F. (1970) What one little ad can do. *Journal of Advertising Research* **10**, 3–13

Brehm, J. W. (1956) Post-decisional changes in the desirability of alternatives. *Journal of Abnormal and Social Psychology* **52**, 384–9

Brehm, J. W. and Cohen, A. R. (1962) *Explorations in Cognitive Dissonance*, New York, Wiley

Broadbent, S. (1981) *Advertising Works*. Institute of Practitioners of Advertising 1980 Advertising Effectiveness Awards. London, Holt, Rinehart & Winston, 78–88

Broadbent, S. (1983) *Advertising Works 2*. Institute of Practitioners of Advertising 1982 Advertising Effectiveness Awards. London, Holt, Rinehart & Winston, pp. 26–41

Broadbent, S. (1984) Modelling with adstock. *Journal of the Market Research Society* **26**, 4, 295–312

Broadbent, S. (1986) 'Two OTS in a purchase interval' – some questions. *Admap* **22**, 11, 12–16

Broadbent, S. (1988) Advertising effects – more methodological issues. *Journal of the Market Research Society* **30**, 2, 225–7

Broadbent, S. (1989) *The Advertising Budget: The Advertiser's Guide to Budget Determination.* Henley, NTC Publications

Broadbent, S. and Colman, S. (1986) Advertising effectiveness: across brands. *Journal of the Market Research Society* **28**, 1, 15–24

Brown, G. (1985) Tracking studies and sales effects: a UK perspective. *Journal of Advertising Research* **25**, 1, 52–64

Brown, G. (1986) Monitoring advertising performance. *Admap* **22**, 3, 151–3

Burnkrant, R. E. and Unnava, H. R. (1987) Effects of variation in message execution of the learning of repeated brand information. In: Wallendorf, M. and Anderson, P. (eds) *Advances in Consumer Research*, vol. XIV. Provo, UT, Association for Consumer Research, pp. 173–6

Campbell, D. T. (1963) Social attitudes and other acquired behavioral dispositions. In: Koch, S. (ed.) *Psychology: A Study of a Science*, vol. 6. New York, McGraw-Hill, pp. 94–172

Castleberry, S. B. and Ehrenberg, A. S. C. (1986) Price changes and price differences. University of Georgia Working Paper

Channon, C. (1985) *Advertising Works 3*. London, Holt, Rinehart & Winston

Channon, C. (1987) *Advertising Works 4*. London, Cassell

Clare, J. E. and Kiser, C. V. (1951) Preference for children of a given sex in relation to fertility. In: Whelpton, P. K. and Kiser, C. V. (1946–58) (eds) *Social and Psychological Factors Affecting Fertility* (5 vols). New York, Milbank Memorial Fund, pp. 621–73

Clore, G. L. and Jeffery, K. M. (1972) Emotional role playing, attitude change, and attraction towards a disabled person. *Journal of Personality and Social Psychology* **23**, 105–11

Cohen, J. B., Fishbein, M. and Ahtola, O. T. (1972) The nature and uses of expectancy-value models in consumer attitude research. *Journal of Marketing Research* **IX**, 456–60

Colley, R. H. (1961) *Defining Advertising Goals and Measuring Advertising Results.* NY, Association of National Advertisers

Collins, B. E., Ashmore, R. D., Hornbeck, F. W. and Whitney, R. E. (1970) Studies in forced compliance: XIII and XV. In search of a dissonance producing forced compliance paradigm. *Representative Research in Social Psychology* **1**

Collins, M. (1971) Market segmentation – the realities of buyer behaviour. *Journal of the Market Research Society* **13**, 3, 146–57

Cooper, J., Zanna, M. P. and Taves, P. A. (1978) Arousal as a necessary condition for attitude change following compliance. *Journal of Personality and Social Psychology* **36**, 1101–6

Condiotte, M. M. and Lichtenstein, E. (1981) Self-efficacy and relapse in smoking cessation programs. *Journal of Consulting and Clinical Psychology* **49**, 648–58

Corlett, T. (1985) Modelling the sales effects of advertising: today's questions. *Admap*, October, 486–500

Cotton, B. C. and Babb, E. M. (1978) Consumer response to promotional deals. *Journal of Marketing* July, 109–13

Cowling, A. B. (1972) Consequences of applying the Fishbein model to advertising planning. *Proceedings of the ESOMAR Madrid Seminar on Advanced Advertising Theories and Research*. Amsterdam, ESOMAR, pp. 41–60

Cowling, A. B. (1973) The use of elicitation technique for producing dimensions of brand choice. *Sixteenth Annual Conference*, Market Research Society of Great Britain

Crocker, J., Fiske, S. T. and Taylor, S. E. (1984) Schematic bases of belief change. In: Eiser, J. R. (ed.) *Attitudinal Judgement*. New York, Springer-Verlag

Crosby, L. A. and Muehling, D. D. (1983) External variables and the Fishbein model: mediation, moderation or direct effects? In: Tybout, A. and Bagozzi, R. P. (eds) *Advances in Consumer Research*, vol. X. Ann Arbor, MI, Association for Consumer Research, 94–9

Curtin, R. T. (1984) Consumer attitudes for forecasting. In: Kinnear, T. C. (ed.), *Advances in Consumer Research*, vol. XI. Provo, UT, Association for Consumer Research, pp. 714–17

Davidson, A. R. and Jaccard, J. J. (1975) Population psychology: a new look at an old problem. *Journal of Personality and Social Psychology* **31**, 1073–82

de Soto, C. and Albrecht, F. (1957) Cognition and social orderings. In: Abelson, R. P., Aronson, E., McGuire, W. J., Newcomb, T. M., Rosenberg, M. J. and Tannenbaum, P. H. *Theories of Cognitive Consistency: a Sourcebook*. Chicago, Rand McNally, pp. 531–8

Dodson, J. A., Tybout, A. M. and Sternthal, B. (1978) Impact of deal and deal retraction on brand switching. *Journal of Marketing Research* **15**, February, 72–81

Dollard, J., Doob, L. W., Miller, N. E., Mowrer, O. H. and Sears, R. R. (1939) *Frustration and Aggression*. New Haven, CT, Yale University Press

Doob, A. N., Carlsmith, J. M., Freedman, J. L., Landauer, T. K. and Tom, S. (1969) The effects of initial selling price on subsequent sales. *Journal of Personality and Social Psychology* **1**, 345–50

East, J. R. (1972) *Uncertainty and Attention Before Choice*. Doctoral thesis, University of Sussex

East, J. R. (1973) The duration of attention to alternatives and re-evaluation in choices with two and three alternatives. *European Journal of Social Psychology* **3**, 2, 125–44

East, J. R. (1984) Methods of pre-testing advertising: a review and a new approach. *International Journal of Advertising* **3**, 347–60

East, J. R. (1985a) *Making Natural Smoking Cessation More Effective*. A report to the Health Education Council, Kingston Polytechnic

East, J. R. (1985b) The determinants of intention to marry among students. Working paper, Kingston Polytechnic

East, J. R., Whittaker, D. and Swift, A. (1984) Measuring the factors that affect product take-up: key beliefs about Breakfast TV in Britain. Working paper, Kingston Polytechnic

Eastlack, J. O. Jr and Rao, A. G. (1986) Modeling response to advertising and pricing changes for 'V-8' cocktail vegetable juice. *Marketing Science* **5**, 3, 245–59

Edwards, W. (1954) The theory of decision making. *Psychological Bulletin* **51**, 4, 380–417

Ehrenberg, A. S. C. (1959) The pattern of consumer purchases. *Applied Statistics* **8**, 26–41

Ehrenberg, A. S. C. (1969) The discovery and use of laws of marketing. *Journal of Advertising Research* **9**, 2, 11–17

Ehrenberg, A. S. C. (1974) Repetitive advertising and the consumer. *Journal of Advertising Research* **14**, 25–34

Ehrenberg, A. S. C. (1988) *Repeat Buying: Theory and Applications*, 2nd ed. London, Charles Griffin & Co. (first published 1972 by North-Holland)

Ehrenberg, A. S. C. and Goodhardt, G. J. (1979) *Essays on Understanding Buyer Behavior*. New York, J. Walter Thompson Co. and Market Research Corporation of America

Ehrenberg, A. S. C. and Goodhardt, G. J. (1986) Jewel in the Crown – Compelling Viewing? *Journal of the Market Research Society* **28**, 1

Ehrenberg, A. S. C., Goodhardt, G. J. and Barwise, P. (1988) Double Jeopardy Revisited. Working paper, London Business School

Eiser, J. R. (1986) *Social Psychology: Attitudes, Cognition and Social Behavior*. Cambridge, UK, Cambridge University Press

Engel, J. F., Blackwell, R. D. and Miniard, P. W. (1986) *Consumer Behavior*, 5th ed. New York, The Dryden Press

Engel, J. F., Kollat, D. T. and Blackwell, R. D. (1968) *Consumer Behavior*. New York, Holt, Rinehart & Winston

England, L. and Ehrenberg, A. S. C. (1986) Pricing experiments 1984. CMaC working paper, London Business School

England, L. and Ehrenberg, A. S. C. (1988) Generalising a pricing effect. Working paper, London Business School

Eskin, G. J. (1985) Tracking advertising and promotion performance with single source data. *Journal of Advertising Research* **25**, 1, 31–9

Evans, J. St B. T. (1980) Current issues in the psychology of reasoning. *British Journal of Psychology* **71**, 2, 227–39

Fazio, R. H. (1985) How do attitudes guide behavior? In: Sorrentino, R. M. and Higgins, E. T. (eds) *The Handbook of Motivation and Cognition: Foundations of Social Behavior*. New York, Guildford Press

Fazio, R. H. and Zanna, M. (1978) Attitudinal qualities relating to the strength of the attitude–behavior relationship. *Journal of Experimental Social Psychology* **14**, 398–408

Fazio, R. H. and Zanna, M. (1981) Direct experience and attitude–behavior consistency. In: Berkowitz, L. O. (ed.) *Advances in Experimental Social Psychology*, vol. 14. New York, Academic Press

Ferber, R. (1954) The role of planning in consumer purchase of durable goods. *American Economics Review* **44**, 854–74

Festinger, L. (1957) *A Theory of Cognitive Dissonance*. Evanston, IL, Row Peterson

Festinger, L. (1964) *Conflict, Decision and Dissonance*. Stanford, CA, Stanford University Press

Festinger, L. and Carlsmith, J. M. (1959) Cognitive consequences of forced compliance. *Journal of Abnormal and Social Psychology* **58**, 203–10

Fishbein, M. (1963) An investigation of the relationships between beliefs about an object and attitudes to that object. *Human Relations* **16**, 233–40

Fishbein, M. (1966) Sexual behavior and propositional control. Paper read to the Psychonomic Society

Fishbein, M. (1972) Some comments on the use of 'models' in advertising research. *Proceedings of the ESOMAR Madrid Seminar on Advanced Advertising Theories and Research*. Amsterdam, ESOMAR, pp. 297–318

Fishbein, M. (1976) Extending the extended model: some comments. In: Anderson, B. B. (ed.) *Advances in Consumer Research*, vol. 3. Ann Arbor, MI, Association for Consumer Research, pp. 491–7

Fishbein, M. (1977) *Consumer beliefs and behavior with respect to cigarette smoking: a critical analysis of the public literature*. A report to the US Federal Trades Commission

Fishbein, M. and Ajzen, I. (1975) *Belief, Attitude, Intention and Behavior*. Reading, MA, Addison-Wesley

Fishbein, M. and Ajzen, I. (1976a) Misconceptions about the Fishbein model: reflections on a study by Songer-Nocks. *Journal of Experimental Social Psychology* **12**, 579–84

Fishbein, M. and Ajzen, I. (1976b) Misconceptions revisited: a final comment. *Journal of Experimental Social Psychology* **12**, 591–3

Fishbein, M. F. and Ajzen, I. (1981) On construct validity: a critique of Miniard and Cohen's paper. *Journal of Experimental Social Psychology* **17**, 340–50

Foxall, G. (1983) *Consumer Choice*. London, Macmillan

Foxall, G. (1984a) Evidence for attitudinal–behavioural consistency: implications for consumer research paradigms. *Journal of Economic Psychology* **5**, 71–92

Foxall, G. (1984b) Consumers' intentions and behaviour: a note on research and a challenge to researchers. *Journal of the Market Research Society* **26**, 3, 231–41

Fredricks, A. J. and Dossett, K. L. (1983) Attitude–behavior relations: A comparison of the Fishbein–Ajzen and the Bentler–Speckart models. *Journal of Personality and Social Psychology* **45**, 501–12

Frost, W. A. K. and Braine, R. L. (1967) The application of the repertory grid technique to problems in marketing research. Paper read at the Market Research Society Conference

Fulgoni, G.M. (1986) Advertising weight testing: the BehaviorScan[R] experience. *Admap* **250**, 136–44

Fulgoni, G. M. (1987) The role of advertising – is there one? *Admap* **262**, 54–7

Fulgoni, G. M. (1988) personal communication

Fulgoni, G. M. and Eskin, G.J. (1981) Use of the BehaviorScan research facility for studying retail shopping patterns. In: Lusch, R. F. and Carden, W. R. *Retail Patronage Theory – 1981 Workshop Proceedings*, University of Oklahoma

Gabor, A. (1988) *Pricing, Concepts and Methods for Effective Marketing* (2nd ed.). Vermont, Gower Publishing

Gabor, A. and Granger, C. W. J. (1973) Ownership and acquisition of consumer durables: report on the Nottingham consumer durables project. *European Journal of Marketing* **6**, 234

Garrick, G. (1986a) Spend *better* advertising dollars, not more. Paper presented to the Advertising Research Foundation Electronic Media Workshop, Hilton, New York, 11 December

Garrick, G. (1986b) What will copy research be like in 1990? Paper presented to the Third Annual ARF Copy Research Workshop, Hilton, New York, 28 May

Gerard, H. B. (1967) Choice difficulty, dissonance and the decision sequence. *Journal of Personality and Social Psychology* **35**, 91–108

Gibson, L. (1983) Not recall. *Journal of Advertising Research* **23**, 1, 39–46

Goddard, J. O. (1978) *Components of Brand Popularity*. Doctoral thesis, University of London, London Business School

Goffman, E. (1959) *The Presentation of Self in Everyday Life*, New York, Doubleday

Goodhardt, G. J., Ehrenberg, A. S. C. and Chatfield, C. (1984) The Dirichlet: A comprehensive model of buying behavior. *Journal of the Royal Statistical Society* **A 147**, 621–55

Goodhardt, G. J., Ehrenberg, A. S. C. and Collins, M. A. (1975) *The Television Audience: Patterns of Viewing*, Aldershot, Hants, Saxon House

Goodhardt, G. J., Ehrenberg, A. S. C. and Collins, M. A. (1987) *The Television Audience: Patterns of Viewing, An Update*. Aldershot, Hants, Gower

Gorn, G. J. (1982) The effects of music in advertising on choice behavior, a classical conditioning approach. *Journal of Marketing* **46**, 1, 94–101

Green, P. E. and Srinivasan, V. (1978) Conjoint analysis in consumer research: issues and outlook. *Journal of Consumer Research* **5**, 103–23

Haley, R. I. (1968) Benefit segmentation: a decision oriented research tool. *Journal of Marketing* **32**, 30–5

Harrison, A. A. (1968) Response competition, frequency, exploratory behavior and liking. *Journal of Personality and Social Psychology* **9**, 4, 363–8

Heider, F. (1958) *The Psychology of Interpersonal Relations*. New York, Wiley

Helson, H. (1964) *Adaptation Level Theory*. New York, Harper & Row

Holmes, J. G. and Strickland, L. H. (1970) Choice freedom and confirmation of incentive expectancy as determinants of attitude change. *Journal of Personality and Social Psychology* **14**, 1, 39–45

Homans, G. C. (1961) *Social Behavior: Its Elementary Forms*. London, Routledge & Kegan Paul

Horst, L. and Jarlais, D. C. (1984) Naturally occurring attitude and behavior changes: content and duration of the change process. *Quarterly Journal of Human Behavior* **21**, 2, 36–42

Howard, J. A. and Sheth, J. N. (1969) *The Theory of Buyer Behavior*. New York, Wiley

Infosino, W. J. (1986) Forecasting new product sales from likelihood of purchase ratings. *Marketing Science* **5**, 4, 372–84

Jaccard, J. J. and Davidson, A. R. (1972) Toward an understanding of family planning behaviors: an initial investigation. *Journal of Applied Social Psychology* **2**, 3, 228–35

Jobber, D. and Kilbride, A. (1986) How major agencies evaluate TV advertising in Britain. *International Journal of Advertising* **5**, 3, 187–95

Jones, E. E. (1979) The rocky road from acts to dispositions. *American Psychologist* **34**, 2 (February), 107–17

Jones, E. E. and Davis, K. E. (1965) From acts to dispositions: the attribution process in person perception. In: Berkowitz, L. (ed.) *Advances in Experimental Social Psychology*, vol. 2. New York, Academic Press

Joreskog, K. G. and Sorbom, D. (1978) *LISREL: Analysis of Linear Structural Relationships by the Method of Maximum Likelihood, Version V, Release 3*. Chicago, National Educational Resources Inc.

Juster, F. T. (1966) Consumer buying intentions and purchase probability; an experiment in survey design. *Journal of the American Statistical Association* **61**, 658–96

Kahle, L. R. and Berman, J. J. (1979) Attitudes cause behaviors: a cross-lagged panel analysis. *Journal of Personality and Social Psychology* **37**, 3, 315–21

Kahneman, B. and Tversky, A. (1972) Subjective probability: a judgement of representativeness. *Cognitive Psychology* **3**, 430–54

Kahneman, D. and Tversky, A. (1973) On the psychology of prediction. *Psychological Review* **80**, 237–51

Kahneman, D. and Tversky, A. (1979) Prospect theory: an analysis of decision under risk. *Econometrica* **47**, 263–91

Kahneman, D. and Tversky, A. (1984) Choices, values and frames. *American Psychologist* **39**, 4, 341–50

Katona, G. (1947) Contribution of psychological data to economic analysis. *Journal of the American Statistical Association* **42**, 449–59

Kau, A. K. and Ehrenberg, A. S. C. (1984) Patterns of store choice. *Journal of Marketing Research* **21**, 399–409

Kelley, H. H. (1967) Attribution theory in social psychology. *Nebraska Symposium on Motivation* **15**, 192–238

Kelly, G. A. (1955) *The Psychology of Personal Constructs*. New York, Norton

King, S. (1984) Setting advertising budgets for lasting effects. *Admap* **20**, August, 335–9

Kish, L. (1959) Some statistical problems in research design. *American Sociological Review* **24**, 328–38

Kitchen, P. J. (1986) Zipping, zapping and nipping. *International Journal of Advertising* **5**, 343–52

Korgaonkar, P. K., Lund, D. and Price, B. (1985) A structural equations approach toward examination of store attitude and store patronage behavior. *Journal of Retailing* **61**, 2, 39–60

Kotler, P. (1972) A generic concept of marketing. *Journal of Marketing* **36**, 46–54. Also in Enis, B. M. and Cox, K. K. (1985) *Marketing Classics*, 5th ed. London, Allyn & Bacon, pp. 52–64

Kotler, P. (1986) *Principles of Marketing.* 3rd ed. Englewood Cliffs, NJ, Prentice-Hall International

Kotler, P. and Levy, S. J. (1969) Broadening the concept of marketing. *Journal of Marketing* **33**, January, 10–15

Kotler, P. and Zaltman, G. (1971) Social marketing: an approach to planned social change. *Journal of Marketing* **35**, July, 3–12

Kristiansen, C. M. (1987) Salient beliefs regarding smoking: consistency across samples and smoking status. *Journal of the Institute of Health Education* **25**, 73–6

Krugman, H. E. (1965) The impact of television advertising: learning without involvement. *Public Opinion Quarterly* **29**, Fall, 349–56

Krugman, H. E. (1972) Why three exposures may be enough. *Journal of Advertising Research* **12**, 6, 11–14

Krugman, H. E. (1986) Low recall and recognition in advertising. *Journal of Advertising Research* **26**, 1, 79–86

Kunst-Wilson, W. R. and Zajonc, R. B. (1980) Affective discrimination of stimuli that cannot be recognized. *Science* **207**, 557–8

Lannon, J. (1985) Advertising research: new ways of seeing, *Admap*, October, 520–4

Lannon, J. and Cooper, P. (1983) Humanistic advertising: a holistic cultural perspective. *International Journal of Advertising* **2**, 195–213

LaPiere, R. T. (1934) Attitudes vs. actions. *Social Forces* **13**, 230–7

Lavidge, R. J. and Steiner, G. A. (1961) A model for predictive measurements of advertising effectiveness. *Journal of Marketing*, October, 59–62. Also in Enis, B. M. and Cox, K. K. (1985) *Marketing Classics: a Selection of Influential Articles*, 5th ed. London, Allyn & Bacon, pp. 408–12

Lichtenstein, S., Slovik, P., Fischoff, B., Layman, M. and Combs, B. (1978) Judged frequency of lethal events. *Journal of Experimental Psychology: Human Learning and Memory* **4**, 551–78

Likert, R. (1932) A technique for the measurement of attitudes. *Archives of Psychology* **140**

Linder, D. E., Cooper, J. and Jones, E. E. (1967) Decision freedom as a determinant of the role of incentive magnitude in attitude change. *Journal of Personality and Social Psychology* **6**, 245–54

Lindzey, G. and Aronson, E. (1985) *Handbook of Social Psychology*, vol. 1, 3rd ed. New York, Random House

Loken, B. (1983) The theory of reasoned action: examination of the sufficiency assumption for a television viewing behavior. In: Bagozzi, R. P. and Tybout, A. M. *Advances in Consumer Research*, vol. X. Ann Arbor, MI, Association for Consumer Research, pp. 100–5

Loken, B. and Fishbein, M. (1980) An analysis of the effects of occupational variables on childbearing intentions. *Journal of Applied Social Psychology* **10**, 202–23

Lutz, R. J. (1976) Conceptual and operational issues in the extended Fishbein model. In: Anderson, B. B. (ed.), *Advances in Consumer Research*, vol. III. Ann Arbor, MI, Association for Consumer Research

Lutz, R. J. (1977) An experimental investigation of causal relations among cognitions, affect, and behavioral intentions. *Journal of Consumer Research* **3**, 197–208

Lutz, R. J. (1978) Rejoinder. *Journal of Consumer Research* **4**, 266–71

McAlister, L. (1985) *The impact of price promotions on a brand's sales pattern, market share and profitability*. Sloan School Working Paper No. 1622–85. Cambridge, MA, Massachusetts Institute of Technology

McAlister, L. (1986) *The impact of price promotions on a brand's sales pattern, market share and profitability*. Sloan School Working Paper No. 86–110. Cambridge, MA, Massachusetts Institute of Technology

McAlister, L. and Totten, J. (1985) Decomposing the promotional bump: Switching, stockpiling, and consumption increase. Paper presented at the ORSA/TIMS 1985 Joint Meeting, 4 November

McArdle, J. B. (1972) Positive and negative communications and subsequent attitude and behavior changes in alcoholics. Unpublished doctoral dissertation, University of Illinois. Reported in Ajzen, I. and Fishbein, M. (1980) *Understanding Attitudes and Predicting Social Behavior*. Englewood Cliffs, NJ, Prentice-Hall

McDonald, C. (1970) What is the short term effect of advertising? *Proceedings of the ESOMAR Congress*, Barcelona, pp. 463–85

McDonald, C. (1986) Advertising effectiveness revisited. *Admap* **22**, 4, 191–203

McIntyre, K. O., Lichtenstein, E. and Mermelstein, R. J. (1983) Self-efficacy and relapse in smoking cessation: a replication and extension. *Journal of Consulting and Clinical Psychology* **51**, 632–3

Mackie, A. M. and Valentine, S. D. (1975) Effectiveness of different fear 'appeals' in road safety propaganda. *TRRL Report 669*, Transport and Road Research Laboratory, Department of the Environment, London

McPhee, W. N. (1963) *Formal Theories of Mass Behavior*. Glencoe, IL, Free Press

McQuarrie, E. F. (1988) An alternative to purchase intentions: the role of prior behaviour in consumer expenditure on computers. *Journal of the Market Research Society* **30**, 4, 407–37

Malec, J. (1982) Ad testing through the marriage of UPC scanning and targetable TV. *Admap*, May, 273–9

Marcel, J. (1976) Unconscious reading: experiments on people who do not know they are reading. Paper presented at the British Association for the Advancement of Science, Lancaster, England

Markus, H. and Zajonc, R. B. (1985) The cognitive perspective in social psychology. In: Lindzey, G. and Aronson, E. *Handbook of Social Psychology*, vol. 1, 3rd ed. New York, Random House, Ch. 4, pp. 137–230

Marsh, A. and Matheson, J. (1983) *Smoking Attitudes and Behaviour*.

An enquiry carried out on behalf of the Department of Health and Social Security. London, HMSO

Mazis, M. B., Ahtola, O. T. and Klippel, R. E. (1975) A comparison of four multi-attribute models in the prediction of consumer attitudes. *Journal of Consumer Research* 2, 38–52

Mead, G. H. (1934) *Mind, Self and Society*. Chicago, University of Chicago Press

Mehrotra, S., van Auken, S. and Lonial, S. C. (1981) Adjective profiles in television copy testing. *Journal of Advertising Research* 21, 4, 21–5

Miller, N. (1959) Liberalization of basic S–R concepts: extensions to conflict behavior, motivation and social learning. In: Koch, S. (ed.) *Psychology: The Study of a Science*, vol. 2. New York, McGraw-Hill, pp. 196–292

Miniard, P. W. and Cohen, J. B. (1979) Isolating attitudinal and normative influences in behavioral intentions models. *Journal of Marketing Research* 16, 102–10

Miniard, P. W. and Cohen, J. B. (1981) An examination of the Fishbein–Ajzen behavioral-intentions model's concepts and measures. *Journal of Experimental Social Psychology* 17, 309–39

Moldovan, S. E. (1984) Copy factors related to persuasion scores. *Journal of Advertising Research* 24, 6, 16–22

Moreton, W. J. and East, J. R. (1983) *Identifying Attitude Factors Associated with Smoking Cessation*. Research Report, Kingston Polytechnic

Morris, L. R. (1987) The research benefits of scanning. In: Bradley, U. *Applied Marketing and Social Research*. Chichester, Wiley, pp. 301–22

Motes, W. H. and Woodside, A. G. (1984) Field test of package advertising effects on brand choice behavior. *Journal of Advertising Research* 24, 1, 39–45

Newcomb, M. D. (1984) Sexual behavior, responsiveness, and attitudes among women: a test of two theories. *Journal of Sex and Marital Therapy* 10, 4, 272–86

Neslin, S. A. and Clarke, D. G. (1987) Relating the brand use profile of coupon redeemers to brand and coupon characteristics. *Journal of Advertising Research* 27, 1, 23–32

Newton, N. and Newton, M. (1950) Relationship of ability to breast feed and maternal attitudes towards breast feeding. *Pediatrics* 5, 869–75

Nisbett, R. E. and Wilson, T. D. (1977) Telling more than we can know: verbal reports on mental processes. *Psychological Review* 84, 231–59

Nuttin, J. M., Jr (1975) *The Illusion of Attitude Change; Towards a Response Contagion Theory of Persuasion*. London, Academic Press

Ogilvy, D. (1963) *Confessions of an Advertising Man*. London, Longman

Ogilvy, D. (1987) Sound the alarm! *International Journal of Advertising* 6, 1, 81–4

O'Herlihy, C. (1976) Making advertising profitable for the advertiser. *Admap*, August, 360–9

O'Herlihy, C. (1983) How econometrics work in practice: 10 years of measuring the sales effects of advertising. *Admap* 19, March, 146–52

Orne, M. (1962) On the social psychology of the psychological experiment: with particular reference to demand characteristics and their implications. *American Psychologist* **17**, 776–83

Osgood, J. F., Suci, G. J. and Tannenbaum, P. H. (1957) *The Measurement of Meaning*. Urbana, IL, University of Illinois Press

Ostlund, L. E., Clancy, J. C. and Sapra, R. (1980) Inertia in copy research. *Journal of Advertising Research* **20**, 1, 17–23

Park, C. W. (1976) The effect of individual and situation related factors on consumer selection of judgmental models. *Journal of Marketing Research* **13**, 144–51

Pavlov, I. P. (1927) *Conditioned Reflexes*. Translated by Anrep, G. V. London, Oxford University Press

Pickering, J. F. (1975) Verbal explanations of consumer durable purchase decisions. *Journal of the Market Research Society* **17**, 2, 107–13

Pickering, J. F. (1984) Purchase expectations and the demand for consumer durables. *Journal of Economic Psychology* **5**, 4, 342–52

Pickering, J. F. and Isherwood, B. C. (1974) Purchase probabilities and consumer durable buying behavior. *Journal of the Market Research Society* **16**, 3, 203–26

Pickering, J. F., Greatorex, M. and Laycock, P. J. (1983) The structure of consumer confidence in four EEC countries. *Journal of Economic Psychology* **4**, 4, 353–62

Pomerance, E. C. (1977) Generalizations from accumulating copy test results. *ESOMAR Proceedings on Research for Decision Making, Oslo*. Amsterdam, ESOMAR

Rajecki, D. W. (1982) *Attitudes: Themes and Advances*. Sunderland, MA, Sinaur Associates Inc.

Ratchford, B. T. (1987) New insights about the FCB Grid. *Journal of Advertising Research* **27**, 4, 24–38

Ray, M. L. and Batra, R. (1983) Emotion and persuasion in advertising: What we do and don't know about affect. In: Tybout, A. and Bagozzi, R. P. (eds) *Advances in Consumer Research*, vol. X. Ann Arbor, MI, Association for Consumer Research, 543–8

Reeves, R. (1961) *Reality in Advertising*. London, MacGibbon

Regan, D. T. and Fazio, R. H. (1977) On the consistency between attitudes and behavior: Look to the method of attitude formation. *Journal of Experimental Social Psychology* **13**, 28–45

Rip, P. (1980) The informational basis of self-reports; a preliminary report. In: Olson, J. C. *Advances in Consumer Research*, vol. VII. Ann Arbor, MI, Association for Consumer Research, pp. 140–5

Rosenberg, M. J. (1956) Cognitive structure and attitudinal affect. *Journal of Abnormal and Social Psychology* **53**, 367–72

Rosenberg, M. J. (1968) Discussion: impression processing and the evaluation of new and old objects. In: Abelson, R. P., Aronson, E., McGuire, W. J., Newcomb, T. M., Rosenberg, M. J. and Tannenbaum, P. H. *Theories of Cognitive Consistency: a Sourcebook*. Chicago, Rand McNally, pp. 763–8

Rosenberg, M. J. and Hovland, C. I. (1960) Cognitive, affective and behavioral components of attitudes. In: Hovland, C. I. and Rosenberg,

M. J. (eds) *Attitude Organization and Change*. New Haven, CT, Yale University Press, 1–14

Ross, H. L. (1982) Recall versus persuasion: an answer. *Journal of Advertising Research* 22, 1, 13–16

Rossiter, J. R. (1987) Comments on 'Consumer beliefs and brand usage' and on Ehrenberg's ATR model. *Journal of the Market Research Society* 29, 1, 83–8

Rowe, D. and Puto, C. P. (1987) Do consumers' reference points affect their buying decisions? In: Wallendorf, M. and Anderson, P. (1987) *Advances in Consumer Research*, vol. XIV. Provo, UT, Association for Consumer Research

Ryan, M. J. (1978) An examination of an alternative form of the behavioural intention model's normative component. In: Hunt, H. K. (ed.) *Advances in Consumer Research*, Vol. 5. Ann Arbor, Michigan, Association for Consumer Research

Ryan, M. J. (1982) Behavioral intention formation: the interdependency of attitudinal and social variables. *Journal of Consumer Research* 9, 263–78

Ryan, M. J. and Etzel, M. J. (1976) The nature of salient outcomes and referents in the extended model. In: Anderson, B. B. *Advances in Consumer Research*, Vol. III. Ann Arbor, MI, Association for Consumer Research, 485–90

Saegert, S. C. and Jellison, J. M. (1970) Effects of initial level of response competition and frequency of exposure on liking and exploratory behavior. *Journal of Personality and Social Psychology* 16, 553–8

Sandell, R. (1981) The dynamic relationship between attitudes and choice behavior in the light of cross-lagged panel correlations. *Reports from Department of Psychology*, No. 581, December. University of Stockholm

Schachter, S. and Singer, J. E. (1962) Cognitive, social and physiological determinants of emotional state. *Psychological Review* 69, 379–99

Schifter, D. B. and Ajzen, I. (1985) Intention, perceived control and weight loss: an application of the theory of planned behavior. *Journal of Personality and Social Psychology* 49, 3, 843–51

Schlegel, R. P., Crawford, C. A. and Sanborn, M. D. (1977) Correspondence and mediational properties of the Fishbein model: an application to adolescent alcohol use. *Journal of Experimental Social Psychology* 13, 421–30

Schmittlein, D. C., Bemmaor, A. C. and Morrison, D. G. (1985) Why does the NBD model work? Robustness in representing product purchases, brand purchases and imperfectly recorded purchases. *Marketing Science* 4, 3, 255–66

Schultz, D. E. (1987) Above or below the line? Growth in sales promotions in the United States. *International Journal of Advertising* 6, 1, 17–27

Schuman, H. and Johnson, M. P. (1976) Attitudes and behavior. *Annual Review of Sociology* 2, 161–207

Scott, C. A. (1976) Effects of trial and incentives on repeat purchase behavior. *Journal of Marketing Research* 13, August, 263–9

Sears, D.O. (1968) The paradox of de facto selective exposure without preferences for supportive information. In: Abelson, R. P., Aronson, E., McGuire, W. J., Newcomb, T. M., Rosenberg, M. J. and Tannenbaum, P. H. *Theories of Cognitive Consistency: A Sourcebook.* Chicago, Rand McNally, pp. 777–87

Sheth, J. N. (1972) Reply to the comments on the nature and uses of expectancy-value models in consumer research. *Journal of Marketing Research* IX, 462–5

Sheth, J. N. and Talarzyk, W. W. (1972) Perceived instrumentality and value importance as determinants of attitudes. *Journal of Marketing Research* IX, 6–9

Shoemaker, R. W. and Shoaf, F. R. (1977) Repeat rate of deal purchases. *Journal of Advertising Research* 17, April, 47–53

Shoemaker, R. W. and Tibewala, V. (1985) Relating coupon redemption rates to past purchasing of the brand. *Journal of Advertising Research* 25, 5, 40–7

Simon, H. A. (1957) *Administrative Behavior.* New York, Macmillan

Simon, J. L. and Arndt, J. (1980) The shape of the advertising response function. *Journal of Advertising Research* 20, 4, 11–28

Skinner, B. F. (1938) *The Behavior of Organisms.* New York, Appleton-Century-Crofts

Skinner, B. F. (1953) *Scientific and Human Behavior.* New York, Macmillan

Smith, E. R. and Miller, F. D. (1978) Limits on perception of cognitive processes: a reply to Nisbett and Wilson. *Psychological Review* 85, 355–62

Smith, R. E. and Swinyard, W. R. (1983) Attitude–behavior consistency; the impact of product trial versus advertising. *Journal of Marketing Research* XX, August, 257–67

Songer-Nocks, E. (1976a) Situational factors affecting the weighting of predictor components in the Fishbein model. *Journal of Experimental Social Psychology* 12, 56–69

Songer-Nocks, E. (1976b) Reply to Fishbein. *Journal of Experimental Social Psychology* 12, 85–90

Speetzen, R. (1984) Which marketing inputs have the greatest influence on market shares? *Admap* 234, 536–41

Steiner, R. L. (1987) Point of view: the paradox of increasing returns to advertising. *Journal of Advertising Research* 27, 1, 45–53

Stewart, D. W. and Furse, D. H. (1984) Analysis of executional factors on advertising performance. *Journal of Advertising Research* 24, 6, 23–6

Sudman, S. and Ferber, R. (1979) *Consumer Panels.* Chicago, American Marketing Association

Sullivan, G. L. and O'Connor, P. J. (1983) Search for relationship between viewer responses to the creative aspects of televised messages and behavioral intention. In: Tybout, A. and Bagozzi, R. P. (eds) *Advances in Consumer Behavior,* vol. X. Ann Arbor, MI, Association for Consumer Research, pp. 32–5

Sutton, S., Marsh, A. and Matheson, J. (1987) Explaining smokers' decisions to stop: test of an expectancy-value approach. *Social Behaviour* **2**, 1, 35–50

Svenson, O. (1974) Coded think aloud protocols obtained when making a choice to purchase one of seven hypothetically offered houses. University of Stockholm

Tauber, E. M. (1975) Predictive validity in consumer research. *Journal of Advertising Research* **15**, 5, 59–64

Telser, L. G. (1962) The demand for branded goods as estimated from consumer panel data. *Review of Economics and Statistics* **44**, August, 300–24

Thaler, R. (1985) Mental accounting and consumer choice. *Marketing Science* **4**, Summer, 199–214

Theil, H. and Kosobud, R. F. (1968) How informative are consumer buying intentions surveys? *Review of Economics and Statistics* **50**, 50–9

Thibaut, J. W. and Kelley, H. H. (1959) *The Social Psychology of Groups*. New York, Wiley

Thomas, K. and Tuck, M. (1975) An exploratory study of determinant and indicant beliefs in attitude measurement. *European Journal of Social Psychology* **5**, 2, 167–87

Thorndike, E. L. (1911) *Animal Intelligence*. New York, Macmillan

Totten, J. C. (1986) Measuring retail sales response to retail sales promotion. Paper presented at the ORSA/TIMS Marketing Science Conference, 13 March

Totten, J. C. and Block, M. P. (1987) *Analyzing Sales Promotion: Text and Cases*. Chicago, Commerce Communications Inc.

Treasure, J. (1975) How advertising works. In: Barnes, M. (ed.) *The Three Faces of Advertising*. London, The Advertising Association, pp. 48–52

Tuck, M. (1977) *How Do We Choose?* London, Methuen

Tversky, A. (1972) Elimination by aspects: a theory of choice. *Psychological Review* **79**, 281–99

Tversky, A. and Kahneman, D. (1974) Judgement under uncertainty: heuristics and biases. *Science* **185**, 1124–31

Tversky, A. and Kahneman, D. (1980) Causals schemas in judgements under uncertainty. In: Fishbein, M. (ed.) *Progress in Social Psychology*, vol. 1, 49–72

Tversky, A. and Kahneman, D. (1981) The framing of decisions and the psychology of choice. *Science* **211**, 453–8

Uncles, M. D. and Ehrenberg, A. S. C. (1987) Patterns of store choice: new evidence from the USA. In: Wrigley, N. *Store Choice, Store Location and Market Analysis*. London, Routledge & Kegan Paul

Uncles, M. D. (1988) *BUYER: Buyer Behaviour Software*. Available from the author. London Business School, Sussex Place, Regent's Park, London NW1 4SA

van Raaij, W. F. (1977) Consumer information processing for different information structures and formats. In: Perreault, W. D., Jr (ed.), *Advances in Consumer Research*, vol. 4, Proceedings of the 1976 Conference of the Association for Consumer Research, pp. 176–84

Vaughn, R. (1980) How advertising works: a planning model. *Journal of Advertising Research* **20**, 5, 27–33

Vaughn, R. (1986) How advertising works: a planning model revisited. *Journal of Advertising Research* **26**, 1, 57–66

Veblen, T. (1899, 1949) *The Theory of The Leisure Class*. London, Macmillan

Vroom, V. H. (1964) *Work and Motivation*. New York, Wiley

Walters, R. G. and Rinne, H. S. (1986) An empirical investigation into the impact of price promotions on retail store performance. *Journal of Retailing* **62**, 3, 237–66

Watson, J. B. (1913) Psychology as the behaviorist views it. *Psychological Review* **20**, 158–77

Watson, J. B. and Rayner, R. (1920) Conditioned emotional reactions. *Journal of Experimental Psychology* **3**, 1–14

Wellan, D. M. and Ehrenberg, A. S. C. (1988) A successful new brand: Shield. *Journal of the Market Research Society* **30**, 1, 35–44

Westoff, C. and Ryder, N. (1970) United States: the Papal encyclical and Catholic practice and attitudes, 1969. *Studies in Family Planning* **50**, 1–7

Wheatley, J. J., Yalch, R. F. and Chiu, J. S. V. (1980) In search of the economists' consumer: the effects of product information, money and prices on choice behavior. In: Olson, J. C. (ed.), *Advances in Consumer Research*, vol. 7. Ann Arbor, MI, Association for Consumer Research, 533–7

White, P. A. (1988) Knowing more than we can tell: 'introspective access' and causal report accuracy 10 years later. *British Journal of Psychology* **79**, 13–45

Wicker, A. W. (1969) Attitude vs actions: the relationship of verbal and overt behavioral responses to attitude objects. *Journal of Social Issues* **25**, 41–78

Wilkie, W. L. and Pessemier, E. E. (1973) Issues in marketing use of multi-attribute models. *Journal of Marketing Research* **10**, 428–41

Wright, P. and Rip, P. (1980) Retrospective reports on consumer decision processes: 'I can remember if I want to but why should I bother trying?' In: Olson, J. C. *Advances in Consumer Researh*, vol. VII. Ann Arbor, MI, Association for Consumer Research, pp. 146–7

Wrigley, N. and Dunn, R. (1984) Stochastic panel-data models of urban shopping behaviour: 2 Multi-store purchasing patterns and the Dirichlet model. *Environment and Planning A* **16**, 759–78

Zajonc, R. B. (1968) Attitudinal effects of mere exposure. *Journal of Personality and Social Psychology Monograph Supplement* **9**, 2 (Part 2), 1–27

Zajonc, R. B. (1980) Feeling and thinking: preferences need no inferences. *American Psychologist* **38**, 151–75

Zajonc, R. B. and Markus, H. (1982) Affective and cognitive factors in preferences. *Journal of Consumer Research* **9**, 2, 123–32

Zajonc, R. B. and Rajecki, D. W. (1969) Exposure and affect: a field experiment. *Psychonomic Science* **17**, 216–17

Zanna, M. P. and Cooper, J. (1974) Dissonance and the pill: an attribution approach to studying the arousal properties of dissonance. *Journal of Personality and Social Psychology* **29**, 703–9

Subject Index

Author Index